Economic Renaissance in the Age of Artificial Intelligence

Economic Renaissance in the Age of Artificial Intelligence

Edited by
Apek Mulay

BEP BUSINESS EXPERT PRESS

Economic Renaissance in the Age of Artificial Intelligence

First published in 2019 by
Business Expert Press, LLC
222 East 46th Street, New York, NY 10017
www.businessexpertpress.com

ISBN-13: 978-1-94784-394-3 (paperback)
ISBN-13: 978-1-94784-395-0 (e-book)

Business Expert Press Economics and Public Policy Collection

Collection ISSN: 2163-761X (print)
Collection ISSN: 2163-7628 (electronic)

Cover and interior design by Exeter Premedia Services Private Ltd., Chennai, India

First edition: 2019

10 9 8 7 6 5 4 3 2 1

Printed in the United States of America.

This book is dedicated to my friend and my mentor
Dr. Ravi Batra

Abstract

Development of Artificial Intelligence (AI) has become a top priority for most leading economies. However, there is an evidence of productivity paradox in today's economy. There is also an evidence that in the last 30 years, growth in productivity from technological innovations has resulted into more income inequality as well as formation of giant oligopolies in the technological sector.

Marshall Goldsmith wrote in his book *What Got You Here, Won't Get You There* that people rely on their past experience to address new challenges. The limitation with this approach is that these new challenges often arise from different contexts and may not be susceptible to traditional approaches.

In the coming era of AI, expanded use of robots, and increased transnational commerce, humanity will face monumental challenges that will differ from those we have faced in the past, including how to avoid mass unemployment due to a rapid growth of automation. In order to survive and thrive in this new era, we will have to think and act differently, so that new ideas can solve not only the problems of the present but also of the near and distant future.

The economic policies of past that have driven the technological progress would further increase disparity because the owners of capital will eventually become the owners of robots. Hence, *Economic Renaissance in the Age of Artificial Intelligence* calls for a total restructuring of the economy based on a new economic treatise that prioritizes creating employment opportunities for human beings over offering free social benefits such as universal basic income (UBI).

This book explores a wide range of new approaches to the economic, social, legal, scientific, technological, financial, architectural, environmental, and humanistic challenges that humanity will face due to increased automation. The new methods and approaches outlined by the various experts in this book will help inform and inspire humanity to create a more balanced world in which science, economics, and the environment can thrive for years to come.

Keywords

Internet of Things (IoT); big data; artificial intelligence (AI); blockchain; sustainability; watershed society; fantacities; collaboration; world constitution; entanglement; self-realization; complimenting economy; business analytics

Contents

Foreword

Apek Mulay has edited an intriguing book. It draws on the foundational work of Indian mystic, macro-historian, and philosopher, Shrii P.R. Sarkar. Almost 60 years ago, Sarkar began the process of envisioning and creating a world after communism and capitalism. Communism has largely disappeared as a vision of the future, while crony capitalism appears to be if not at its end, certainly in its dying stages as inequity continues to increase within nations and between nations. Sarkar imagined a world with far greater efficiency, far greater productivity, far less inequality, living with nature and enhanced by amazing new technologies—"mind in technology," if you will—what we know today as the beginning of artificial intelligence (AI). This would be a planetary civilization where the boundaries would be functional not sentiment-based as in today's nation-states. However, this was not a utopian vision in that it was a no-place, but a Eutopian vision, a good place. Contradictions do not magically disappear; however, exploitation decreases and the world gets better and better.

What seemed far away 60 years ago no longer seems distant. Discussion of global governance, a universal basic income , an Internet of everything, dramatic advances in robotics all challenge the current world capitalist system and the mind-set that sustains it.

But how would this system actually work? It is this question that many contributing authors seek to answer. What would a universal basic income look like? Is it even possible? Would it create security or a culture of incapacity? What legislation is required to encourage cooperatives? Do we need a global constitution? How do we create an economy where the "money flows"? Can we, should we, move from dark green to bright green (ecology with AI), or more important, are structural changes in the world economy. These and many other similar questions are tackled and answered by the contributing authors.

This book is rare in many ways. First as suggested earlier, it fills in the details to Sarkar's alternative vision of the future where technology creates less inequality with higher productivity. Second, it takes macroeconomics seriously. Mulay is an economist and to his credit, he has created a community of thought leaders who move between economics, sociology, law, and futures studies. Issues of taxation and the employment implications of robots are not lost sight of. Indeed, solutions from new taxation regimes to blockchains to constitutional amendments are offered. And inner issues, for example, the implications of meditation and spiritual consciousness on post-capitalism are met head on.

Thus, the text both attempts to optimize our life in current reality—the world as we know it—how can we create more value for all, how can we be happier, and how can we create a more just planetary civilization after capitalism. The present and the emerging possible future are both addressed.

This is a unique time in our human history. There is much to appreciate, even though horror is everywhere. As we transition to a new society we need visions and operational suggestions as to what to do next.

Professor Sohail Inayatullah
UNESCO Chair in Futures Studies. USIM, TKU, USC
New book, Asia 2038. http://metafuture.org/2018/04/12/new-book-asia-2038-2018/
Upcoming public workshops http://metafuture.org/coursestraining/forthcoming-speeches-workshops-and-training/

Preface

Andy Haldane, the chief economist for the Bank of England, has been very critical of the current state of macroeconomics. In his 2016 speech titled "The Dappled World," Haldane argued that the unexpected global downturn that began in late 2007 has left behind "a crisis in the economics and finance profession." The reasoning behind Haldane's belief that it poses a deep intellectual crisis for macroeconomics is that the field of macroeconomics, as it has developed since the work of John Maynard Keynes in the 1930s, was to prevent just the sort of severe downturn that started in 2007 called as "The Great Recession."

According to Haldane, macroeconomics was developed with a specific, real-world purpose, and a negative purpose to boot: to stop anything like the Great Depression from ever happening again. Given this goal—to avert systemic crises and downturns—the credit crunch and the Great Recession were an intellectual disaster for the profession of macroeconomics because economic disasters destroy lives of so many.

Haldane talks about the need for macroeconomics to learn from other disciplines to seek "a different perspective on individual behavior and systemwide dynamics." He argues that the profession has "borrowed too little from other disciplines" and hence it has become "a methodological monoculture," with the associated risks that everybody in the field can be wrong in the same way and at the same time. Many topics have already been covered in my previous volume titled *New Macroeconomics*. Haldane finds compelling evidence in a survey of American professors of social science, who were asked whether "interdisciplinary" knowledge was better than knowledge "obtained by a single discipline." To Haldane's surprise, 57 percent of economists, who were polled, either disagreed or strongly disagreed, which means that economists literally think they have nothing to learn from anyone else. Haldane believes that the field of macroeconomics also suffers from its rigid hierarchies and its lack of gender and racial diversity. Thus, Haldane concluded that economics remains an insular and self-referential discipline.

Haldane isn't the only prominent nonacademic economist to think there are profound problems in macroeconomics. Even the chief economist at the World Bank, Paul Romer, believes that the biggest weakness in the field is the omission of finance and role of money from economic models. Indeed, it is hard for non-economists to understand why the dominant macroeconomic models (including the ones used by central banks) made no allowance for how money works—especially not for the fluctuations in how much of it is around. These things have been taken into consideration in my self-published book titled *Mass Capitalism: A Blueprint for Economic Revival.*

While my previous book *New Macroeconomics* focused on the importance of wage-gap theory and how it could solve several problems in the field of macroeconomics, *Economic Renaissance in the Age of Artificial Intelligence* involves expertise from several different professionals to offer a free market solution as a blueprint due to its "interdisciplinary" approach. The solutions offered in this volume are a compendium of interdisciplinary approaches to the field of macroeconomics, provided by professionals and thought leaders from diverse academic and business backgrounds. They are a broader macroeconomic solution to a crisis brewing due to an uncertainty created by a rapid growth in the field of artificial intelligence (AI) technology.

The disconnect between macroeconomic planners and technology experts has resulted in a knowledge gap, which has proven to be a disaster for both fields. While technology experts have been pushing for doles such as universal basic income (UBI) to sustain technological advancements, the macroeconomic planners are worried about the overall economic stability with the expected huge unemployment of workers with growth of AI and other related technologies. Thus, there is a deep intellectual crisis brewing in the field of macroeconomics to find a way to ensure full employment for the economy and sustain the current technological progress. Some of the very well-known technology experts such as Elon Musk also claim about a possibility of having World War III due to rapid advancement of AI and on the other hand, Russian President Vladimir Putin opines that the first global leader in AI would "become the ruler of the world" and it in no surprise that China is determined to steal the AI crown from the United States. Thus, there has been a lot of tumult and turmoil within the profession of macroeconomics.

In addition to the replacement of human jobs by automation and AI-related technologies, there is also an evidence of depression among today's workforce. Human beings have become increasingly addicted to drugs and there is a clear evidence of increased gun violence in society. The addiction of human beings to social networks has also decreased productivity at work. On top of it, the technological progress of Moore's law is coming to a grinding halt due to reduced purchasing power of citizens and less percentage of workforce in the United States making a choice to pursue STEM (science, technology, engineering, and math) education. On top of everything, human beings have reduced their social interaction because of getting glued to their electronic gadgets. All these are the result of the progress of technology much faster than the progress of society.

It needs to be mentioned that our human civilization has an intimate relation with science and technology and hence both (civilization and science) should progress together. But where scientific progress supersedes the progress of civilization, there the civilization meets its Waterloo. This has been evident based on historical research for ancient Egypt and ancient Greece. So long as the scientific progress of these two countries did not supersede the progress of civilization, civilization prospered very well. But when the ingredients of personal enjoyment grew up in abundance, the civilization of both countries got destroyed, because science had occupied a higher position than civilization. Hence, when considering Industry 4.0 and Industry 5.0, it is important that entire civilization progresses on par with science. Else, progress of AI and IoT (Internet of Things) technologies without an overall progress of our human civilization is sure to lead to a disaster. While my previously published volumes viz. *Mass Capitalism* (2014), *Sustaining Moore's Law* (2015), *How Information Revolution Remade the Business and the Economy* (2016), and *New Macroeconomics* (2018) focused on offering free market solutions to reduce the wage gap in order to achieve a sustainable technological progress, there are several other ideas from other disciplines and their contributions to the profession of macroeconomics in order to make this blueprint complete so that progress of civilization is on par with the progress of science.

In 2013, a study from Oxford University researchers, viz. Michael Osborne and Carl Frey, predicted that 47 percent of U.S. jobs could be replaced by automated technology in the next 10 to 20 years. While some of the well-known billionaires such as Facebook founder Mark Zuckerberg; SolarCity, SpaceX, and Tesla founder Elon Musk; billionaire entrepreneur Richard Branson; Y Combinator President Sam Altman; and Slack CEO Stewart Butterfield have endorsed UBI, others like self-made millionaire Grant Cardone and former Vice President Joe Biden reject UBI and call giving free doles as un-American. In fact, Joe Biden also said that. "I believe we can—we must—build a future that puts work first."

Economic Renaissance in the Age of Artificial Intelligence believes in putting work first and hence it draws its inspiration from a new economic treatise called as the progressive utilization theory, which was propounded in 1959 by late Indian scholar, Shri Prabhat Ranjan Sarkar. In the quest of achieving exponential growth in technological progress in present society, increased automation risks displacing human beings and necessitates doles such as UBI in order to eliminate the problem of unemployment. However, UBI will result in higher income taxes on employed workforce as well as a much larger intervention of government into the economy. Hence, free markets can certainly not be achieved when there is an acute problem of unemployment created with increased automation in every sector of economy. To achieve free markets where the role of government is small and taxes on individuals are low, the macroeconomic policies call for a total restructuring of the economy. It needs major reforms in trade policies, monetary policies, reforms in democracy, reforms in supply chains, reforms in business models, revamping of the financial industry as well as having sound policies for creation of a sound money supply.

Free markets should also ensure that there is a maximum circulation of currency, resulting in a multiplying effect, eliminating trade and budget deficits, minimizing the size of government as well as ethical political leadership that restores confidence in civilian democracy, ensures establishment of sound fiscal policies, and results in growth of innovation as well as brings about much needed constitutional reforms as per the changes in time and space. With the changes in time and space, new forms of currencies such as crypto-currency have now come into existence and newer technologies such as blockchains have the potential to revolutionize the Internet that we have known for so long. However, the turmoil in crypto-currency market shows that the fintech revolution has a long way to go from becoming useful for everyday transactions. The goal of fintech revolution should be to support a good monetary policy such that wages keep pace with productivity of workforce. When all these good ideas come together, what comes out of it is a totally new socioeconomic system, which ushers a productive utilization of technology for bettering lives of all human beings. This book is essentially a comprehension of such new ideas in order to provide a free market solution to an imminent monumental crisis to entire human society that would result from a rapid progress of AI.

This book is divided in following five parts, viz. technological background (which includes Chapters 1 through 3) forms Part I, social, environmental, and ethical aspects form Part II (which includes Chapters 4 through 6), Part III is on policy options (which include Chapters 7 and 8), spiritual implications are covered in Part IV (which includes Chapters 9 and 10), and economic issues are covered in Part V (which includes Chapters 11 and 12) followed by concluding Chapter 13.

Chapter 1 is all about IoT. The IoT is beginning to permeate every facet of our world and take hold in all major industries. The introduction of IoT technologies into manufacturing and large industrial-scale machinery is fostering a new economy nurtured by these technologies. The IoT enables machines to communicate with one another as well as with their human counterparts. This provides improved safety, security, and efficiency. IoT will have wide-reaching economic impacts. These advances go beyond just manufacturing and will spread into farming, city planning, energy management, and more. This expansion will create a boom of technological, economic, and global benefits. It is predicted that this growth will be comparable to the industrial revolution. If so, it will increase the GDP around the world, and provide new economic, technical, and employment opportunities to citizens globally. As with previous revolutions, it is expected that the IoT revolution will drive up average incomes and living standards, particularly in industrially advanced economies.

Chapter 2 is about big data and AI, which are revolutionizing the economy with new business models and the business processes with "intelligent systems" reducing the dependence on human resources. Though AI has been in existence for three to four decades now, it is the evolution of processing power technology and gigabit Internet speeds that has made this possible. These technologies have opened the doors for new opportunities that are going to change the business models and workforce such as new business paradigms, knowledge economy, and speech recognition. It is therefore imperative to understand how these systems and technologies function at a high level in order to be ready to work with these new-age systems.

In Chapter 3, we discuss upcoming revolutions in financial technology in the form of blockchains and the importance of a gold standard for a sound global financial system. In the modern era, we are pounded with new systems and processes where technologies are created faster than we can digest. Blockchain is one such technology, which is most advanced, error free, eliminates frauds in payment systems, international money transfer, and cross-border payments. Blockchain technology can use a gold-backed cryptocurrency and is very likely to become the most used technology on the planet. If any individual, corporate, government, or a nation is looking for a strategy to protecting their assets, they should be looking at implementing blockchain technology.

Contemporary cities as economic actors are technological marvels yet also unsustainable monsters in the making. In Chapter 4, we explore the idea that if cities are to coexist in any kind of beneficial way with the unintended consequences of modernism, they will need to reject the distortions that neoliberal macroeconomics imposes together with those elements of the Western way of knowing that underpin that worldview. It argues that the alternative requires a new kind of macroeconomics, a praxis that is both holistic and pragmatic about diverse rapid transitions that are postcapitalist, postextractivist, and postgrowth in their intention.

In Chapter 5, we discuss about green technology, including environmentally friendly robots that will be an integral contributor to a more sustainable economy. The most important innovation toward a more sustainable future, however, will not be green technology, but rather a greener economic system. Capitalism itself is the main hindrance toward greener technology innovations and a greener economy. What the world now needs is a restructured economy in which capitalism's excessive greed for profit and resources will be curbed and balanced with economic restructuring, decentralization, and technological innovations serving an economy in dynamic balance with nature.

The AI revolution promises to dramatically expand our socioeconomic capabilities and achievements. AI-operated robots are irreversibly transforming how work is accomplished and what role humans play. The game-changing potential of AI eclipses previous inventions that channeled earlier stages of human socioeconomic development. Whether AI opens new possibilities for humans or bankrupts the entire human enterprise depends on which aspects of current human behavior becomes the primordial foundation of AI development. Will the human capability for collaboration be the core of AI, or the human capability for predation? In particular, will AI be deployed to inspire and evolve collaborative business models and organizational paradigms, or to cement and entrench predatory ones? The choice is up to humans to make and will prove decisive for eons and this is precisely what we shall explore in Chapter 6.

Climate change is causing massive planetary decline. At the same time the technological revolution is displacing millions. Can universal income divert human capital to needed planetary change? 12,000 years of civilizational rise and collapse assert basic laws of sustainability. Huge hierarchical urban centers always collapse; but when they are decentralized, populations thrive. When the laws of the watershed are followed, we return to resilience. In Chapter 7, we discuss why technological advancement must accompany the redirection of human capital to these eternal laws.

In a highly automated world, new legal structures will be needed to address critical issues of the day. Throughout history as societies have grown more complex, so have the problems that faced them. By the mid-20th century, human survival was threatened by global war and the United Nations was formed in response. In Chapter 8, we discuss how in the age of AI, economic justice and environmental sustainability will be key challenges requiring a new global constitutional structure to address them.

In Chapter 9, we explore how recent scientific discoveries in quantum physics leave no doubt that nonlocality is a basic feature of physical reality. This fact indicates that our customary way of viewing consciousness and mind needs to undergo radical change—away from the morbid, local perspective of materialism, to a view grounded in both spirituality and empirical science. In this modern view, consciousness is considered the fundamental "ground substance" of creation, which is nonlocal and causal and not merely an incidental byproduct of the brain. Furthermore, we explore how phenomena such as extrasensory perception (ESP), out-of-body and near-death experiences, as well as mental states affecting physiological changes prove that mind is nonlocal and cannot be equated with the brain. Nonlocality in the physical and mental realms negate the materialistic worldview but is entirely consistent with spiritual worldview. This worldview describes a universe that is whole, in which the "parts" we observe emerge from a hidden transcendent reality.

Chapter 10 on meditation and consciousness takes us on a fascinating inner journey of biopsychology and elucidates the important role of sentient lifestyle and meditation in helping us to control our emotions and lift the mind unto the highest state of supreme consciousness. The meditative pursuits also help us to develop attitudes that enable us to control technology for greater welfare and enable us to function as better leaders—whether in business, at home, in politics, or in any other public domain. What emerges from this pursuit is a new mindset of "liberating human intellect" in order to bring about lasting inner peace as well as a progressive social, economic, and political order.

Chapter 11 describes how America, once an envy of other nations, has been hollowed, thanks to poor leadership, lack of creative thinking, and outright greed of power and wealth. All dynamic systems including organisms and human economic systems that provide stuff for our existence must learn to bring harmony, balance, and complementarity between the opposites to thrive, prosper, and transcend. All humanity has been now connected, thanks to discoveries of modern technologies. We need to also accept the fact of the primacy of human mind (which is nonlocal) over the matter. Intellect is mere a tool to discover the ever-changing truth for greater good. United States and other countries need to change from educating people based upon only materialism to the education of the heart learnt from historical experience.

In Chapter 12, we discuss the importance of having a free market economy and why the existing business models need reforms to ensure that there is no need of UBI. The new regulations such as General Data

Protection Regulation (GDPR) as well as other data protection laws enacted across the world are changing the dynamics of operation of global businesses. In this chapter we discuss the business models that are necessary to envision a fully automated free market economy. This chapter also highlights the importance of business analytics and how to achieve much more accurate predictions using data analytics. Besides it also throws light on the importance of achieving a sustainable technological progress by integrating science with spirituality.

In Chapter 13, we summarize the contents in all chapters and introduce the reader to the law of social cycle and progressive utilization theory. We also mention about how these new ideas would be envisioned for a bright future of humanity.

Acknowledgments

I owe my greatest intellectual debt to a great neo-humanist, the late Shrii Prabhat Ranjan Sarkar, whose books on progress utilization theory have given me new ideas to provide solutions to the problem of the day faced by human society. While *New Macroeconomics* offered a new look of the profession the reader, this book offers an interdisciplinary approach between several professions to offer a comprehensive blueprint with different ideas to achieve progress of civilization on par with the progress of science.

This venture would not have been possible without the encouragement that I received from the acquisitions editor of Business Expert Press, Scott Isenberg. I would also like to extend my sincere thanks to my contributing authors from different professions and from different parts of the world including Satinder Paul Singh (technology consultant from Germany), Sreenivas Adiki (director of big data from United States), Shrikant Shete (managing director from Australia), Dr. Michael McAllum (chief steward from Australia), Roar Bjonnes (environmentalist from the United States), Dr. Stephen Willis (collaboration expert from the United States), Dr. Matt Oppenheim (anthropologist from the United States), Craig Runde (attorney from the United States), Dr. Steven Richheimer (scientist from the United States), Dr. Shambhushivananda (rector from Sweden), and Navin Doshi (philanthropist from the United States).

Last but not least, I am very grateful to Dr. Sohail Inayatullah (UNESCO chair of future studies) for foreword to this book.

PART I
Technology Background

CHAPTER 1

Internet of Things: A Revolutionary Economic Opportunity

Satinder Paul Singh

Introduction

Internet of Things (IoT) refers to physical and virtual objects that have unique identities and are connected to the Internet to facilitate intelligent applications that make energy, logistics, industrial control, retail, agriculture, and many other domains "smarter."[1] IoT is a new revolution of the Internet that is rapidly gathering momentum driven by the advancements in sensor networks, mobile devices, and wireless communications, networking, and cloud technologies. Experts forecast that by the year 2020, there will be a total of approximately 50 billion devices/things connected to the Internet (Figure 1.1). Economically, the IoT could have a significant impact in the years ahead. According to analysis from the McKinsey Global Institute,[6] the potential economic impact of the IoT in 2025, including consumer surplus, could be anything between $3.9 and $11.1 trillion. Elsewhere, Accenture has estimated that the industrial IoT could add $14.2 trillion to the global economy by the year 2030.

Applications for IoT exist in fields such as connected industry, smart city, smart energy, connected car, smart agriculture, connected buildings, connecting health, smart retail, and smart supply chain; manufacturing, software engineering, Internet security, and so on (Figure 1.2). It is set to create a revolution in every sector of the global economy and about to transform the global economy. This new wave of connectivity is going beyond laptops and smartphones; it's going toward connected cars, smart

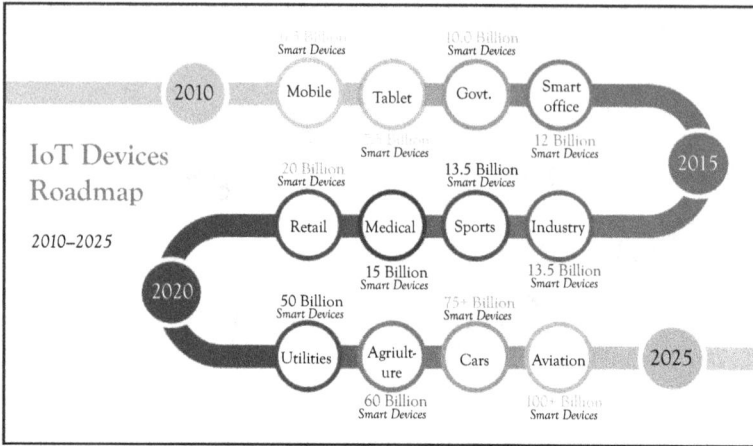

Figure 1.1 IoT devices roadmap

Figure 1.2 IoT as a network of connected devices

homes, connected wearables, smart cities, and connected health care. Basically, the IoT revolution is nothing but a connected life.

Call it the IoT, machine data, or sensor-driven analytics, but the world has yet to untap its potential, the advent of IoT has enabled a natural resource-a rich seam of data that can transform every aspect of operational performance. There is a lot of data generated from Internet searches, website visits, social networking activity, streaming videos, electronic health care records, sensor networks, large-scale simulations, and so on.

The challenge companies face is to access the resource of machines that predate IoT concepts and deliver tangible value, not only to their business but to the wider economy.[3]

This chapter is organized into three main sections, comprising of a total of five subsections. Section I covers the sizing of the opportunity given by IoT. A taxonomy of IoT systems is proposed comprising various IoT levels with increasing levels of complexity and various implications for semiconductor and software companies. Section II introduces the reader to the technological and ecosystem challenges aspects of IoT to companies with a view toward rapid prototyping of complex IoT applications. Section III introduces the reader on how chip and software service companies can really build a solid strategy to seek value beyond silicon using advanced data analytics. They may need to consider more radical approaches to improve the value captured, including a shift to new business models. Also, the impact of machine learning, artificial intelligence, and blockchain on IoT will be discussed.

IoT could change the landscape of the electrical, mechanical, and service industries. Following are few lists of some of the effects it could achieve:

- *Provide greater control over production*
    1. Reduced costs
    2. Expanding production becomes easier, raising revenues
- *Facilitate linking manufactured products to services*
    1. Monitors engines in real time, reducing unexpected maintenance
    2. Extends lifetime of products
    3. Supports zero defect or zero downtime guarantees
- *Speed up production or service development*
    1. Actively identifies issues in products while they are produced
    2. Reduces errors and poorly produced products, eliminating time lost

Biggest trends shaping the long-term technology landscape:

- The Resurgence in semiconductor startups
- Machine learning becoming ubiquitous in the real world
- The end of Moore's Law and the coming mainstream availability of 'exotic' wafer processes
- Increased verticalization of the mega semiconductor consumers (e.g. Apple)
- China becoming a premier market for introducing new technology

Sizing the Opportunity: Change the Business Models

The IoT signals a major change in business models for many businesses. IoT will help companies create new value streams for customers, institute processes that speed time to market, triage market performance, and respond rapidly to customer needs. Fitness trackers like Fitbit and Jawbone already aggregate data about our fitness habits and health stats and share these with their strategic partners.[1] There are plenty of organizations keen to get their hands on that kind of data for marketing and other purposes. The most important thing when considering how the IoT will affect your business is to think bigger—much bigger.

It is not simply about what products you can make "smart," provide business efficiencies, or how you might sell that data to customers and associates. The IoT will change the playing field, and every business needs to consider its implications.

Real-time information: A significant part of the IoT is not so much about smart devices as it is about sensors. These minute innovations attached to everything from yogurt cups to the cement in bridges will record and send data into the Cloud. Analytics allows businesses to collect increasingly specific feedback on the use of a product or equipment when these break and even what users might want in the future.[2] With IoT, organizations can capture data about their processes and products in a timely fashion to create new revenue streams, improve operational efficiency, and increase customer loyalty. The need to dig deep and provide well-informed recommendations based upon real-time data is set to rise astronomically. At first, in-house staffers or consulting firms might perform such services.

IoT: A Techno-Economist Derivation

An alternative way to look at an IoT product is like an intranetworking of sensors and an internetwork of external systems connected to provide data to the software-defined product and analytics. The cost of these connections rises linearly, but the resulting value from the data they collect rises exponentially—nicely fitting Metcalfe's law:

$$V \propto n^k \text{ or Value} \propto (\text{Total connections})^k$$

Smearing this observation along the IoT tech range, which gets more and more networked, springs a different way to explain why the consequence economy will be so enormous.

The value of an IoT product is relational to the number of data sources in the system:

$$V(\text{IoT product}) \propto (\text{data sources})^k$$

The value of an IoT product line is proportional to the number of IoT products in the system:

$$V(\text{IoT product line}) \propto (\text{IoT products})^k$$

The value of an IoT ecosystem is proportional to the square of the number of IoT product lines in the system:

$$V(\text{IoT ecosystem}) \propto (\text{IoT product lines})^{2k}$$

And finally, the value of an outcome economy is proportional to the square of the number of IoT ecosystems in the system:

$$V(\text{Outcome Economy}) \propto (\text{IoT ecosystems})^{4k}$$

Figure 1.3 Business intelligence obtained from data analysis

Using substitution, we get:

$$V\,(\text{Outcome Economy})\ \alpha\ (\text{sources of data})^{8k}$$

Or put an alternative way, the value of an outcome economy is highly exponentially related to the number of data sources within it.

Economies are going to be amalgamations of product, service, and outcome economies. Those that are more outcome based will outpace those that are more product or service based. However, the biggest macro-level significance is that the new economy is all about data—data that are transformed into valuable information by the IoT.

The combination of IoT, data analytics, and behavioral science enables us to reach the highest level of empirical power in the DIKW (data, information, knowledge, and wisdom) pyramid framework (Figure 1.3). We can use data mining to extract information from data and knowledge engineering to extract knowledge from information. But to transform knowledge into wise behavioral predictions, we need to exploit new sources of personalized data offered by the IoT.

Future Jobs in IoT Connected Economy

What are the IoT jobs of the future as companies strive to implement IoT strategies?

Over time, however, business professionals well-versed in the specific skills will handle these. Intelligent software would be deployed to perform analysis for business-minded end-users. Efficient, intelligent operations would be the outcome. Our phones used to be for making phone calls. Today, consumers expect a lot more from the device they carry in their pocket. Therefore, though strange or unnecessary at first glance to have a smart tennis racket, an IoT-enabled frying pan, or a smart yoga mat, these are just the first forays into the world of the IoT. Today's smart grid already supplies data to utility companies and allows organizations to make on-the-fly decisions on pricing, logistics, sales, and support, deployment, and so forth.

With IoT on the rise, companies will be expecting and training their employees to cover skills that weren't much in demand before such as:

- *The CIoTO / CDO: chief IoT officer / chief data officer*
  - The need of ready access to data access will increase concomitantly with increased data volumes overall.
- *The IoT business designer*
  - Individual responsible for determining unexplored business models and processes are likely to command a premium.
- *Circuit designers, hardware designers, microcontroller programmers*
  - For developing semiconductor solutions (things) for IoT products
- *"Fuller stack" developers*
  - Employers will value developers who can offer everything from user experience (UX) to Cloud skills, and everything in between
- *IoT architects*
  - Compensating for the increasing architectural complexity of IoT stacks
- *Data designers/data scientists/statisticians*
  - Looking to extract value from huge amounts of data generated by IoT devices.
- *Machine learning specialists*
  - For developing machine learning (historical data) applications.
- *Security consultants*
  - Security professionals will be needed to guard against breaches in data protection, and to offer us some peace of

mind that our data is not being accessed by those we would
prefer not to access it

- *Mechatronics engineers*
  - For developing human–physical interactions.
- *App developers*
  - For developing IoT applications for smart "devices"
- *Electrical installation engineers*
  - For installing and maintaining IoT infrastructure (nodes)
- *Analytical skills*
  - Analytics employees will need baseline computer skill as
    well as familiarity with data processing frameworks like
    Hadoop.
- *Software development*
  - Boeing is requiring programmers to work on simulations
    and analytics.
  - Rapid development of new services in Cloud ecosystems;
    testing and development of new software for applications
- *Infrastructure management*
  - Big data lakes require familiarity with virtualized
    environments.

There will also be changes to business models as more and more companies adopt the trend.

- *As-a-service to mechanical or electronic products*
  - Rolls-Royce: power by the hour
  - Michelin: kilometer by the hour
- *Guarantees of high-level performance*
  - Rolls-Royce: zero-based disruption
  - FANUC: zero downtime

How Can Businesses Profit from the Economy of Things?

Companies across industries must grasp the scale of IoT transformation
that will occur over the next decade and get ready for its impact.[5] These
questions can help identify useful steps that executives across industries
could take:

- *What is your plan to manage products with IoT instrumentation and real-time insights?*
- *How will your IoT device generate new value through improved asset utilization, risk management, and efficiency?*
- *In what ways can your organization analyze IoT data and act on the resulting insights to monetize physical assets before the rest of the industry catches up?*
- *How will you define your role(s) in new marketplaces that emerge in the new economy of things?*

Understanding the IoT Business Value Proposition: Where Changes Will Happen

IoT is creating new opportunities for business in five main ways:

- *New business models*: The IoT will help companies create new value streams for customers, institute processes that speed time to market, triage market performance, and respond rapidly to customer needs.
- *Real-time information on mission-critical systems*: With IoT, organizations can capture more data about their processes and products in a timely fashion to create new revenue streams, improve operational efficiency, and increase customer loyalty.
- *Diversification of revenue streams*: The IoT can help companies create new services and new revenue streams on top of traditional products, for example, vending machine vendors offering inventory management to those who supply the goods in the machine.
- *Global visibility*: The IoT will make it easier for enterprises to see across the business regardless of location, including tracking effectiveness and efficacy from one end of the supply chain to the other.
- *Efficient, intelligent operations*: Access to information from autonomous end points, as today's smart grid already supplies to utility companies, will allow organizations to make on-the-fly decisions on pricing, logistics, sales, and support deployment, and so on.

Figure 1.4 shows eight verticals[5] identified which are directly benefitting using Internet of Things.

Retail operations have until now had relatively few functions fully connected. Sure, the point of sales systems connected to inventory management systems and security systems have become intertwined with video, audio, and sensory technology. Overall, this is mostly at the individual store level and provides little opportunity for retail franchises to manage. The "customer is king" and the king demands an excellent consumer experience; the IoT can play a central role in delivering it. When customers call, retail agents will know who they are, their buying history, and what they might want to purchase next. The IoT allows for innovation, a lift in sales, and a happier customer base. During manufacturing at an automobile manufacturing facility, there are dozens of tools connected to networks and storage devices, but often, this information is kept in discrete silos. The IoT will deliver this information to a central intelligence forum, where it can then be used to quickly improve processes and achieve operational goals. Medical hospitals collect massive amounts of data. What if that information was connected to a central or aggregated intelligence management structure allowing deep, complex analysis? Sure, hospital staff handles the distribution of drugs and monitoring of blood pressure. With the IoT, this data will be channeled into actions to dramatically improve care, reduce the length of hospital stays including minimizing re-admission to hospitals, and lower the transmission of diseases and infection rates (*source*: Kate E. Pickett).

Automotive-Certain industries have such a great deal of information, change and connection to the IoT that automotive gets its own subsection. AT&T has published information about the future for automotive, including that nine of the top 10 fleet management providers in the United States make use of IoT connectivity from AT&T, and they predict that there will be 9.7 million active fleet management systems in use in North America by 2019. Most vehicles will have IoT connection; vehicles for transporting goods and people, work and commercial vehicles will be "smart" vehicles. What would these smart vehicles do? Smart vehicles would make use of data in a more analytical fashion. They would integrate new data sources to realize efficiencies, including predictive capabilities for performance, maintenance, and operations. A future

Transportation	Healthcare	Housing and hospitality	Industry
• Accident avoidance • Car sharing • Private hire and taxi platforms • Driverless cars • Public transport fleet and route management • Telematics • Traffic jam reduction	• At-home recovery and rehabilitation • Chronic disease monitoring • Medicine consumption optimization • Non-observance reduction • Early identification of diseases or risk factors • Smart pharmaceutical R&D • Time Savings from better treatment	• Energy savings • Fire alarm • House automation • Remote burglar alarms • White and brown goods • Telematics • Smart kitchen in restaurants • Smart energy in hospitality	• Express and parcel delivery • Smart construction • Smart logistics • Container tracking • Rail car tracking • Fleet management • Smart manufacturing

Retail and wholesale	Utilities	Primary sectors	Public administration
• Stockout and theft reduction • Smart logistic fleet Management • Automatic checkout • Express and parcel delivery • Sports articles	• Smart grid • Smart water • Smart gas	• Precision farming: Crop management • Precision farming: Livestock management • Smart extraction (oil and gas, mining)	• Public administration efficiency • Street light control • Waste management • Education classroom management

Figure 1.4 IoT application in vertical segments

scenario is the automotive management market dominated by several providers with installed IoT bases. IoT is paired with big data within the auto industry, as illustrated by AT&T with its vast experience in the U.S. transport market. The IoT already accounts for about 2 million vehicle units in North America.

The full portfolio of AT&T includes basic fleet tracking needs and a consultative selection of more advanced solutions. Vehicle fleets commonly adopt telematics systems from AT&T to improve management efficiency, proof of delivery, and driver productivity.[7] Applications streamline dispatch, routing, tracking, and reporting. AT&T alone expects to have 10 million connected cars by 2017. At least 27 airlines also use AT&T's Cargo View that monitors 280,000 containers globally. IoT has a bright future with vehicles, including driverless cars and taxis, tracking of shipments, locations of planes, cargo, air and road freight, fleets, as well as providing navigation and vehicle upkeep to ensure safety. Applying IoT to fleets and individual vehicles will decrease Department of Transportation violations and motor accidents and save significantly on insurance costs. The IoT will further provide cost-effective software updates to vehicles, resulting in huge returns and savings. Then, of course, there is the field of autonomous self-driving vehicles. This topic could make a whole book on its own. However, for the purposes of our chapter, its sufficient to know that fully autonomous vehicles, capable of driverless operation and safe travel, will be a reality by 2019. In terms of business

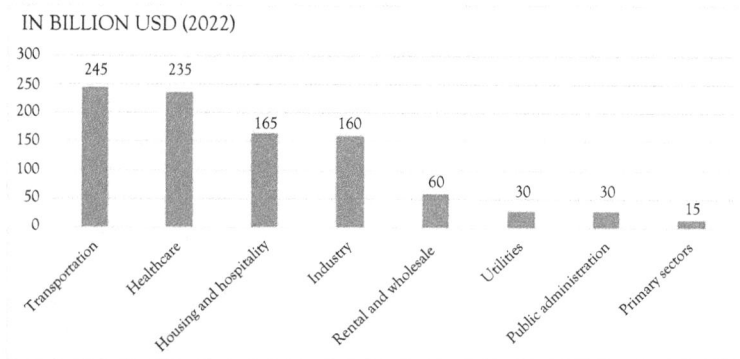

IN BILLION USD (2022)

Figure 1.5 IoT's GDP impact by various sectors in vertical segments

Source: IMF Statistics.[4]

opportunity, automotive is one of the best fields right now. IoT has the capability to disrupt and explode the growth of the automotive industry, particularly with autonomous vehicles. Vehicles do not just include cars, trucks, and airplanes, but marine vehicles too!

Figure 1.5 shows the impact on Gross Domestic Product (GDP) by various sectors in vertical segments by implementing the Internet of Things.

Implications for Semiconductor and Software Companies: The Race for More Standardization and Lower Cost

Semiconductor leaders in the market that want to address their challenges and capture the IoT's enormous growth potential might be tempted to move ahead quickly, but this would be a mistake. The IoT is unlike any high-tech segment that they have previously served, and their traditional strategies may not succeed with the new customer base. With so much at stake, semiconductor companies need to re-evaluate all aspects of their businesses and make some radical changes. From a strategic perspective, three tactics will be particularly important.

Finding the Right Niches

There may be many profitable IoT niches within the fragmented market, and semiconductor companies will need to identify and quickly serve the most promising ones. As noted earlier, the use of a platform approach to cover multiple niches will be critical, since R&D costs may otherwise be prohibitive. When companies are selecting the right niches, one of the most important considerations are their own capabilities and expertise. For instance, a semiconductor player that has strong ties to consumer electronics companies and possesses full system integration capabilities might decide to focus on wearables and smart-home devices, providing all appropriate chips as well as software/algorithms, devices, and servers or other infrastructure. By contrast, a company with specific expertise with high-reliability integrated circuits and security might want to focus on medical electronics and industrial automation, providing a full IoT solution in this area. In some cases, companies may need to form alliances to cover all the desired niches. For example, a small player specializing in connectivity might form collaborative partnerships with another semiconductor players or IoT companies to offer a full solution, thereby allowing it to serve as many verticals as possible without developing any additional in-house capabilities.

How would you identify application- and vertical-specific growth pockets?

- Perform an in-depth assessment of market opportunity and the requirement for each IoT vertical/application.
- Identify growth pockets that fit well with specific products/capabilities of each semiconductor company.
- Make bold moves if required to enter a specific application vertical.

Developing a Solid Strategy to Seek Value Beyond Silicon

When developing and marketing new products, semiconductor companies must identify the features their customers' value most and incorporate them into their products and services. To do so, they should think about solutions that include software, services, and other offerings, rather than maintaining their traditional focus on chips. Semiconductor companies should also consider even more radical changes as they attempt to move beyond silicon, including shifting to a completely new business model—for instance, one that focuses on usage-based pricing. To mitigate risks and avoid moving too far from their core competencies, semiconductor companies should carefully test any new approaches before widespread rollout. For example, they could create a team to test it in a niche application market and then undertake a broader rollout with more applications.

- Understand application and vertical-specific value drivers for the end user (How does the consumer of enterprise derive value).
- Identify opportunities beyond silicon (e.g., system integration, software) to generate value for the customers.
- Test alternative business models to capture more of the generated value (e.g., usage based).

Revisiting (and Revolutionizing) the Corporate Operating Model

Since the IoT presents new challenges, semiconductor companies should consider an overhaul of their operating model, with a focus on organizational changes. For instance, most semiconductor companies now include a limited number of large business units, a focus on direct sales and field-application engineers, and an emphasis on application-specific R&D programs. A more appropriate structure for the IoT might emphasize multimarket sales approach and a greater reliance on channel partners, such as distributors, as part of the go-to-market strategy. Other possible areas for improvement include the following:

- *R&D*: As noted earlier, R&D should focus on platform development, rather than the creation of application-specific solutions, since it allows companies to cover multiple products while controlling costs. In some cases, companies may be able to license another company's intellectual property to build a platform—for instance, for image processing— thereby gaining access to new technologies while reducing development costs.
- *Investments*: Rather than making a limited number of large portfolio bets under the direction of a business-unit lead, companies should make small bets on many different applications in diverse markets. This diversification approach will help companies avoid the common mistake of allocating most funds to core products, rather than using them to develop new applications.
- *Change management*: Management should focus on helping staff build new skills, such as those related to software development, if they decide to cultivate such capabilities.

Bringing IoT into Your Organization's Change Management: Product Lifecycle Management

The IoT has the potential to make an impact across the product lifecycle. In the innovation phase, companies can imagine new business models, new products, and new services. In the definition phase, companies can benefit from a better understanding of customer needs to develop new products and services. They can also improve existing products and services. Data fed back from products in the field can be fed into the development of the next generation of products. Product developers can review feedback information about reliability problems, failure rates, and customer complaints corresponding to specific usage conditions and product performance levels. They can analyze information about typical component lifetimes, average repair and replacement rates, disposal costs, and actual disassembly costs and times.

All of the previous information can be used to improve future components and products. Data about the product's performance reliability, availability, maintainability, and safety during realization and use can be used to avoid repeating errors and reduce development time and effort. Designs that have been successful in existing products could be re-used. Re-using successful designs should reduce development time. And due to the use of a proven design, there would be fewer breakdowns and changes during product operation. Increased customer satisfaction should result from a more reliable product. In the realization phase, for example on the company's shop floor, if a component is incorrectly positioned for assembly, its position can be automatically corrected. Components can be tracked through manufacturing and assembly so that anything that goes wrong can be corrected quickly. In their use phase, products can be tracked throughout their lifetime. Immediate support can be provided, if needed.

The IoT offers opportunities to get a better understanding of the way products to behave over the lifecycle. This can be used to optimize the use and maintenance activities of the product. For example, the collection and analysis of data from a fleet of commercial vehicles enables a different maintenance schedule for each vehicle based upon its specific usage conditions. Engine components can be monitored for fatigue. Compared to maintenance at fixed intervals, this can lead to a reduction in downtime and maintenance costs. The number of component breakdowns can be reduced. Maintenance practices for all sorts of household appliances, ranging from water heaters to refrigerators, can be improved, shifting from intervention after breakdown to predictive maintenance. As a result, there would be a fewer component failures, reduced maintenance intervention, and reduced maintenance costs. The IoT also enables remote upgrade of a product's control software. This reduces downtime compared to a traditional approach of taking the product to a service center for an upgrade. In the retire/recycle phase, products and components could be tracked, identified, and treated in an environmentally correct way. Based on information about production dates, maintenance dates, repaired parts, replaced parts and usage conditions, better decisions can be taken about which components to dispose of, which to re-manufacture, and which to re-use.

How Big Data Is Powering the IoT Revolution

The disruptive IoT technology needs new infrastructures, including software and hardware applications as well as an operating system; enterprises must handle the influx of data that begins flowing in and examine it in real time as it evolves by the minute. That is where big data arrives in the picture; big data analytics tools have the capacity to handle large volumes of data generated from IoT devices that create a continuous stream of information.[9] But, to differentiate between them, IoT provides data from which big data analytics can extract information to generate insights required of it. However, IoT conducts data on a completely different scale, so the analytics solution must accommodate its needs of processing and rapid ingestion followed by a fast and accurate extraction.

There are many solutions available that provide near real-time analytics on large-sized data sets, and necessarily change a full-rack database into a small server that processes up to 100 TB, so small amount of hardware is needed. The analytics database of next generation leverages Graphics Processing Unit (GPU) technology, thus enabling even more downsizing of the hardware, that is, 5 TB on a laptop or a big database in the car. This largely helps IoT organizations correlate the evolving number of data sets, which helps them adapt to changing trends and acquire real-time responses, solving the challenge regarding size and compromising on the performance.

Consequence of Moore's Law

Moore's law impacts mostly electronic costs before impacting data pricing, we find that, as could be expected, the collection and the use of data see their costs alleviated from one generation of semiconductors to the next through Moore's law. Hence the prospect for collecting data gets more attractive from one semiconductor generation to the next. Data generated increases exponentially, partially because of Moore's law and wider use of computers, but also because population increases exponentially.

Meanwhile, Moore's law allows us a lot more power to process data in ways that were not possible before. There is no reason to doubt that devices connected to IoT will soon be flooding in the mass market. We will see compact, connected sensors and actuators make their way into everyday consumer electronics, household appliances, and general infrastructure. Network and semiconductor manufacturers will no doubt benefit from this movement, but big data vendors should also be cheering. With all things connected to the Internet that opens up more real-time data inventory to sell. Figure 1.6 shows the estimated revenue for hardware and for the services and software combined. As indicated, the combined services and software revenue are expected to reach $2 trillion by 2022. As per European Commission data of 2017 census shows (Table 1.1) different IoT units installed based on various categories like Consumer, Generic business and Vertical businesses.[4]

Social media is one area that is witnessing data explosion. Because of the vast amounts of data available if your account for every site on the web, we need new methods to process data and begin finding meaningful

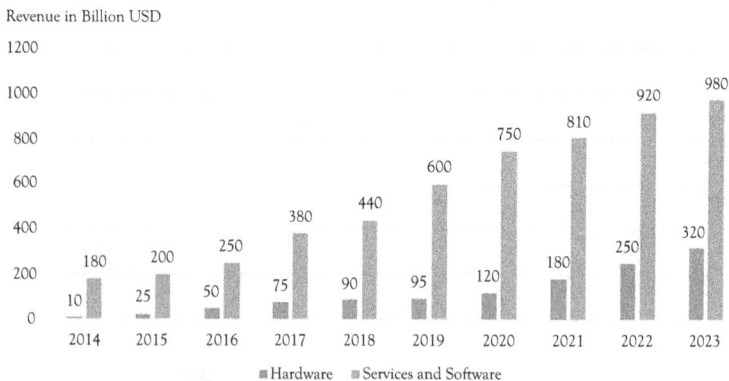

Figure 1.6 Enterprise estimated revenue from IoT

Source: IoT-European Platform Initiative statistics.[4]

Table 1.1 IoT units installed based on category (excluding automotive)

Category	2014	2015	2016	2017
Consumer	2277	3023	4024	13,509
Generic business	623	815	1092	4408
Vertical business	898	1065	1276	2880
Grand total	3807	4902	6392	20,797

Source: European Commission Data 2017.

conclusions as this data is highly unstructured.[3] This cycle of innovation and the new technologies at the heart of it will enable individuals, businesses, and society to gain greater value from the flood of big data, at much the same rate that Moore's law has predicted for the underlying evolution of technology itself in the last half century.

Machine Learning/Artificial Intelligence and IoT: Understanding the IoT Business Value Proposition

Machine learning (a subset of artificial intelligence) uses supervised learning techniques on historical data to make cognitive decisions. The greater the quantity of historic data, the better the decision-making capabilities of the algorithm. This philosophy makes IoT the ideal use case for machine learning as the data generated by the devices are usually very frequent.[10] The following are a few common scenarios where machine learning works together with IoT to enable business optimizations:

- *Anomaly monitoring*: Azure machine learning can be used to detect anomalies in time series data, in data feeds sent by the IoT devices that are uniformly spaced in time. Anomalies like spikes and dips, positive and negative trends, can be detected using a machine learning algorithm monitoring the live stream of device feeds.
- *Predictive maintenance*: Predictive maintenance directly impacts the costs to an organization, which makes it one of the most popular machine learning solutions. The ability of machine learning algorithms to foresee possibilities of a

device failing, remaining life of an equipment, and causes of failure can enable the business to optimize operational cost by reducing the maintenance time significantly.

- *Vehicle telemetry*: The capability of machine learning solutions to ingest millions of events from vehicles to improve their safety, reliability, and driving experience makes it a desirable technology to adopt for transportation and logistics industries.

How IoT Has Made Machine Learning More Effective

Despite the much-vaunted merits of machine learning, the effectiveness of its algorithms can still heavily rely on what data is fed into them. An abundance of relevant data can impressively fuel a machine learning algorithm much like useful clues can help a detective to reach wiser conclusions. It is exactly for this reason that IoT can make an ideal use case for the technology. A wide range of IoT devices can generate data at a very high frequency, which can then be placed into a machine learning algorithm. For example, information provided from devices on which a firm strongly relies can help that firm foresee how those devices could falter or how long they might remain functional with the aid of machine learning. These revelations can then assist the business in trimming maintenance time. Transportation and logistics industries can also be attracted to machine learning. This is because machine learning can source extensive data from vehicles to assist in enhancing the safety and reliability.

Blockchain, IoT, and Supply Chain

Chapter 3 discusses blockchains in extensive detail. They are the core technology behind cryptocurrencies like Bitcoin, Litecoin, ether, and others. You can imagine blockchains as decentralized databases.[8] In a general database, you need a central authority for data integrity. This can become a bottleneck for running efficient and fast services. In a blockchain ecosystem, data is stored on decentralized nodes and there is no need for central authentication. Mathematical algorithms ensure the integrity of data. In recent years, there has been a shift in customer expectations. Customers have become used to high-quality products delivered fast at cheaper prices. So, commodity producers and distributors are looking for ways to improve their supply chains. They must reduce operating costs, manage risks, improve product quality, and provide better customer service. As a result, companies are looking for better solutions. Besides, decentralizing the supply chains, a combination of the Blockchain and IoT can improve supply chains in the following ways:

- End-to-end real-time control and visibility
- Data-driven insights
- Regulation compliance
- Enterprise resource planning (ERP) integration
- Global supply chain automated transactions

In an IoT context, security is always a challenge. There is always a fear of some possible hacks. Security needs to be addressed when we think of automating important processes using IoT technology. The Blockchain is also seen to secure the IoT. There are smart contracts expected to execute between devices. During the execution of smart contracts, responsibility issues may crop for the actions taken by devices. Blockchain technology can help fix these responsibility issues and hence smooth execution of smart contracts. Blockchain, in general, will help to improve the trust between devices and interested parties. Existing IoT solutions are expensive because of the high infrastructure and maintenance cost associated with centralized Clouds, large server farms, and networking equipment. The sheer amount of communications that will have to be handled when there are tens of billions of IoT devices will increase those costs substantially. A solution to this business problem could be decentralized IoT infrastructures. Blockchain technology can help the decentralization of IoT networks.

Challenges for The Internet of (Economic) Things Ecosystem

It is projected that by the year 2020, approximately 20.8 billion things will be utilized around the globe, as the IoT continues its expansion; and as a result, we will also witness major safety concerns and cybersecurity issues, as hackers would break into traffic systems, the power grid, and any other system that is linked and contains sensitive data that can shut down an entire city. In Chapter 9, we discuss how quantum physics has a robust solution to the threats posed to cyber security. Internet security platforms such as Z-scaler provide IoT devices with protection against unauthorized access of data with a Cloud-based solution. You can route the traffic via the platform and implement policies for the devices so that they won't interact with unnecessary servers. Big data and IoT share a closely knitted future. It is evident that the two fields will generate new solutions and opportunities that will have a long-lasting impact.

Security and privacy: There is no doubt that IoT will improve our lives, and that big data and related analytical techniques such as predictive analytics and machine learning will provide a lot of value to many organizations. But like most other advanced technologies, they are also subject to a misuse. This leads to a rather important discussion on the potential risks with IoT and sophisticated data analysis.

Hackers and physical dangers: With the billions of IoT devices of the future, there is a risk that a malicious hacker could take control of a device or steal data from it. This may not be too much of a problem for an Internet-connected light bulb or bathroom scale, but what about power plants, self-driving cars, or medical devices? The harm or destruction could be enormous. In fact, severe and worrying examples have already been demonstrated. In my mind, the biggest problem for IoT in the coming years is security, as many product developers either do not have the skills to make a secure and hacker-resistant product, or don't care to try. Some of the solutions to these cybersecurity issues will be permanently resolved with advancements in quantum computing as discussed in Chapter 9.

Organizational (cultural change): This may be the biggest obstacle. Change is hard but necessary, especially for established organizations that, for decades, have been so successful with their existing business models, practices, and processes. It isn't easy for information technology (IT) and operational technology (OT) to come together and cooperate, as it isn't very easy for vendors to embrace common open standards, but it has been done in past and its benefits are undeniable. Change is mostly a question of communication, leadership, retraining, and keeping an open mind. Opportunities as large as IoT provide a strong incentive for everyone to cooperate.

Government: IoT benefits the government in the form of smarter cities, Government also has a role to play in regulating and agenda setting, ensuring that IoT develops and grows by applying regulations in some areas but also by means of easing regulatory impediments in other areas to encourage new business models based on IoT.

IoT and the Co-Economy

IoT will emerge as the first step in bringing about a co-economy where:

- People and organizations cooperate and collaborate in more and different and deeper ways;
- Devices communicate with any device;
- Openness rules;
- Proprietary becomes a temporary experience; and
- Customers are free to choose based on what they want and need, rather than being constrained by the attributes of the thing—be it physical, logical, or virtual.

IoT technologies are impacting the supply chains with the following key transformative trends (Figure 1.7), in the order of increasing potential of positive business impact.

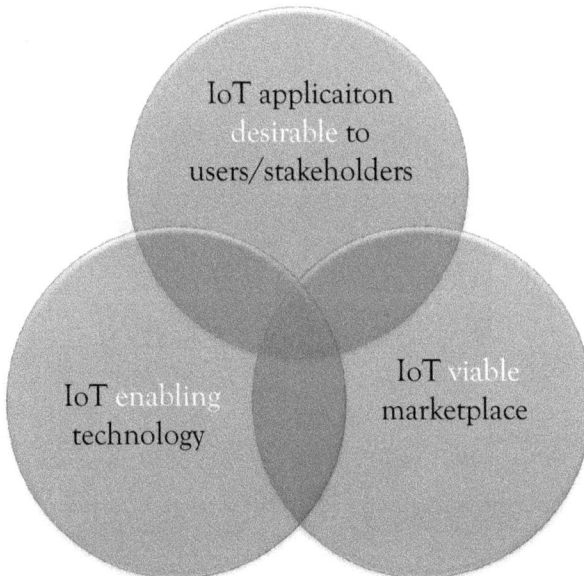

Figure 1.7 IoT ecosystem

Optimizations in Individual Supply Chain Functions

Each individual supply chain function such as manufacturing, transportation, logistics, and service are realizing operational improvements due to IoT technologies. For example, the manufacturing sector is witnessing significant bottom-line reduction due to real-time visibility into business key performance indicators (KPI) such as overall equipment effectiveness (OEE), zero unplanned downtime, and predictive maintenance. The transportation and logistics sectors are benefiting from significantly lower downtime due to real-time monitoring of trucks, on-time arrivals due to location tracking and intelligent routing, reduction in liabilities due to driver behavior monitoring, and reduction in in-transit damages due to cargo monitoring.

Interconnecting the Supply Chain (Digital Thread)

Today, individual functions in the supply chain operate in their own silo. Interconnection of the entire supply chain in a seamless digital thread delivers a new level of business benefit (Figure 1.8). For example, when an increase in the product demand causes warehouse inventory levels to drop at a rate faster than usual, a new manufacturing order can be automatically planned and released. Shipments can be automatically planned

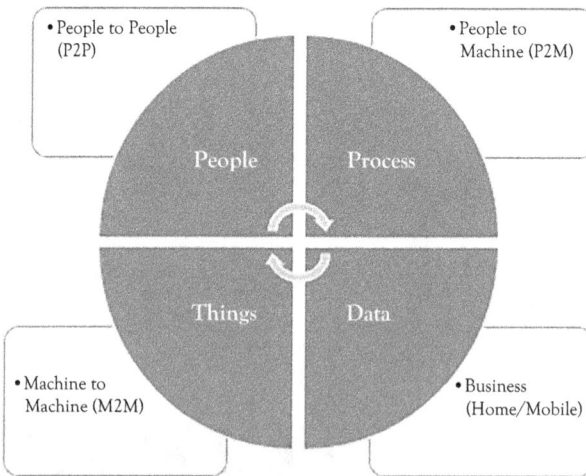

Figure 1.8 Internet of everything

and communicated to third-party logistics companies in real time, and product demand planning can be re-evaluated to consider the surge in the demand signals.

New Business Models: Servitization

Perhaps the most disruptive impact IoT technologies have on the supply chain is that it enables new business models. Servitization, or selling products as a service, as a major trend that is disrupting many industries. Stemming from IoT-based monitoring and predictions, companies can sell a service with a pay-as-you-go model, instead of selling a product. For example, an engine manufacturer can sell engine-hours of operation with uptime guarantees, instead of selling an engine and annual maintenance contracts. This allows their customer to shift their expense models from capital expenditure (CapEx) to operational expenditure (OpEx) and change their consumption patterns in a fundamental way.

A "Perfect Storm" of Technology, Economy, and Culture

IoT is bringing together three key elements—technology, economy, and culture to form what can be popularly described as a "perfect storm." Whereas a lethal brew of elements is typically associated with a dangerous storm, IoT's wide open opportunities can be embraced by any organization that wants to be involved. In the process, we're all experiencing a massive rebalancing of key economic, social, environmental, and privacy/security priorities.

The IoT is the next industrial revolution, and it will transform the way we live forever. Quite possibly, IoT will be as disruptive as the Internet itself, in particular, when combined with big data and predictive analytics. Products in almost all industries will become smart and provide services previously unimaginable. We will also be able to monitor and understand systems to an unprecedented level, with many benefits as a result. Comfort, safety, health, and the environment will all benefit greatly. On the negative side, there are a lot of security, privacy, and ethical questions arising from the widespread use of IoT devices and advanced

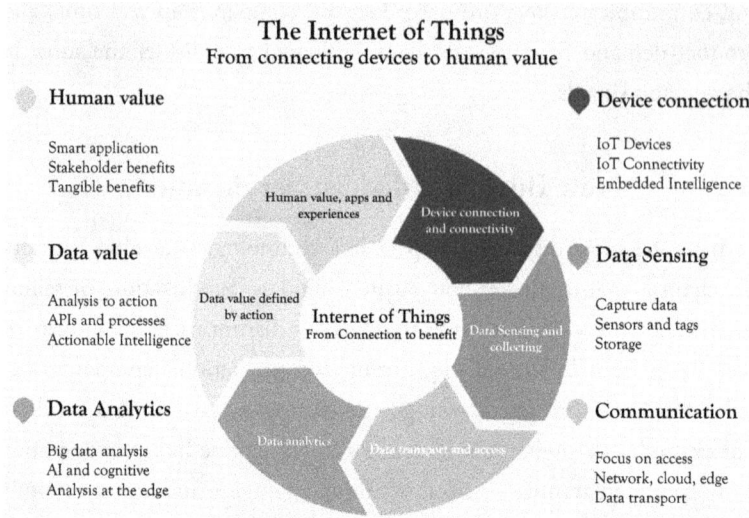

Figure 1.9 Ergonomics of IoT systems

data analytics. We could be monitored at each step we take, everywhere. It will never again be possible to be anonymous and leave no digital footprint. Figure 1.9 explains the complete new impact on the human race by changing dimensions with new ergonomics defined by IoT.

Like all advances in history, new technology provides many benefits, but if used in the wrong way, it could create a lot of harm. The same goes for IoT, big data, and predictive analytics. Utilized in the right way, they will greatly improve our quality of life and the environment. But used in the wrong way, individuals, malicious organizations, or even the state will be able to control us like never before. We are currently in the early years of IoT adoption, and standardization issues are limiting initial success. Once the market enjoys a more limited set of well-established interoperability standards that all the main suppliers embrace and agree upon, IoT will deliver even more value. One thing is for sure: the world will never be like it was.

As connected devices have proliferated, and networks have penetrated into remote regions, the potential for IoT solutions and growth in the IoT ecosystem has increased. If IoT solutions can improve enterprise adopters' fundamental business values, not only savings and risk management but also revenue growth and innovation, demand and new uses for connected devices will grow. At a higher level, IoT has a role to play in helping companies create more sustained value through moving from a one-time transaction focus to a continuous, relationship focus with customers, suppliers, workers, and assets. While technical issues that affect reliable connectivity and performance still exist, enterprises will be more willing to adopt IoT solutions if they can see significant, lasting benefits to the business that outweigh the real and perceived risks of connection. Participants in the IoT ecosystem will need to work together to create solutions that improve enterprise adopters' business performance, not just in the short term but sustained over time. In so doing, they will unlock the business value for enterprise adopters and grow the IoT market for everyone. The potential for the next stage of IoT is unbounded and it will be shaped by the decisions that participants in the IoT ecosystem make today.

The Real Challenge and What's Next

IoTs greatest challenge isn't technical; it's the economic and business challenge. The lack of standardization and strong enough security are technological challenges, but we can and will solve them. But they won't be solved, nor will IoT get past its hype and its early adopters, until the IoT helps companies make more money. This also needs a good purchasing power in the populace.

Just as the Internet is part of every business, so too will be the IoT, which is its natural technical evolution. The revolution comes from how anyone chooses to use it in your business. Given the IoT is coming, all businesses must plan for it. Companies should develop their IoT plan, this will reduce competitive risk and prepare companies to decide when to spend the time and resources needed to leverage the IoT to develop their IoT business and product line.

Conclusion

IoT creates new business models that can attract more and different revenue-generating customers, while offering new service delivery options boost customer satisfaction and convenience with lower support costs. Remote service and support both increase in efficiency and lower costs. New go-to-market strategies can open markets that previously couldn't effectively address. The wealth of information, about your products and your customers' use of those products, collected through IoT can help you develop new and much improved offerings and attract more and different customers. Some of this knowledge, as well as the data itself, can generate revenue, as partners and even customers are increasingly willing to pay for pertinent, timely, and actionable information as a service.

IoT makes possible the profitable transition to a service model and the corresponding ability to digitize the production environment. A digital economy can vastly facilitate the service model, and the payoff can be tremendous. Clearly, IoT touches all aspects of the customer–partner relationship. In the IoT economy, participant won't always be either the provider or the customer. The bi-directional nature of IoT impacts the buying as well as the selling, the usage as well as the manufacture and distribution of products and services. In effect, IoT will a broader impact on the entire value chain.

References

[1] Behmann, F., and K. Wu. 2015. *Collaborative Internet of Things (C-IoT): For Future Smart Connected Life and Business*. John Wiley & Sons.

[2] *Precision: Principles, Practices and Solutions for the Internet of Things*.

[3] *It's Not About the Technology: Developing the Craft of Thinking for a High Technology Corporation*.

[4] Definition of a Research and Innovation Policy Leveraging Cloud Computing and IoT Combination—Final Report; Luxembourg, Publications Office of the European Union; 2014.

[5] Hughes, A. Manufacturing Metrics in an IoT World. Measuring the Progress of the Industrial Internet of Things (www.lnsresearch.com).

[6] McKinsey Global Institute Analysis. June 2015. *The Internet of Things: Mapping the Value Beyond the Hype*, 125. McKinsey Global Institute (MGI). www.mckinsey.com/mgi

[7] *The ThingWorx Guide to the Internet of Things* (http://thingworx.com/ thingworxanalytics).

[8] Bahga, A., and V. Madisetti. 2017. *Blockchain Applications: A Hands-On Approach*.VPT.

[9] Schmarzo, B. 2013. *Big Data—Understanding How Data Powers Big Business*. John Wiley & Sons.

[10] Bell, J. 2014. *Machine Learning—Hands-on for Developers and Technical Professionals*. John Wiley & Sons.

CHAPTER 2

Impact of Big Data and Artificial Intelligence on Economy

Sreenivas Adiki

Introduction

Big data and artificial intelligence (AI) are revolutionizing the business processes that impact internal business units and end customers. Although AI has existed since the past three to four decades, it is the power achieved by processing and storage technologies due to rapid advancement of Moore's law that makes a difference in the way business processes are being automated to reduce operational costs today. An example of the potential impact of AI technologies on the economy is the decline in the number of jobs for those employed in the customer services industry.[15, 19, 28, 29, 30]

Another upcoming disruptive application of AI that is being heavily invested by Fortune 500 companies like Google, Apple, and Uber is the self-driving technology platforms that primarily depends on processing data in real-time and make intelligent human like driving decisions. Additionally, the economy is also being affected by prominent use of AI bots[20] such as Amazon Echo, Google Home, and Apple Home Pod, which are changing the way people interact with systems for information, support, and e-commerce services. Majority of the data generated by the interactions between people and information systems are coming from crowdsourcing or third-party sources like social media, blogs, and feedback interactions.

Experts forecast that AI-based conversational analytics market[15, 17, 20] will be worth more than $600 billion by 2022. Such tremendous growth in data, be it structured, semistructured, or un-structured, is creating enormous opportunities for companies to understand customer behavior from different perspectives and model services based on these insights. Notably, all types of companies need unconventional tools to interact with these data sets and natural language processing (NLP) technologies seem to be the forerunner of processing unstructured data, as users are most comfortable with voice interaction rather than written queries.

Virtual assistants are on the rise due the technological advancements over the past five years, which are powered by NLP and machine learning algorithms. Further, with huge amount of data that is stored on big data platforms, there is a tremendous focus on deep learning to understand the context of the conversations and generate the natural language response. [13, 1, 2, 34]

AI-based deep learning platforms are creating new opportunities for firms in the following areas:

1. New business models: firms with 60:40 workforce to virtual assistant ratio.
2. Knowledge economy: Workforce that needs to be skilled on how to collaborate with virtual assistants, AI bots, and robots.
3. AI systems with the ability of speech recognition: based on context, situation, and emotion. In other words, "a human-like system."

The focus of this chapter is to understand big data and conversational AI systems that have fundamentally changed the paradigm of how data has been processed, stored and accessed. The second last Chapter 12 of this book provides some insights about the emerging business paradigms in an automated economy.

Big Data Systems

It is interesting to know how big data technology was conceptualized before moving on to understand large-scale data processing and storage. Though John Mashey[14] is credited for coining the term "big data" during late 1990s, Roger Magoulas[16] of O'Reilly Radar used this term extensively when Web 2.0[16] was shaping up. It essentially meant a large set of data that was impossible to process with the existing set of tools at the time.

Around 2004 and 2005, Google published the MapReduce[4] paradigm that was aimed at processing all the World Wide Web data that was stored in their data center. Nevertheless, this paradigm was the basis of implementation of "Hadoop Distributed File System (HDFS)[10] and MapReduce"[4] by Yahoo team (under the leadership of Doug Cutting) as a special purpose project called "Nutch," later renamed as "Hadoop."

The project was eventually released as an open source project in 2007 under the Apache Project Foundation. This release was the first major milestone in the evolution of big data platforms and gave a real-life implementation of processing huge data volumes. Though Hadoop originally, was composed of HDFS[10] and MapReduce[4] components written purely on Java technologies, it quickly evolved into a massive distributed parallel processing systems with the addition of YARN[49] and other tools such as Pig[50] and HIVE,[51] which made it easier for the business users to work with the Hadoop ecosystem using SQL and procedure languages.

The availability of these tools facilitated the process of worldwide adoption of Hadoop by technology community and new companies emerged, which started to commercialize big data platforms; noted among these are Hortonworks, Cloudera, and Map-R.

During the last decade, many new tools and frameworks were developed around the Hadoop ecosystem under Apache Project umbrella. Few examples of these tools include Sqoop (a data transfer utility for moving data between relation databases and Hadoop), Impala (analytical database using C++), Mahout (a distributed linear algebra framework), Giraph (a data store processing engine as graphs), Oozie (a job scheduling and monitoring tool on Hadoop), Zookeeper (a distributed configuration and coordination), and NoSQL databases like HBase (a columnar data store that can store very large tables—billions of rows).

The next most significant milestone was the development of the Lambda architecture, which facilitated both real-time and batch processing on the same platform. The development of Lambda architecture led the coexistence of stream processing frameworks like Storm, Spark, Flume, and Flink with batch processing frameworks such as MapReduce. The addition of these frameworks to the Hadoop ecosystem further increased the adoption of big data platforms during the last five years, wherein many large organizations started to invest into strategic projects to gain deeper and analytical insights of their data using machine learning.

One such project example is the real-time recommendations of products or services, which was derived out of huge amounts of data generated through online shopping by customers. Other noted projects consist of real-time fraud detection of credit-card transactions, large-scale image processing for suspect identification, and real-time object detection in driver-less vehicles, to mention a few.

Internet of things (IoT)[44]—machine-to-machine data transfer in real time with thousands of devices connected—are riding on capabilities of flexibility and scalability of big data platforms. The insights from these data sources have improved the quality of manufacturing to a significantly greater percentage, leading to a higher processing efficiency and cost reductions. In general, big data technologies have started to impact every industry in today's economy and have created new "economies of scale," thereby reducing the cost of production of goods and services. Big data and AI have triggered a digital revolution where "customer experience" has become the key performance indicator (KPI) for all organizations.

For instance, millennials and Gen Z have already embraced chat bots and interactive media for carrying out transactions over phones and tablets. Like every other technology, even big data and AI will have to evolve further into smart systems to deliver a human-like experience. The reference architecture depicted in Figure 2.1 provides a reasonably good example of the components of big data architecture and serves as a reference for the details provided in the infographic (Figure 2.1).

A brief introduction of each of the architecture layers can help the audience understand the intended functionality that is fulfilled by the respective component.

Data Ingestion

Data ingestion addresses both streaming and nonstreaming data sources using a distributed parallel processing paradigm and set of application

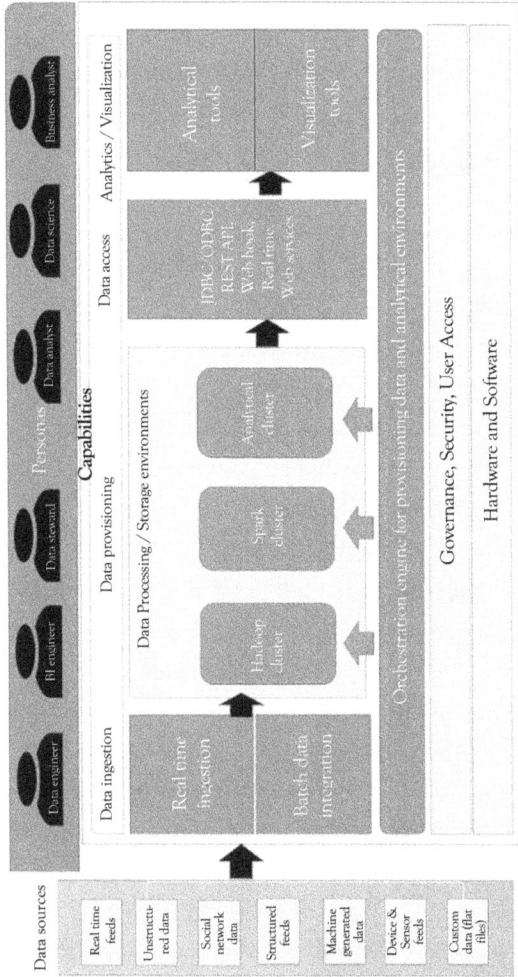

Figure 2.1 Big data reference architecture based on Lambda architecture

programming interfaces (APIs)), integrated with the Hadoop ecosystem. These APIs and tools are designed to handle data from data sources— JSON (Java Script Object Notification), XML (Extensible Mark-up Language), HTML (Hyper Text Markup Language), text, images, streams, RDBMS (Relational Data Base Management Systems), EXCEL, CSV (Comma Separated Variable), and delimited data files—that are classified into semistructured, unstructured, or structured data formats, while considering the 3V's (volume, velocity, and veracity) of data.

Data Processing and Provisioning

Data is processed using two types of processing paradigms: MapReduce for batch data processing and stream processing for real-time data. In its simplest form, MapReduce refers to two distinct tasks that need to be performed by Hadoop programs. The Map job processes the desired data and converts it into another set of data whereby individual data elements are broken down into key–value pairs (also known as tuples). Map operations are "read and write" intensive and are distributed across a cluster of nodes on Hadoop, thus achieving the required performance.[4]

The second task of MapReduce is the Reduce job, which takes the output of the Map job and combines the similar keys and aggregates the values to derive a new set of tuples (key/value) pairs. MapReduce jobs are always performed in a sequence: the map being the first and the reduce following the map job. An intermediate task between Map and Reduce, also known as Shuffle and Sort, distributes and sorts all the data belonging to the same key to the right worker node on the cluster. This operation reduces the processing time required by the Reduce job, and it becomes very effective for the Reduce job to aggregate and publish the data.

Stream processing deals with ingestion and processing of data in real time using distributed "in-memory" parallel processing techniques to achieve a massive processing scale of billions of events that are typically stored in big data systems. Stream processing paradigm consists of processing a given sequence of data (a stream) with a series of operations that are applied to each element in the stream. The operations are computed in memory and the results are stored in optimized data structures that are then consumed by the dashboarding tools. The resultant data is later stored in the big data systems for machine learning and data mining activities.

Apache Spark, Storm, and Flink are the currently used frameworks that support stream processing at scale. A brief description of these popular frameworks is as mentioned below.

(a) Apache Spark is open source cluster-computing processing framework built for speed, ease of use, and analytics. It contains a built-in set of over 50+ operators that can be used to write applications either in Scala, Java, or Python programming languages. Spark Streaming is an extension of the core Spark API that provides high-throughput, fault-tolerant stream processing of ingested data streams. The other three modules that exist on top of the core API are SparkSQL (used for structured data processing using SQL language), SparkMib (a machine library that provides scalable algorithms and speed), and GraphX (a graph computation engine built on top of Spark that enables users to interactively build, transform, and reason about graph-structured data at scale).[5]

(b) Storm is an open-source distributed real-time computational system that reliably processes unbounded streams of data. It is scalable, fault-tolerant, and guarantees processing of ingested data. Storm topology is a graph of "spouts" and "bolts" that are connected with stream groupings. A spout is a resource of streams in a topology and reads tuples from live steams of data that is reliable or unreliable based on the requirements of replay.[41]

Bolts are used to process the data using different functions such as filtering, aggregations, joins, and interact with big data stores. There are eight different built-in stream groupings that are used to define how that stream should be partitioned among the bolt's tasks.

(c) Flink is another parallel stream processing framework that competes with Spark and is also an Apache Software Foundation project. The core of Flink is a distributed streaming dataflow engine. It provides a low-latency and high-throughput latency engine as well as support for event-time processing and state management. Programs can be written in Java, Scala, Python, or SQL (Structured query language) languages and are automatically compiled and optimized into dataflow pipelines that are executed on the distributed cluster.[43]

Orchestration Engine

The orchestration engine is a key component of reference architecture, as it provides a workflow to spin off the required environment based on the user persona. The personas are defined by business units based on requirements such as "self-service" capability to spin-off desired environments and execute the developed code or package. A typical multitenant hierarchical structure is shown in Figure 2.2.

The master or superadministrator is the only user who has full control of the orchestration engine. The superadministrator creates a "tenant administrator" user for each business function. It is then the tenant administrator's job to create and map all the other users to the required environment based on the persona. A sample hierarchy of tenants and users is shown in Figure 2.2 to provide a clear overview of how a multitenant orchestration framework functions.

Big data systems generally integrate with lightweight directory access protocol (LDAP) based active directory systems that supports business and function-based on user groups that are managed at a single location instead of application specific servers. This allows the organizations to delegate the authentication, authorization, and accounting for every user from a centralized server.

Metadata and Lineage

Metadata is, essentially, "data" about data. Every system that stores data for a specific business requirement maintains a repository of the business entities and attributes with clear definition of each attribute and its associated datatype. HCatalog[52] is a metadata and table management system for a broader Hadoop ecosystem. It enables data storage in any format, be it structured, semi-structured, or unstructured. The HCatalog,[52] coupled with "schema on read" nature of the Hadoop system, enables data science teams to quickly perform data exploration and data discovery. HCatalog[52] also enables developers to share the metadata across Hadoop tools like Pig, HIVE, and MapReduce. Furthermore, it integrates with Oozie workflow tool.

Apache Atlas[53] provides metadata management and governance capabilities for data assets created by applications and business users.

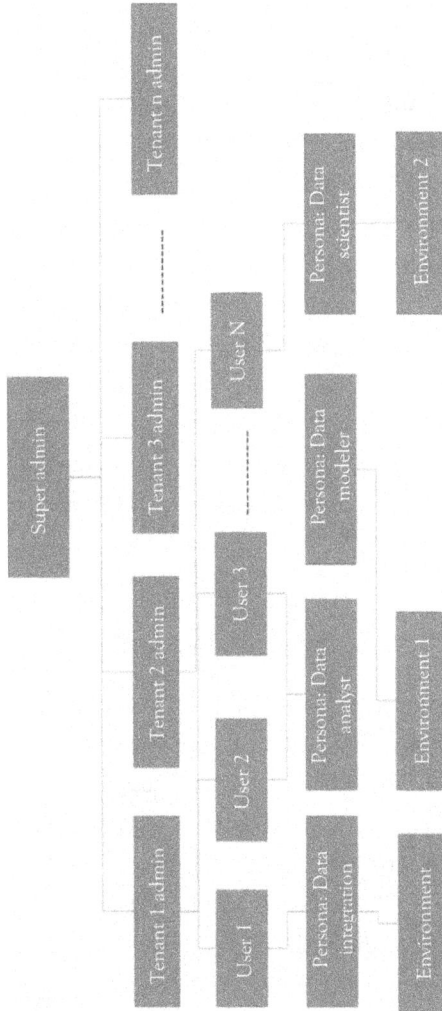

Figure 2.2 Hierarchy of tenants and users

Atlas, also an Apache Project, provides a centralized repository for the metadata like Hive Metastore, Kafka[54] topics, HBase tables, and so on, and is equipped with powerful searching capabilities as well as full text search. In addition to storing comprehensive details about metadata and the ability to use REST APIs to work with the instances, it also provides an intuitive user interface to view lineage of data, as it moves through various processes.

Another important feature of metadata is its ability to dynamically classify the attributes such as personal identifiable information (PII), Sensitive, Expire_on_Date with the data stored, enabling seamless data discovery and security enforcement by tools such as Ranger,[56] which is discussed in the Security and Audit section.[3]

Cloudera navigator[55] is another tool promoted by Cloudera that supports the metadata features described earlier. However, this is specific to Cloudera distribution of Hadoop only, unlike Atlas, which is an Apache Foundation Project. Both Atlas and Navigator Audit services automatically capture events from the Hadoop file systems, databases, and authorization components of the platform and provide interfaces to query those events for audit purposes.

Security and Audit

Authentication, authorization, and accounting (Audit) are the fundamental aspects of a security framework. The focus of any good framework is deeply centered around user, storage, and access level security for data, both at rest and in motion. As big data and AI technologies have the capability to process data in motion, security is a critical key performance indicator for vulnerability assessments, in order to protect the users and the data associated with the business unit. Hence, security that cuts across all layers of the reference architecture is fundamental to any system that has adopted the "secure by design" principle.

As these systems store huge amounts of data for processing, user, data, and access classifications become a critical aspect of information security right from the beginning. The security framework in the world of big data needs extensions not only to the security incident and management (SIEM) system, but also to the intrusion detection systems (IDS) and intrusion prevention systems (IPS). The need for these extensions stem from the big data platforms processing and storage models. Some of the critical extensions that are required are discussed as follows:[33]

(a) *Massive scalability*: Secure data transfer is a critical operation during the data ingestion process, when the internal data sources are combined with the external sources of information. Anomaly detection is another important aspect of data transfer to significantly reduce information security issues such as hacking.

(b) *Longer retention and storage*: Security logs are very important to be stored for longer duration of time so that it can be used for data mining and deep learning analytical algorithms to learn more about vulnerabilities on a bigger scale. Long retention helps detect hidden patterns of fraud, which can be used for further research in improving the performance of security algorithms.

(c) *Visualization of analysis*: Security experts have always been using reporting and visualization tools to understand the analyzed data and take actions based on certain rules, which are configured on a "rules base security tool" to trigger alerts based on the type of security vulnerability and threat assessment.

However, with the advent of big data technologies, security systems have expanded the scope to address the unstructured data (images, https, blogs, voice, videos) trojans, before ingesting into HFDS. New visualizations have been developed to trigger the actions based on the vulnerabilities related to variety of data.

(d) *Context and location*: The location of information and an understanding of context associated with the information is an important requirement before ingesting the data. This is because of the device and the associated event locations, unlike the customers, are not stationary but constantly on move. Such contextual security assessment is unique to big data and AI systems.

To address this issue, attribute-level security is suggested by experts and needs a different kinds of security solution such as blockchain, advanced encryption standard (AES) 256-bit encryptions used in protecting personal sensitive information. Moreover, attribute-level security assessments also need enormous processing power, which is available today with graphic processing unit (GPU) and Hogel processing unit (HPU) processing systems.

(e) *Multinetwork and multiprotocol data*: With the advent of IoT, data can now be collected using various protocols such as Wi-Fi (802.11x), ZigBee, Bluetooth, loRA, Sigfox, and so on, in addition to the following traditional protocols: UDP/TCP, http/https, EDI, radio (4G/5G), and customized network protocols. The security dimension has changed significantly due to the aforementioned complex networks that generate petabytes of data. Kerberos is one such security mechanism that is widely implemented to address authentication mechanism.

Kerberos provides a single sign-on mechanism that uses a ticket-based key authentication mechanism, and it is used extensively along with SPNEGO protocol, which is supported by all major browsers for extending Kerberos to web-based applications working with large-scale distributed systems. It is quite common to use lightweight directory access protocol (LDAP) based systems as the back end for Kerberos, although other forms of authentications such as SAML, OAuth, and HTTP exist.

Authorization deals with answering questions related user authorization and functionality and is typically implemented using the access control list (ACL) of UNIX and fine-grained role-based access control solutions like Apache Ranger / Knox (Hortonworks) and Apache Sentry (Cloudera and Map-R). These solutions are also used to implement attribute-level security discussed earlier.

The data-level security is addressed using AES-256-bit encryption cryptography for storage and transportation of data to and from the big data systems. Blockchain is a new technology that is showing enormous potential to secure the data in a highly distributed environment, and it is currently being implemented in cryptocurrency solutions such as Bitcoin, Ethereum, and so on, which have gained enormous attention in the financial industry. We shall discuss more about blockchain in Chapter 3.

Audit trail is essential to keep track of all the activities in the big data systems, since audit trails consist of various services, which are implemented as per the user requirements. All major Hadoop distribution such as Hortonworks, Cloudera, or Map-R provide audit capabilities, where the audit logs are monitored through the common management interfaces such as Ambari, Cloudera Manager, and Map-R control system respectively. These logs are either available on the local file system or HDFS. Likewise, Centrify is another comprehensive product platform for security and audit.

Hardware and Software

Infrastructure plays a key role in implementing massive big data platforms. Technologies such as OpenStack, VMWare, Docker Swarm, and Hypervisors are used to scale the infrastructure using infrastructure as a service (IaaS) paradigm. The ability to dynamically scale to thousands of nodes based on compute or processing power or adding a new node is the key to handle dynamic growth of data. Virtual Machines and Dockers provide the capability to package the software into images and run on any environment and has paved the way for Platform as a Service (PaaS). These tools have also increased the capability to package custom applications into simple deployable container that can be scaled based on the load. Containerization provides the flexibility to lift and shift the application with the required compute to other environments seamlessly and is a key technology adopted by leading technology companies. All these capabilities have led to the development of Anything as a Service (XaaS) model that has created enormous opportunities for companies to start building applications with a few hundreds of dollars using services provided by cloud vendors.

AWS, Google, IBM, and Microsoft are the leading vendors of <X>aaS (anything as a service) market and prominent big data vendors such as Hortonworks, Cloudera, and Map-R are using cloud providers to spin-off Hadoop ecosystem based on the dynamic changes in business requirements. Other specialized vendor products that focus on verticals like telecom, banking, insurance and so on also use one of the aforementioned Cloud vendors to provide "as a service" environments for their prospects. The key, however, is to build a commercial model that can scale both on premise and on Cloud, and specialized vendors offer have come up with hybrid models that address this space as organizations prefer to embrace a seamless transition path from on-premise to private cloud.

Analytical and Visualization

Traditional analytical tools such as SAS, SPSS, and R have limitations of working with limited data. This led to the development analytical libraries such as SparkMLib that address the analytical processing of large data sets instead of extrapolating with the sample data in traditional tools. However, these traditional tools have also evolved to work with big data systems with extensions to Hadoop; however, these are yet to address the distributed processing model that SparkMLib provides. Spark framework has also integrated R and Python to take advantage of the enormous libraries that have been developed by various experts making it easier for data scientists who have been working with them over the years.

The next paradigm that is catching up fast is analytics (ML/AI) as a service, wherein the analytical models are built, deployed, and are consumed as an API using any language of choice such as Python, JavaScript, Java, C#, and so on. However, these analytical models should be compliant with predictive model markup language (PMML) or portable format for analytics (PFA) format in order to be consumed by API. There is lot of research being conducted on extending PFA to customized machine learning models that are built by data scientists and are not added to the standard machine libraries such as R, Python, or SparkMLib.

New generation visualization tools with drag-and-drop capabilities integrated with R and python analytical libraries provide interactive capabilities on top of business intelligence reports and dashboards, which otherwise were not possible a few years ago. Another way of interaction with users that is fast catching up is the conversational bots or virtual assistants are deployed on customer-facing portals and customer care organizations. These bots are serving thousands of customers with support queries across industry verticals such as banking, insurance, telecom, retail, and e-commerce.

Although these chatbots or virtual assistants are designed using a question–answer model based upon predefined business processes, yet they drive approximately 20 to 25 percent of the support queries today. With tremendous progression in technology during recent years, the prospects of human-like conversation with ability to understand context, situation, and emotion is potentially becoming closer to reality. The next section talks about conversational AI ecosystem at a broader level to understand the working components.

Conversational Artificial Intelligence

Humans, by nature, like to converse in the language that they are most comfortable with, especially when using various form factors like mobile phones, tablets, pads, laptops, and desktop computers. There is lot of special emphasis and on-going research in the field of human–computer interaction (HCI) to understand how humans interact with all kinds of mobile devices and computers. Similarly, a lot of research that is being aggressively pursued is the ability of machines to understand the natural language with respect to intent, context, situation, and emotion. This has led to the development of a new stream called conversational AI, which have manifested into chatbots, virtual assistants, and augmented/mixed reality solutions.

These, coupled with the big data technologies, have not only increased the speed of processing but also have provided the capability to store billions of semistructured and unstructured data on commodity hardware. For real-time applications, special-purpose hardware units with GPUs and HPUs systems are used to identify the intent, context, and situation of the conversations and then deliver the intended experience based on deep learning models.

Figure 2.3 depicts a high-level overview of a conversational system that can be used to build chatbots or virtual assistants.

Conversations are mostly unstructured data consisting of either voice, free-form text, emoticons, videos, or images. Therefore, it becomes critical to capture and understand the intent before generating the right response using machine learning models deployed on conversational AI

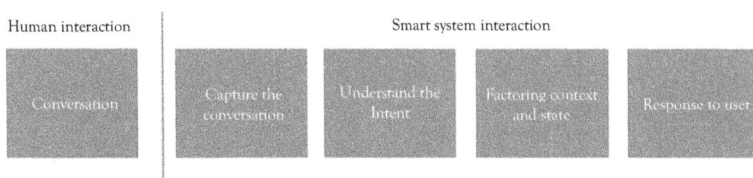

Human interaction | Smart system interaction

Conversation | Capture the conversation | Understand the Intent | Factoring context and state | Response to user

Figure 2.3 Conversational system framework

systems. However, the system's response is as good as data used for training the model before deploying in real-time scenario. As such, the system also has an inbuilt mechanism to self-learn from conversations, when deployed into the field over a period of time eventually delivering the results with a desired level of accuracy. Each type of conversation, that is, voice, text, image, and videos need different kinds of technologies and techniques that are listed in Table 2.1 for a quick understanding of the same.

NLP[26, 23, 6, 7, 8, 9, 12, 13] is a well-defined data science discipline, which is being researched since the past two decades and has a structure processing paradigm as listed in the following. Each of these steps are in turn research disciplines for various organizations and primary educational institutions across the world. However, the focus in this chapter is to provide a simple overview of the same with the references cited at the end for those who are interested in enhanced reading.

(a) Phonology

Phonology is the process of understanding of how words are pronounced in a sequence, which are part of the sentence. The process consists of breaking the sentence into words, called as tokenization, and then apply phonetics to sequence the understanding of pronunciation. This is useful to identify the differentiations between the same language. The output of the phonology is language detection (applicable to multilingual systems) and a list of tokenized words that are devoid of unnecessary punctuation and special characters.

(b) Morphology

Morphology concerns with the structure and the meaning of words that have been tokenized. It is important to understand the structure of the word to be able to separate the nonword tokens such as punctuation and identify the "atomic" words or "morphemes." This step is important as there is a syntactic way of combining the morphemes to form the word. These words are analyzed into parts of speech (POS) also known as POS tagging in NLP, used for building the POS tree, which is an input to syntactic analysis. Most popular techniques that are used in the morphological analysis are POS tagging and affixation.

Table 2.1 Conversations, technology components and analytical models

Conversation type	Technology components	NLP Analytical Models/Algorithms used for understanding	Comments
Voice	Voice file identification, voice-to-text conversion.	Hidden Markov Models, Linear discriminant analysis, Artificial neural networks, Deep neural networks and recurrent neural networks, automatic speech recognition models based on "listen, attend, and spell"	Algorithms reduce human speech into a structured ontology.
Text	Language detection Language understanding	N-Gram based text categorization, Markov model, Tri-gram frequency vectors, support vector machines, naïve Bayes, to name a few Deep learning models based on attention memory networks	Optical character recognition, Apache OpenNLP, Google, Microsoft, Facebook, and Apple are leading players.
Videos	Video file detection Video play format Object (logo, face, product) detection and classification Action recognition Cross-camera person re-identification	Neural nets, naïve Bayes classification. Deep convolution neural networks, tensor flow, Keras, Theano Segmentation and classification using support vector machines	OpenCV, Google, Microsoft, Apple, Facebook, Amazon and apache are leading players.
Images	Image detection Image identification	Neural nets, naïve Bayes classification Deep convolution neural networks, tensor flow, Keras, Theano Segmentation and classification using support vector machines	
Emotion icons	Emoticon recognition and classification	Deep neural networks, word2vec, k-means classifications	Twitter users are one of the largest bases that use emoticons for conveying sentiments.

(c) Syntactic analysis

Syntactic analysis deals with analyzing the words to determine the relationship between two or more words. Parts of speech tags like N (noun), V (verb) , A (adjective), P (preposition), DET (articles), and so on. from the morphological analysis are used to build a structural description of the sentence. The goal of this process is to form a structure that defines the units represented by the flat list of words. The output is a parse tree that represents the hierarchical structure of the sentence with each leaf node representing a word that has been analyzed starting with the root "S" (sentence). For example, the parse tree for conversation "Mike printed the file" is shown in Figure 2.4.

(d) Semantic analysis

The first step in this process is to look up for the meaning of the word(s) in subject-specific lexicon to determine the correct word based on the context using the disambiguation techniques. This is done by association technique, wherein each word in the question is associated with the context of the other word that are in the conversation. For example, a place or location mentioned in the conversation is associated with the demographic lexicons that are available on the Internet. There are various kinds of lexicons available that are built based on the topic of interest. For instance, English language lexicon, sports-specific lexicon, health care-specific lexicon, and so on.

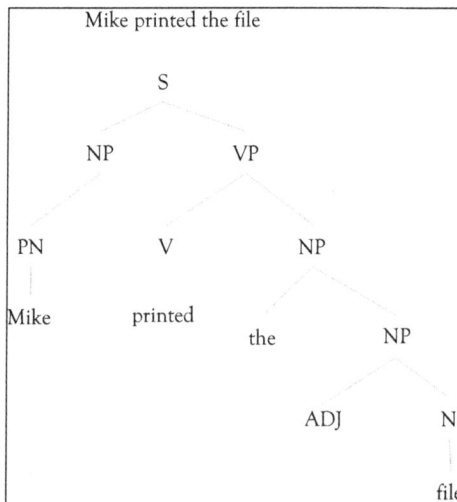

Figure 2.4 Parse tree for conversation "Mike printed the file"

To quote a specific example, sentiment analysis is based on the corpus of words, such as "good," "excellent," "very good," and "fantastic" for positive sentiment and "bad," "not good," "pathetic," and "very bad" for negative sentiments, with scores for each word or pair of words, indicating the strength of the sentiment. Different machine learning algorithms are used to accurately identify the meaning of the word and thereby used for classification into the right sentiment. The output of the semantic analysis is a set of business classifiers as defined by the problem statement. However, the conversations should be subjected to discourse analysis to identify the right classification for the conversation.

(e) Discourse analysis and integration

The output of the semantic analysis is analyzed for the relationships between the sentences to derive the coherence. Discourse analysis may be defined as the process of analyzing the conversation to understand the social interactions. This includes the conversations before and after the current conversation that is analyzed. The output of the discourse integration is the identification of the object–predicate and the subsequent references to the objects and is useful for building the right contextual understanding of the conversation. For instance, restaurant reviews such as "Food was good and was served at the right time; however, the ambience was not so attractive" leads to positive sentiment for the food lovers but neutral sentiment for the overall experience.

(f) Pragmatic analysis

Pragmatic analysis deals with the translation from the knowledge-based representation to a command or response to be executed by the machine. The result of this execution is the right response to the end user based on the advanced machine learning and deep learning algorithms. To reiterate, intent followed by context, situation, and emotion are critical toward building an accurate, human-like conversational AI system. Though machine learning techniques listed in Table 2.1 have come a long way in understanding the intent and to a certain extent the context of conversation, yet a tremendous amount of research is still going on to interpret the right context and situation.

It is common knowledge that with every piece of new technology comes a new set of challenges. For example, it will be interesting to see how AI bots will replace human agents providing support services, while still being empathetic. Another interesting aspect is the chatbot's perception of context, situation, and emotions with respect to the demographics of the customers. As the technology advances into the next decade, AI bots will converse with us as receptionists, store assistants, and office clerks in a true human-like experience.

Emerging Business Paradigms

Let us now turn our attention to the new business paradigms that have emerged with the advent of these new technologies. One such paradigm that has gained popularity is "conversational commerce," which was coined by Chris Messina. It represents the shift in chat bot or virtual assistant–based customer to brand interactions, along the customer journey life cycle. A very personalized and human-like interaction is possible, since bots are required to not only handle product/ services marketing, but also gather feedback about the products and personal interests.

Some of the industries that are impacted due to conversational bots or virtual assistants are listed next. However, the list is not exhaustive, since new business paradigms could change the face of the economy and thus originating macroeconomics of supply and demand (Table 2.2).

Table 2.2 Impact on employment in various industries due to conversational AI systems

Business area	Industries impacted	Impact on employment
Customer support	Banking, telecom, electronics and computer manufacturers, retail, insurance, large companies' internal support	About 30–40 percent of call volume is now handled by virtual agents. Thus, many customer support jobs are in peril.
Commerce (Selling)	e-Commerce, retail, FMCG, electronics	Sales jobs where touch, see, and feel experience is not important. Most of e-commerce will transform to conversational commerce.

Sales & Marketing	Telecom services, retail, e-commerce	Marketing activities handled by virtual assistants based on the customer relationship management (CRM) processes and are focused on selling services and customer experience. This trend will impact jobs in marketing.
Health care	Assisted health care services for care professionals	Doctor appointments, pills/medicine management (care professionals), diagnosis assistance.
Logistics	Delivery of packets/goods	Impact on delivery jobs due to drones, driverless vehicles.
Information and communications technology (ICT)	Automation of IT support, IaaS, PaaS, and SaaS	Reduction in support jobs due to automation and smart assistants.
All industries	Office and administrative support	Most affected due to AI and automation.

Conclusion

To conclude, technologies like big data and conversational AI are going to have a profound impact on the economy, be it positive, through the creation of new job types, or negative, through the elimination of jobs requiring direct human involvement namely food delivery, banking, or transportation. Industry experts estimate that, on average, the AI-driven economy will be worth approximately $15.7 trillion by 2035 and will generate new business opportunities as well as impact the existing job market, before stabilizing with a predicted fourth industrial revolution based on big data and AI.[15, 47]

Macroeconomics in the age of AI is going to fundamentally change the rate of growth, gross domestic product, unemployment, and inflation. The subsequent chapters in this book will detail some important solutions to the potential problems with human unemployment created by an AI-driven economy.[47]

References

[1] Krishnamurthy, J., and T. Kollar. 2013. "Jointly Learning to Parse and Perceive: Connecting Natural Language to the Physical World." *Transactions of the Association for Computational Linguistics* 1, pp. 193–206.

[2] Hu, M., and B. Liu. August 2004. "Mining and Summarizing Customer Reviews." In *Proceedings of the Tenth ACM SIGKDD International Conference on Knowledge Discovery and Data Mining*, 168–77, ACM.

[3] Li, H., Z. Chen, A. Mukherjee, B. Li, and J. Shao. 2015. "Analyzing and Detecting Opinion Spam on a Largescale Dataset Via Temporal and Spatial Patterns." *Proceedings of the 9th International AAAI Conference on Web and Social Media (ICWSM-15)*, Oxford, UK.

[4] Dean, J., and S. Ghemawat. 2004. "MapReduce—Simplified Data Processing on Large Clusters." *OSDI'04: Sixth Symposium on Operating System Design and Implementation*, 137–50. San Francisco, CA, https://static.googleusercontent.com/media/research.google.com/en//archive/mapreduce-osdi04.pdf

[5] Zaharia, M., M. Chowdhury, M.J. Franklin, S. Shenker, and I. Stoica. 2010. "Spark: Cluster Computing With Working Sets." *Hot Cloud* 10, no. 10, p. 95.

[6] Negi, S., S. Joshi, A.K. Chalamalla, and L.V. Subramaniam. December 2009. "Automatically Extracting Dialog Models from Conversation Transcripts." *2009 Ninth IEEE International Conference on Data Mining*. IEEE.

[7] Bordes, A., S. Chopra, and J. Weston. 2014."Question Answering with Subgraph Embeddings." arXiv preprint arXiv:1406.3676.

[8] Sordoni, A., M. Galley, M. Auli, C. Brockett, Y. Ji, M. Mitchell, and B. Dolan. 2015. "A Neural Network Approach to Context-sensitive Generation of Conversational Responses." arXiv preprint arXiv:1506.06714.

[9] Chakrabarti, C., and G.F. Luger. 2015. "Artificial Conversations for Customer Service Chatter Bots: Architecture, Algorithms, and Evaluation Metrics." *Expert Systems with Applications* 42, no. 20, pp. 6878–97.

[10] HDFS—Hadoop Distributed File System. http://hadoop.apache.org/ and https://en.wikipedia.org/wiki/Apache_Nutch and https://en.wikipedia.org/wiki/Apache_Hadoop#Hadoop_distributed_file_system

[11] O'Malley, O., and A.C. Murthy. May 2009. "Hadoop Sorts a Petabyte in 16.25 Hours and a Terabyte in 62 Seconds." [online] available at http://developer.yahoo.net/blogs/hadoop/2009/05/hadoop_sorts_a_petabyte_in_162.html

[12] Lokman, A.S., and J.M. Zain. 2010. "Extension and Prerequisite: An Algorithm to Enable Relations Between Responses in Chatbot Technology." *Journal of Computer Science* 6, no. 10, p. 1212.

[13] API.ai: Voice-enabling and NLP Engine. https://docs.api.ai/docs/reference

[14] John Mashley has been credited for being the first to spread the term and concept of big data in the 1990s. https://en.wikipedia.org/wiki/John_Mashey

[15] Big Data Analytics and Hadoop Market Accounted for $8.48 billion in 2015 and is expected to reach $99.31 billion by 2022 growing at a compounded annual growth rate (CAGR) of 42.1 percent from 2015 to 2022. Rise of big data and growing need for big data analytics and rapid growth in consumer

data are some of the factors fueling market growth. Lack of skilled workers and lack of security features in the Hadoop framework are restraining the market growth. Venture capital funding is the major opportunity for vendors in big data analytics and Hadoop market. http://sbwire.com/press-releases/hadoop-big-data-analytics-market-2018-global-trend-segmentation-and-opportunities-forecast-to-2025-927935.htm

[16] Refers to Roger Mougalas Coining the Word Big Data Shortly After Web 2.0. https://datafloq.com/read/big-data-history/239

[17] http://nordic.businessinsider.com/9-tech-trends-2017-billions-2016-10/ Market for Conversational Platforms Will be $600.1 billion by 2021 Referred in the Above article. https://www.inbenta.com/en/blog/report-specialized-digital-assistants-and-bots-a-600-billion-market-by-2020/

[18] "Based on Analysis by the International Institute for Analytics (IIA), IDC, and New Vantage Partners—Regarding the Market for Big Data Analytics. The Big Data Analytics Market Will Soon Surpass $200 billion." https://forbes.com/sites/gilpress/2017/01/20/6-predictions-for-the-203-billion-big-data-analytics-market/#5e4fb32d2083

[19] IDC says that worldwide revenues for big data and business analytics will grow from $130.1 billion in 2016 to more than $203 billion in 2020, at a compound annual growth rate (CAGR) of 11.7 percent. In addition to being an industry with the largest investment in big data and business analytics solutions (nearly $17 billion in 2016), banking will see the fastest spending growth. https://idc.com/getdoc.jsp?containerId=prUS41826116

[20] https://inbenta.com/en/blog/report-specialized-digital-assistants-and-bots-a-600-billion-market-by-2020/

[21] https://medium.com/chris-messina/2016-will-be-the-year-of-conversational-commerce-1586e85e3991

[22] Dr. Mariana Neves, June 6, 2016—Discourse Analysis. https://hpi.de/fileadmin/user_upload/fachgebiete/plattner/teaching/NaturalLanguage Processing/NLP2016/NLP07_DiscourseAnalysis.pdf

[23] Afantenos, S., E. Kow, N. Asher, and J. Perret. September 2015. "Discourse Parsing for Multi-party Chat Dialogues." *Empirical Methods on Natural Language Processing, Lisbonne (EMNLP 2016)*, Portugal, Association for Computational Linguistics (ACL).

[24] Chris Messina. https://medium.com/chris-messina/conversational-commerce-92e0bccfc3ff

[25] Sordoni, A., M. Galley, M. Auli, C. Brockett, Y. Ji, M. Mitchell, and B. Dolan. 2015. "A Neural Network Approach to Context Sensitive Generation of Conversational Responses." arXiv preprint arXiv:1506.06714.

[26] What Is Natural Language Processing and Generation (NLP/NLG)? by Ben Dickson. https://bdtechtalks.com/2018/02/20/ai-machine-learning-nlg-nlp/

[27] Why Is Edge AI Important? by Ben Dickson. https://bdtechtalks. com/2017/08/14/edge-artificial-intelligence-fog-computing/

[28] The AI Revolution: The Road to Superintelligence by Tim Urban. https:// waitbutwhy.com/2015/01/artificial-intelligence-revolution-1.html

[29] Welcome, Robot Overlords. Please Don't Fire Us? by Kevin Drum. https:// motherjones.com/media/2013/05/robots-artificial-intelligence-jobs-automation/

[30] Race Against the Machine, by Erik Brynjolfsson and Andrew McAfee. https://amazon.com/Race-Against-Machine-Accelerating-Productivity/ dp/0984725113#reader_0984725113

[31] How to Tackle Big Data from a Security Point of View by Peter Wood. https://computerweekly.com/feature/How-to-tackle-big-data-from-a-security-point-of-view

[32] Introduction to Big Data Security Analytics in the Enterprise, by Dan Sullivan. https://searchsecurity.techtarget.com/feature/Introduction-to-big-data-security-analytics-in-the-enterprise

[33] Big Data Security Analytics: Harnessing New Tools for Better Security, by Scoot Crawford. https://searchsecurity.techtarget.com/magazineContent/ Big-data-security-analytics-Harnessing-new-tools-for-better-security

[34] Practical Natural Language Processing by Jaganadh G. https://slideshare. net/jaganadhg/c-uo-k

[35] Apache Sqoop™ is a Tool Designed for Efficiently Transferring Bulk Data Between Apache Hadoop and Structured Datastores Such as Relational Databases. Refer to http://sqoop.apache.org/ for more details

[36] Apache Impala-Apache Impala is the Open Source, Native Analytic Database for Apache Hadoop. http://impala.apache.org

[37] Apache Giraph is an Iterative Graph Processing System Built for High Scalability. http://giraph.apache.org

[38] Oozie is a Workflow Scheduler System to Manage Apache Hadoop Jobs. http://oozie.apache.org/

[39] ZooKeeper is a Centralized Service for Maintaining Configuration Information, Naming, Providing Distributed Synchronization, and Providing Group Services. http://zookeeper.apache.org

[40] Human–computer interaction (HCI). Human–computer Interaction (HCI) is a Multidisciplinary Field of Study Focusing on the Design of Computer Technology and, in Particular, the Interaction Between Humans (the users) and Computers. https://interaction-design.org/literature/topics/human-computer-interaction

[41] Apache Storm is a Free and Open Source Distributed Real-time Computation System. http://storm.apache.org

[42] Flume is a Distributed, Reliable, and Available Service for Efficiently Collecting, Aggregating, and Moving Large Amounts of Log Data. http://flume.apache.org

[43] Apache Flink is a Framework and Distributed Processing Engine for Stateful Computations Over Unbounded and Bounded Data Streams. https://flink.apache.org/flink-architecture.html

[44] The Internet of Things (IoT) is the network of physical devices, vehicles, home appliances, and other items embedded with electronics, software, sensors, actuators, and connectivity, which enables these things to connect and exchange data, creating opportunities for more direct integration of the physical world into computer-based systems, resulting in efficiency improvements, economic benefits, and reduced human exertions. https://en.wikipedia.org/wiki/Internet_of_things

[45] A Security Product Firm for Various Industries and Technologies Including Big Data. www.centrify.com

[46] Everything as a Service (XaaS) on the Cloud: Origins, Current and Future Trends—Yucong Duan; Guohua Fu; Nianjun Zhou; Xiaobing Sun; Nanjangud C. Narendra; Bo Hu—<X>aaS—Anything as a Service—XaaS is a general, collective term that refers to the delivery of anything as a service. It recognizes the vast number of products, tools and technologies that vendors now deliver to users as a service over a network—typically the Internet—rather than provide locally or on-site within an enterprise.

[47] AI-driven Economy. http://visualcapitalist.com

[48] Likely Transition Areas and Declining Areas: Reference for the Need for Human Labor. https://forbes.com/sites/quora/2017/01/18/how-much-will-ai-decrease-the-need-for-human-labor/#5c5d88b775c0

[49] YARN – Yet Another Recognition Negotiator - Apache Hadoop YARN is the resource management and job scheduling technology in the open source Hadoop distributed processing framework. One of Apache Hadoop's core components, YARN is responsible for allocating system resources to the various applications running in a Hadoop cluster and scheduling tasks to be executed on different cluster nodes. Refer to https://hadoop.apache.org/docs/current/hadoop-yarn/hadoop-yarn-site/YARN.html for more details.

[50] Apache Pig is a platform analyzing large data sets and the Pig language is used for analysis of the data sets. Refer to https://pig.apache.org/ for more details.

[51] Apache HIVE – A data warehouse software that facilitates reading, writing and managing large data sets on distributed storage using SQL (structured query language). Refer to https://hive.apache.org/ for more details

[52] HCatalog – It is a table and storage management layer for Hadoop that exposes tables of HIVE metastore with read and write capabilities using tools such as Pig and MapReduce. https://cwiki.apache.org/confluence/display/Hive/HCatalog

[53] Apache Atlas – Data governance and metadata management framework for Hadoop. Refer to https://atlas.apache.org for further reading

[54] Apache Kafka – is an open source stream processing software platform from Apache Software Foundation. https://kafka.apache.org

[55] Cloudera Navigator – **Cloudera Navigator** is a data governance solution for Hadoop, offering critical capabilities such as data discovery, continuous optimization, audit, lineage, metadata management, and policy enforcement. More information at https://www.cloudera.com/products/product-components/cloudera-navigator.html

[56] Apache Ranger™ is a framework to enable, monitor and manage comprehensive data security across the Hadoop platform. Refer to https://ranger.apache.org for further reading.

CHAPTER 3

Blockchain: The Future of Fintech Innovation

Shrikant Shete

Introduction to Blockchain Technology

Blockchain is an open or shared digital ledger, with a constantly updated list of transactions. It is supported by a peer-to-peer network that is either public or private. Every member on the community network represents a "block" (Figure 3.1). This creates a permanent unique audit trail. There is no single point of failure. There is no way to make modifications to the transaction record.

Blockchain is a fintech that disrupts the common technology in use by the banking and financial systems. So it is easy to say that within the financial technologies, the blockchain technology has unleashed a

Figure 3.1 Blockchain technology

potential to replace banking services almost completely. Banking in the future will be much more comfortable for its users. It will be easy to store records of transactions by financial technologies that use blockchain systems, which are much more affordable, easily accessible, and create nondestructible transactions and records that are secure, trusted, and could be verified when needed.

How Does the Blockchain Technology Work?

We shall start with a request for transaction in a financial system:

1. Someone requests a transaction.
2. This requested transaction is sent to a peer-to-peer network consisting of blocks.
3. Validating the transaction is the next process. This network blocks validates the transaction and verifies user status, using the software or algorithms.
4. The validated transaction can contain a cryptocurrency used for the speed of the transaction and other records.
5. Once the transaction is verified, it is combined with more transactions, which creates a "block" of records or data for the ledger.
6. The new block thus created cannot be altered and remains permanent.
7. This is added to the existing blockchain. It is important to note that every time a new block is created and added to this chain, it must refer to the earlier block to validate itself and so the name blockchain.
8. The transaction is now complete.

We shall now try to understand how the new technology scores over the conventional methods and if it is cost-competitive. We shall also take a fresh look at its application in financial technologies (fintech).

Advantages of Blockchain Technology over Conventional Methods

By principle, blockchain is a decentralized technology. The technology is now the most sought-after financial technology just due to its inherent characteristics. It is discussed at every corporate institution, every financial institution, government, and all are trying to evaluate the use of blockchain. We shall soon see how the blockchain technology correlates to all the aspects of business other than fintech.

For banking and financial institutions, payments and money transfers (digital money transfers to be precise) are used daily worldwide. The traditional methods take long time, have complicated processes, prone to frauds, and use human factor to eliminate errors while blockchain technology offers easy error-free, multiple use in cross-border payments and transaction settlements. By its inherent characteristics, the transactions are very fast due to the underlying technology it uses. The software and algorithms make use of cryptocurrencies to transmit the money with high speeds so that when payments are transferred, the receiving end gets the equivalent value of money in other currency almost instantly. Thus, it can be observed that the very nature of blockchain-based payments and transfers help the financial system to generate the other currency without any fluctuations.[1]

We shall now take a broad outlook on the blockchain technology and how it can eliminate all the "gaps" in the traditional banking systems.

Blockchain Technology and Its Use in Banking and Financial Services

The blockchain technology in payments and money transfer services can be used specially by financial institutions and exchange centers for cross-border payments. These can be international bill payments or just cash payments, which depend on the user and the algorithms in use. Financial institutions can use blockchain technology extensively for international money transfer, international remittances, and simple foreign exchange settlements. We foresee very high transactions in cross-border payments, in which the blockchain technology stands out to be the outstanding revolution in Hi-Tech.

We divert our focus toward different areas of operation where we get a substantial advantage of the blockchain technology.

Advantages of Blockchain Technology Over Card Methods in the Financial Systems

We face costs of high magnitude when we use the current methods of transactions. The current mode of transactions is costly, and are done through card organizations such as VISA, Mastercard, UnionPay, and others. These modes of transactions have stabilized over a substantial time period and even today it is observed that about 85 percent of the transactions are done by this traditional and old banking transfer methods. These organizations by virtue of being in markets for a long period of time are more familiar to the users and hence an aggressive introduction of fintech technologies such as blockchain has become imperative. In cross-border transaction systems, these new technologies are revolutionary in the sense that they can help reduce costs, make operations easier, and are highly secure. If we penetrate just 50 percent of the transactions in the financial systems using the blockchain technology by year 2020, we shall observe phenomenal results, never observed in history. This is possible because the transactions can be done very fast in a fraction of time normally used by old banking and card methods.

Moreover, the time taken for the old methods vary with the exchange rates at the receiving end. The transactions are costly and charged anywhere in the range from 1.5 to 3.5 percent and these are the official transactions. For large amounts of money, these old methods of transmission and payments get obsolete as the transaction charges with blockchain hardly exceed 1 percent on the higher side.

We shall now take a look at the risks using the old systems currently in use and get a bird's eye view on how the blockchain technology can help transform the financial system.

What Are the Risks Associated with the Old Systems and How Are They Eliminated with Use of an Advanced Blockchain Technology?

By this time, we are all aware that all the international cards, old banking transactions have high risks of fraud. This is eliminated in the blockchain technology by creating blocks where regulatory body represents itself on the either side of block. The card and old banking transactions have low success rates since the fraud control measures are deployed very stringently. Whenever there are requests for multiple transactions in a single day from a single location of similar amounts, it triggers the fraud control measures, which do not allow the transactions to take place. This causes system failure. Yes, a system failure.

For example, there are overseas merchant acquirers of payments who send goods but get stuck in receiving payments from the parties most of the times. These circumstances lead the online merchants to go to arbitration, court of law, which do not offer a complete solution but possibly if they are adequately insured, they find respite in settlements. But in doing so it consumes long time, waste of money, and resources.

We now have a look at some more hurdles we face in the conventional systems and then offer the solutions to these hurdles.

More Disadvantages in Traditional Banking and Card Technologies and How to Eliminate Them

The conventional banking systems are highly deficient. Out of the many ineffective systems, the disadvantage with the traditional banking is that if the transaction has to be cancelled and the sender wants the money back, then the processes are long enough for the card holders, banks, and financial institutions to return the money. Whereas in a blockchain technology, since the transactions are recorded in every block, it is much easier to check the amount of money involved in the transaction and take appropriate decision.[2]

Some digital payment systems offer to deal with the third-party payments and returns. However, with the revolutionary fintech blockchain technology, the relation is established between the two sides, the sender and the receiver. This is the most trusted, authentic system and changes the way people do business on the Internet.

As defined, blockchain is a distributed decentralized ledger and will have a significant impact on the transactions and financial institutions. As noted before, the risk of systems failure is completely eliminated and this is the most important risk blockchain can reduce or eliminate from the transactions done by any institution.

It is imperative that we take an overview of the disruption within the banking and financial systems.

How Does the Blockchain Technology Revolutionize Banking and Financial Institutions?

It is important to note that before the introduction of blockchain technology, due to system errors and system failures, many transactions have gone unnoticed in the existing conventional technology. We could never track the source of funds, neither was it possible to track the quality of funds and the receiver's use of funds. Now, with the introduction of blockchain technology, we have a decentralized ledger as shown in the

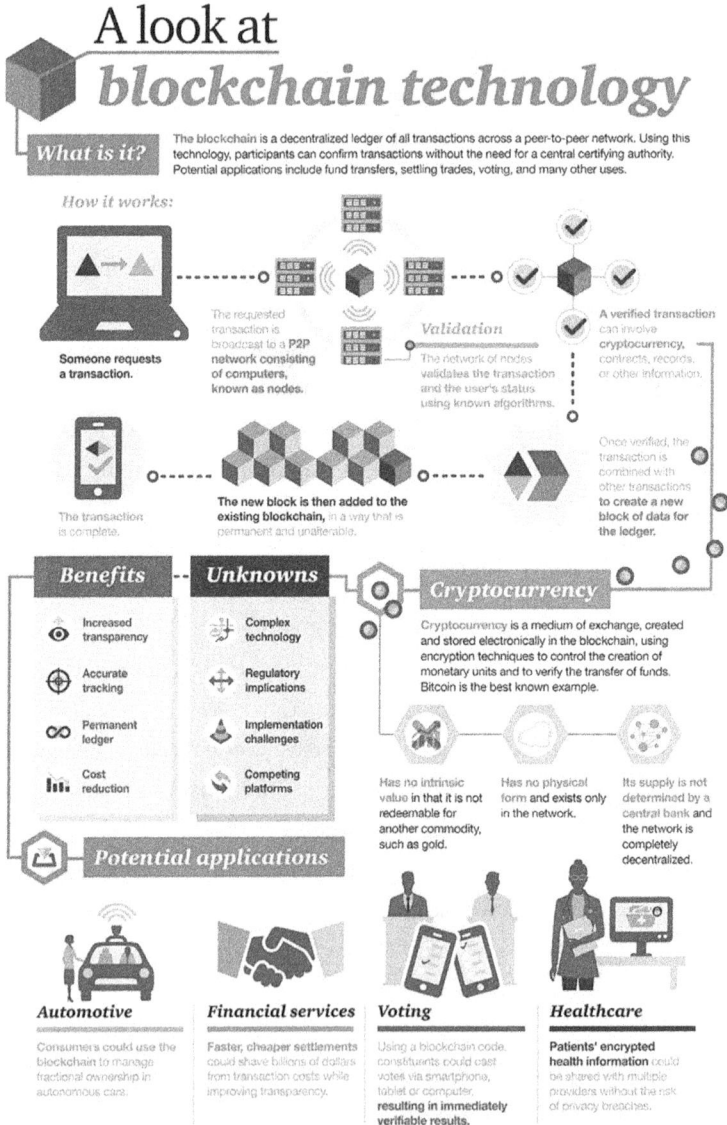

A look at
blockchain technology

What is it?   The blockchain is a decentralized ledger of all transactions across a peer-to-peer network. Using this technology, participants can confirm transactions without the need for a central certifying authority. Potential applications include fund transfers, settling trades, voting, and many other uses.

How it works:

Someone requests a transaction.

The requested transaction is broadcast to a P2P network consisting of computers, known as nodes.

Validation
The network of nodes validates the transaction and the user's status using known algorithms.

A verified transaction can involve cryptocurrency, contracts, records, or other information.

The transaction is complete.

The new block is then added to the existing blockchain, in a way that is permanent and unalterable.

Once verified, the transaction is combined with other transactions to create a new block of data for the ledger.

Benefits

Increased transparency

Accurate tracking

Permanent ledger

Cost reduction

Unknowns

Complex technology

Regulatory implications

Implementation challenges

Competing platforms

Cryptocurrency

Cryptocurrency is a medium of exchange, created and stored electronically in the blockchain, using encryption techniques to control the creation of monetary units and to verify the transfer of funds. Bitcoin is the best known example.

Has no intrinsic value in that it is not redeemable for another commodity, such as gold.

Has no physical form and exists only in the network.

Its supply is not determined by a central bank and the network is completely decentralized.

Potential applications

Automotive
Consumers could use the blockchain to manage fractional ownership in autonomous cars.

Financial services
Faster, cheaper settlements could shave billions of dollars from transaction costs while improving transparency.

Voting
Using a blockchain code, constituents could cast votes via smartphone, tablet or computer, resulting in immediately verifiable results.

Healthcare
Patients' encrypted health information could be shared with multiple providers without the risk of privacy breaches.

Figure 3.2 An overview of blockchain technology and services

Figure 3.2, which creates a trusted transaction, which is most authentic and the type of blocks vary with every transaction.

So, it is easy to identify, track the source of funds, the quality of funds, and use of funds by the receiver. The new technology is low cost, error free and such transactions can never go unnoticed, since they are seen by the constituents and stored in a block as a permanent record. Hence, blockchain technologies would find major use in payments and payment systems, but it would not be restricted to these three transactions viz.

1. Cross-border payments;
2. International money transfers and securities transactions; and
3. Domestic money transfers.

Let us get an overview of a typical scenario:

Merchant end: Receiving end scenario
This is the place where the payment reaches from the paying customer. There are two types of payment possibilities in this case for a blockchain technology: online and offline method. When a client pays digitally, the merchant receives the legal currency simultaneously and instantly.

The client can pay digital currency to the merchant through a digital wallet and the payment institution on receiving the request from sender sells the same amount of digital currency at the current price and this guarantees no loss of exchange rates and the merchant receives payment in legal currency.

What Are the Advantages, Improvements, and Cost Effectiveness of This New Technology?

Every new technology introduced comes with costs attached to it. But these costs are much lower in blockchain technology and are much more effective than the conventional technologies that have been used so far. Unless the blockchain technology offers competitive and lower costs, the adaptability to the financial systems shall be low. In the era of big data and IoT, we are very concerned about the safety of our transactions and data privacy. These problems can be permanently solved with use of quantum computing as explained later in Chapter 9.

How Are the Costs Reduced? How Does the Blockchain Technology Ensure Safety?

The preceding processes improve cross-border payments, domestic payments and international transfers, and bill payments:

1. Transaction fee as mentioned earlier does not exceed 1 percent and mostly it is lower than 1 percent. It is very cost effective than the existing card systems, conventional online payments, or traditional banking systems.
2. Merchants, utilities, or any organization receives money in very short time duration and error free every time.
3. One important advantage of this system is that the orders paid in digital currency are irrevocable and therefore eliminates risks.
4. The payments with blockchain technology do not carry fraud control technology of credit and debit cards or traditional banking institutions and hence they do not influence payments.
5. Blockchain is absolutely risk free and is embedded with a fraud control mechanism, which secures the transfer of funds. So, we are using a very safe, secure, and trustworthy mechanism, which is the blockchain technology.

Digital Currency   Legal Currency

Customer ------→ Wallet --------------------→ Payment Institution ----------------------→Merchant

+

Exchange

This is the place where we introduce digital cash for transaction with the benefits of Blockchain Technology in the above processes.

Figure 3.3 Process for blockchain digital cash payments

6. Payments and money transfer of any value, are 100 percent successful with this technology.

7. How the costs are reduced using the blockchain technology? As shown in Figure 3.3, the format of payment for institutions or banking and financial institutions is very simple. The institutions do not find any need to set up overseas banks or long-distance branches. The blockchain offers better settlement systems, which eliminates the constraints of card organizations. This results in lower operating costs, lower overheads and simple service network reducing the cost of transactions substantially.

8. Recently we have seen that the data theft worries are getting worse. With the existing card technology and even with old banking technology, the data is open to theft. We have seen many instances of forged and copied cards, and chips are cracked by the hackers and criminals. Banks are thus prone to theft of the customer's data, which is open and available to anyone in the bank.

Blockchain technology guarantees that the users are safe because their data is safe in blocks. The user has to ensure safety of login id and

How a blockchain transaction works

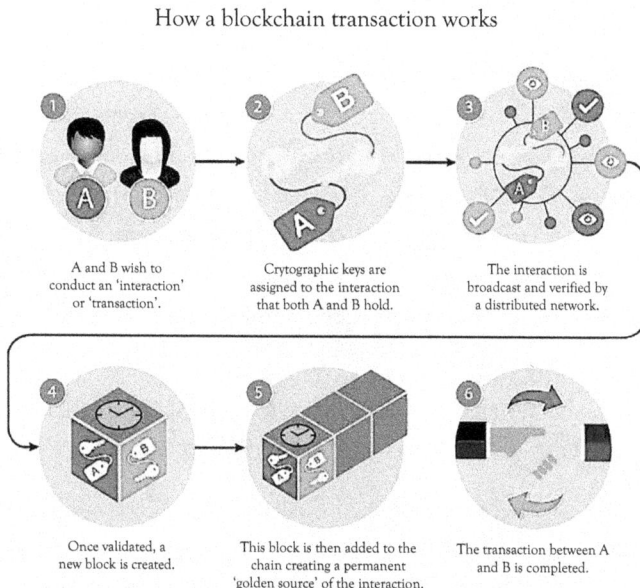

| A and B wish to conduct an 'interaction' or 'transaction'. | Crytographic keys are assigned to the interaction that both A and B hold. | The interaction is broadcast and verified by a distributed network. |

| Once validated, a new block is created. | This block is then added to the chain creating a permanent 'golden source' of the interaction. | The transaction between A and B is completed. |

Figure 3.4 How blockchain transactions work

passwords. And a normal change of passwords regularly keeps the criminals away. In a blockchain, the risk of theft and frauds is extremely low. This is because the constituents of a block are already alerted where the money is traveling as shown in Figure 3.4.

Other Applications of Blockchain Technology

Let us now observe if blockchain technology can be used in other applications and what are those applications. We shall also observe if blockchain could reduce costs and eliminate errors and risks. It should be noted that the blockchain is an underlying technology behind several other applications besides payments and digital money transfers. Just as payments are digitally transferred from issuer to the receiver, similarly the records of the following can be stored on a blockchain:

1. National Security Numbers / Social Security Numbers;
2. Driving licenses;
3. Passports;
4. Mobile numbers;
5. Tangible assets;
6. Intangible assets;
7. Medical papers; and so on.

Blockchain is an open or shared digital ledger and constantly updates its list in real-time transactions. Blockchain could help maintain a never-ending historical trail. As we keep progressing through newer generations and adopt newer technologies, there could be a disruption in the traditional methods of transactions or records. As given before, with the help of blockchain technology, it is easy to value assets, transfer assets, sell or buy assets as well as valuate new assets and keep their records.[1]

Absorption or Acceptance of Blockchain Technology Globally

We studied previously how the blockchain technology can make cards and banks completely obsolete in major transactions. However in some cases, the traditional banking methods will still apply but the entire banking transaction costs could be reduced by almost 90 percent if the blockchain is adopted as a financial technology by banks and other financial institutions. There are regulatory compliances in different countries and the new blockchain technology is getting absorbed, understood, and implemented. Blockchain technology also makes card transactions obsolete in money transfers and payments so that the new technology when implemented can win war against credit cards frauds, risks, hackers as well as money launderers.

Gold Standard for Financial Industry with Blockchain Technology

Now, let us explore how blockchain technology could be linked to gold standard and how it could have gold standard for cryptocurrency in order to ensure that there is more stability in financial industry. We shall discuss the importance of gold standard for stability of country's financial system in Chapter 11. The importance of restoring gold standard has also been elaborated in greater depth by economist Apek Mulay in his book *Mass Capitalism: A Blueprint for Economic Revival*. In December 2017, we witnessed the launch of Shariah gold standard. It was announced in Bahrain by the Accounting and Auditing Organization of Islamic Financial Institutions (AAOIFI) and the World Gold Council. The standard is the first ever set of guidelines for people looking to invest in gold-based fintech Products. It also a positive for those looking to invest in real estate, land, and keep records of any transactions and any number of transactions within financial and nonfinancial products.

According to the research by Goldcore, international bullion workers who supply precious metal bullion delivery and storage in United States, the potential for Islamic investment is vast. According to Goldcore, if one percent of Islamic finance goes into gold, demand could increase up to a massive 1000 tons a year. In 2016, gold production set its third successive record ever, with around 3,222 tons or 103 million Oz. being produced.

Adoption of Gold-Backed Cryptocurrency

The adoption of a Shariah standard was less of an issue for individual investors than it was for institutions, that offer gold-based instruments says Mr. Ibrahim Mohammed, chief executive of Gold Guard, a

Dubai-based bullion investor. In early 2018, Gold Guard together with OneGram, a Dubai-based blockchain issued the first Sharia-compliant gold backed cryptocurrency. Bullion is stored inside a vault inside Dubai Airport Free Zone.

The demand came from not just the Muslim world, but also from Europe. The level of interest from the investors in Europe is surprising, especially from the UK, where investors have been searching for secure vehicles to hedge against the devaluation of British pound. This is a clear evidence of the fact that Sharia instruments are appealing to a wide audience. And perhaps even more significantly, it shows that Dubai is growing as a center of trust for the investors looking for safety in an uncertain global economy. Today, Dubai is being viewed as a place offering security to investors and it is very encouraging to see that these investors are going to Dubai just because blockchain technology protects their assets.

There is a growing concern about the payment systems in many parts of the world specifically in the Middle East. Payments in the Middle East region has posed some challenges since the payment options there are quite different from other areas of the world. The success of ecommerce and online payments are redefining the Payment Systems in the Middle East region. Blockchain Technology is all about to restructure the unorganized payment systems in Middle East where they still await a reliable and popular payment method as ecommerce, fintech and online Payments grow.[3]

In Blockchain Technology, the Banks themselves become one of the constituents of the block to validate the transactions. That makes the financial systems most secure, reliable and authentic. There will be a major revolution in payment systems in the Middle East with the launch of Blockchain technology.

Legal Approach for the Blockchain with the Banks and Financial Institutions

The regulatory bodies for blockchain include:

1. Central banks of every country
2. Banks in various locations of a country
3. Financial institutions in various locations of a country

The regulatory bodies have often posed challenges to blockchain technology, but in real sense this is an unstoppable technology since it is transparent and based on gold standard, which helps maintain a stability of cryptocurrency. The algorithms are known to mainly the fintech companies as compared to the banking institutions, and hence it is essential that the banks and financial institutions align their activities with the fintech offering blockchain technologies.

Change is inevitable, whether it is technological advancement with smartphones, Internet of Things (IoT) devices, or blockchain financial technology. It is a moment that will impact every human being's life. It is just the kind of revolutionary technology that will uplift the human lifestyle and human living standards with a combination of *Mass Capitalism*'s sound monetary policy, economic decentralization achieved with blockchain technology and gold standard for cryptocurrency. This is the change that world has been waiting for a long time. Blockchain is also the innovation that entire humanity has been waiting for whether it is technological innovation or financial innovation.

Conclusion

Blockchain technology will bring about a complete change of the banking systems within the next decade because it is the first time that economists, global finance community is feeling that the banking systems need strong security alongwith a fundamental and structural change. This change is inevitable, the bankers either have to upgrade their skill toward advancement in fintech innovations or close their financial activities in favor of blockchain. This will definitely be gradual. But the change is inevitable!

References

[1] Kershen, J. 2016. *Blockchain: The Future of Internet Innovation – Ideas, Application and Use of Blockchain Technology.* CreateSpace Independent Publishing Platform (ISBN 1533490678, 9781533490674).

[2] Wattenhofer, R. 2017. *Distributed Ledger Technology: The Science of Blockchain.* CreateSpace Independent Publishing Platform (ISBN 1544232101, 9781544232102).

[3] ISTIZADA Arabic and Middle East Marketing Solutions: ISTIZADA online. http://istizada.com/blog/middle-east-online-payment-methods/

PART II

Social, Environmental, and Ethical Aspects

CHAPTER 4

Monsters of Our Own Making

Michael McAllum

Unraveling Toward

The core contention of this chapter is that cities are in part both representations of macroeconomic activity and also—particularly since the advent of globalization—economic actors in their own right. It asserts that the effect of this mostly successful globalization activity has been to create a set of circumstances that make cities unsustainable and potentially monstrous. This chapter therefore explores ways in which "the city," both as a representation and as an actor, needs to be re-thought consequently acting as a contributor to the conversation on a "new macroeconomics." However, the considerations that follow make the case that future cities need to emerge from a pragmatic rather than a theoretical view of the world, and therefore there is, in a sense, no such thing as a "new macroeconomics" today. Notwithstanding this contention, the assertions in this chapter need to be seen as part of an "unraveling toward" an understanding of what might be, rather than as some kind of proposed end point. It suggests that if macroeconomic thinking fails to move outside the dominant Western world view of individualism, rationalism, dualism (dialectics), objectification, and economism, it will be insufficient as a framework for confronting and ultimately resolving the existential threats that face contemporary humanity. It is in this spirit that the following ideas are presented.

Context

Every city is, in part, a physical manifestation of the economic systems that emerged during its formation. These socioeconomic agglomerations exist as a pragmatic realization of all current activities required for value exchange, and they evolve, or have evolved, partly as a consequence of population growth, and partly though investment in particular future aspirations by the most influential of their citizens. Over the last three decades, the role of cities (as representations and actors) has been influenced and shaped by the globalization, world-making ethos of today's dominant macroeconomic worldviews; the introduction of technologies that have enabled boundaryless geographic activity; and the powerful actors who most benefit from those worldviews.

But these contemporary urban settlements are, for the most part, conceptually and architecturally defiant statements of a Western-centric, neoliberal-economic, techno-determinist, industrialized orientation that pays little or no regard to either ecosystem considerations or the provision of social foundations for many communities. The result is that the world's cities now share and face a set of complex problems that, if not addressed in the near term, will almost certainly lead to rapid decline. In this sense then, they are monsters of our own making, and how we learn to coexist with the consequences of these creations is a question that is existential in nature. It will require an ontological (rethinking) and practical reframing of how we relate to cities as desirable habitations and "place spaces" of beneficial activity and exchange. Thus, as this chapter will argue, an emergent praxis (theory and practice) will necessarily form part of any viable economic renaissance, if indeed disciplines of any kind remain relevant as ways of knowing.

Actors and Monsters in a Westernized World

While the emphasis of this chapter is on the nature of this reframing, there are three foundational statements that assist in contextualizing the argument. The first asserts that the city is an economic actor and therefore is an integral part of any economic renaissance. The second contends that while every city is different (and this diversity is important) they are, for the most part, representations of a colonizing Western worldview. The third briefly traverses the evidence that suggests most cities, despite their attraction, are indeed becoming "monstrous," even though for the lucky few, the scale of this monstrosity is largely concealed behind a veneer of sophistication and elegance.

The concept of exchange is central to all economic theory and it can be argued that cities by their very nature bring into being particular forms of exchange, and then represent those forms in their artifacts, institutions, place making, and activities. The Japanese critical theorist Kojin Karatani[15] asserts that cities, as manifestations of emergent sedentary cultures, need to develop modes of exchange in order to maintain social cohesion. In this sense then cities are, by definition, macroeconomic. He contends that there are essentially four modes of exchange that often coexist, with one normally being dominant over the others. These include exchanges based on reciprocal gift giving; plunder-based exchanges that require the offering of protection for the dominant (plundering) community; commodity exchanges; and a higher dimensional, yet-to-be-realized communal mode of exchange that, in its nature, has some similarities to exchanges based on gift giving.[10]

Basing macroeconomics of the future on the nature of exchange at once frees thinking from the confines of Samuelson's circular flow diagram—which relates only to commodity exchange and its disregard for energy and "other externalities"—and the largely opinion-based, neoliberal economic narrative "about the efficiency of the market, the incompetence of the state, the domesticity of the household and the tragedy of the commons."[24] Such a reorientation also opens up the possibility of "world making," other than that which relates to fictional market equilibriums, continuous growth, work, inflation, and interest rates (Ibid, loc. 547). As a reframing, it shifts the debate from one that always asserts the primacy of the economic lens to one that considers how deeply embedded and integrated exchange activity (only some of which is economic) is in the fabric of human activity and history, especially in the cities where the majority of the world's population now lives. It also points to the idea that rethinking exchange is foundational to any economic renaissance.

If the mechanistic consequences of "circular flow" are the default basis for the analysis of cities, then the expectation is that the world's megacities and second-tier cities will drive a new era of growth through the primacy of connection or exchanges, based on the continued globalization of people (tourism), goods, data, and services. Indeed, some postulate that "cities in the 21st century are mankind's most profound infrastructure; they are the human technology most visible from space, growing from villages to towns to counties to megacities to super-corridors stretching hundreds of kilometers."[16] But this lens assumes that, while the sheer speed in the growth of both numbers and size of cities is completely disruptive, shifting the locus from Europe and North America to China and the Indian subcontinent,[6] there is a sameness in the character of these cities that simply replicates the nature and behavior of those already established in the industrial era.

However, there is little to justify this view. For instance, with the exception of parts of China—where, as it seeks to move a further 100 million from the countryside to new cities by 2020, the government investment in sameness is considerable—the mechanistic orderliness of the "ideal metropolis" that a universal macroeconomics requires seems missing in action. Rather, the growth of emerging cities more typically resembles a planet of slums, where "there is little or no planning to accommodate these people [who are attracted to what the city can provide] or provide them with services."[35] In parts of Nairobi and other African cities, for instance, the most common method of sewage disposal is a plastic bag (the flying toilet) thrown as far away from the individual as possible. This behavior is due to "the inaccessibility of toilet facilities especially during late hours and is due to uneven distribution and lack of convenience often resulting in insecurity."[20] Elsewhere, despite the promise of renewables, energy poverty—when combined with energy theft—has made investment in utilities unattractive. In other places (e.g., Mexico City, Chongqing, and Rio), poor or no infrastructure produces congestion nightmares that make Khanna's Connectography almost impossible. All of this comes together in the Gulf of Guinea (Lagos) megasprawl, a conglomeration that is so chaotic and inefficient that it has the dubious distinction of having the largest single footprint on earth.[5]

While this litany could go even further, from a macroeconomic perspective there are two points to be made. The first is to assert that that the monolithic idea of the city is insufficient for the diversity that now confronts us, even though the ethos of "development" still encourages investment into projects that make as many cities as possible in the image of the Westernized ideal. The second is to suggest that the processes of value exchange within that diversity cannot be reduced to oversimplified market concepts, or indeed a universally applicable theory. Consequently, however poorly, what is being designed and created are culturally and geographically specific assemblages, with only passing similarity to each other: a pluriverse of cities, not a universe of cities.

In this chaotic and complex pluriverse, there are a number of patterns that most cities share. First, almost all are completely dependent on either their immediate hinterlands, or on goods and services imported from elsewhere. In that sense they are not sustainable in their own right. Rather, they are statements of a technological triumphalism that asserts that humans can create settlements existing independently from the ecosystems in which they are nestled.

Second, while there is an emergent crisis on a global scale, with respect to freshwater availability, air quality, food availability, and global warming that is a systemic consequence of contemporary neoliberal-driven economic activity, at a localized level these same issues are beginning to have monstrous effects for cities designed with the expectation that extreme events are the exception, rather than the norm. For example, at the time of writing, the South African city of Cape Town has become the first modern city to confront just one of the dire consequences of global warming–induced climate variability: authorities may have to turn off the taps that provide the city with water, what locals have come to know as Day Zero. It may not come to pass, but the assertion of nature over humanity is palpable. Elsewhere other potential Day Zero type events have emerged. A few solutions towards sustainability are offered in Chapter 7.

Vast regions have come to a standstill as the polar vortex moved toward northern countries as a result of Arctic warming.[17] In war-torn regions like Syria, many consider that the influx of young men into cities seeking to escape regional drought and famine is one of the most significant contributors to the instability that follows. The litany of sorrow will most likely expand. This exponential increase in the number of extreme or Day Zero type events is now part of confronting a new normal for cities that were not designed to accommodate these levels of disruption. As such they will become increasingly problematic if, as the science posits, cumulative feedback effects of climate change from human activity (also called as global warming) have already locked in a 2°C increase by 2050 into the system.[26]

Third, in the making of cities, despite their apparent efficiencies, the general orientation is "humans first, nature second." While this is consistent with the economic theory of externalities, it at once brings into focus the macroeconomic conundrum. How can cities survive the adverse consequences of the very processes that have made them successful? To whit: the industrialization and commoditization of all valued goods and services (especially an increasing monoculture concentration of foodstuffs); the evident toxic by-products of modern production processes (think plastic in the sea); or the creation of investment and value exchange processes that demand continued growth and an almost religious attachment to an economic model that is mostly in denial about the adverse systemic effects of its application, and thus continues to drive climate change from human activity past safe limits?

Recent technological developments that radically reduce costs in both supply and demand create yet another contradiction, in that their success destroys the viability of parts of the marketplace without, it seems, creating new forms of activity that allows those displaced to find alternatives at the rates required to keep the system stable.[25] These contradictions are beginning to manifest themselves in the contemporary fabric of cities; as retailing goes online, blockchain-type technologies facilitate distributed, rather than centralized, transactions, and robotics begins to replace all kinds of work that can be standardized and systematized.

Finally, perhaps the "monster in the making" is not in consequences themselves, but in the mental seductions that are integral to the whole economic model. For the most part, we call these seductions consumerism; that is the art of persuading ourselves and everyone else that the acquisition of material things and particular lifestyles will make life and living so much better. While these microeconomic seductions of a macroeconomic ideal are often illusory artifices without foundation (more stuff makes you happier), the growth in credit dependence is, on a global scale, feeding a culture of extravagance that is at not only contrary to the notions of thrift and self-restraint around which earlier societies organized themselves, but is now also an essential foundation for the financial institutions that exist at the heart of the system itself.[34]

Additionally, the incentives for those that profit from these seductions is to, as far as possible, extend the values that would otherwise have a normality to them. Hence individualism becomes hyperindividualism with an overemphasis on the ego; objectification becomes hyperobjectification through incentivizing extreme specializations that argue that nothing is important if it can't be measured; and finally, economism morphs into the unfettered right to make money at any time in almost any circumstance (what we now describe as neoliberal economics). This relentless pursuit of "affluenza" has one other consequence for cities: it subordinates the role of citizen to the role of consumer. In so doing, it makes it difficult to institute value-exchange entities and processes that are not based on consumerism.

The monster, therefore, presents in many ways. It is evident in physical dysfunctions (polluted waterways for instance); social breakdowns (slums, drugs); widening inequities and inequalities[4]; the fragility of many apparently successful functioning parts when confronted by anything other than optimal operating conditions[32]; and in the contradictions inherent in the successful functioning of the system itself. However, the rapid uptake of network-based and renewable technologies (a new kind of technological triumphalism) is rapidly undermining and distorting many of the premises that are vital to the functioning of the current economic model and the supposedly vibrant and viable cities (the original technological triumphalism) that emerge as a consequence. If this is so then the question is: what's next?

New Forms Require New Thinking

That all is not well with modern cities has not gone unnoticed among those who care about such things. City leaders have, over the past two decades, invested in programs and projects to make their cities more appealing to the creative classes (creative cities), smarter (smart cities), greener (green cities), more diverse, and so forth. However, recent studies show that these endeavors not only principally "serve the corporate agendas of multinational consultancies and technology companies" but that they "suffer from a fragmented evolution along disciplinary lines and the field has yet to adequately address many of these limiting biases."[33] In short, despite the considerable amount of money spent on them, these concepts and projects cannot possibly generate the new thinking and new forms required to sustain viable cities. This is because they are situated within conventional understandings and worldviews and thus are more likely to be part of the problem rather than part of the solution.

The idea of new forms extends to language as well. It has been the practice (certainly in conventional economics) to use language rhythms and cadences that are succinct, even terse. These, either intentionally or otherwise, convey suggestions of mechanism, efficiency, and scientific rigor. All these of course are consistent with and reinforce the dominant model of progress that economics has been servant to. But now the world of cities and for that matter economic activity is much too complex, chaotic, and contradictory to simply be reduced to the system models of the machine. Thus new language, cadences, and rhythms must be used that are more nuanced, emergent, and more accommodating of the uncertainty that is likely to be the steady state of the future. For some, this will seem confronting for it destabilizes at a very deep almost poetic level the worldviews that have been central to most conversations in the last 50 years.

Outlined in the following are seven alternative ways of thinking about cities and their potential diverse forms. They are not intended to be exhaustive. Nor are they intended as a typology (typologies privilege a disciplinary bias). Rather, they are indicative of the design and practice potential that might be released if other forms are engaged. In brief, these are as follows:

- Cities have their own voice, and if cities are indeed an economic actor their voice must be incorporated into an economic renaissance.
- Larger cities as systems cannot be completely known to us, and as such, we never quite know what the effect of our actions might be.
- Cities are complex systems in the making that should not be seen as simply representative of a set of policies, economic activities, infrastructure bundles, or energy systems.
- The design of cities requires rethinking, not through applying noncontextualized theory, value systems, and beliefs, but rather from knowing that emerges pragmatically from the unique circumstances being considered.

- Cities should not be seen as convenient agglomerations of activity through which nonlocalized actors can extract the maximum value, while leaving only a residue behind. Rather, they should be seen as post-extractavist incubators of value creation and exchange that, through their interrelationships with other incubators, act in such a way that the systems so created within each of them, and between them, becomes more self-sustaining and self-regenerating.
- Network-based technologies and the shift from fossil fuels to renewables are redefining the way cities think about time, form, and space in ways that both create new opportunities yet also undermine those whose successes are based on place-dependent, competition-oriented conceptions of time, form, and space.
- Cities will always be different from each other because they establish their own uniqueness through the (positive or negative) pathways to the future they create in the "between" or "liminal" spaces.

The City Has Speech

In modernism and economics the city is seen as an object that we can either create, or do whatever we want to, especially if that interest is economic. It is not seen as an actor in its own right. However, the sociologist Saskia Sassen[30] argues "not so." She contends that cities should be treated in the same way we treat corporations—as systems that exist in their own right. Like corporations, cities have interests that should be protected, even though they are always in the making, and they are more than the constitution of their physical parts. This means cities have norms and identities that often affect how conflicts are resolved and how a strengthened "civicness" emerges. This establishes them "as strategic sites for major economic processes and for new types of political actors including non-urban processes and actors." (Ibid: 211) Sassen goes further to suggest that in ways that are nonverbal a city can, and does, speak to us through "its capability to alter, to shape, to provoke, to invite, all following the logic that aims at enhancing or protecting the city's complexity and its incompleteness" (Ibid: 214).

We collectively experience what the city is saying as we interact with its pressure points (rush hour), its reactions to stresses (storms), and its myriad ways of exchanging value and the interdependencies that creates, that all manifest in the coexistences that the city demands, both of humans and nonhumans. For instance, how much better would water quality be in many of the world's cities if the city was able to say, "I have a right to be pure," and be able to defend that right in the same ways that individuals and corporations can. This idea may not be as far-fetched as it first seems. In 2017, New Zealand's Whanganui river was granted by the Parliament the status of a person in law.[21] This de-objectification seems completely alien in the context of macroeconomic theory and is certainly disruptive to those interests that try to make one city merely a carbon copy of the one next to it. Strangely, however, it is completely understandable and reflected in the language and lived experience of city inhabitants everywhere. Hence, considering the city to be an economic actor with interests beyond economics and with a voice that is its own should be one of the conceptual foundations for a viable future economic renaissance.

Hyperobjects

The philosopher Timothy Morton reinforces the idea that megacities and second-tier cities can never be objectively known. He considers them along with entities such as black holes, global warming, and the global economy to be hyperobjects. These are systems that we cannot really objectify (although we try to) because we cannot see them in their entirety, or at a distance that would allow this to happen. These hyperobjects "occupy a high-dimensional phase space that results in them being invisible to humans for stretches of time."[19] This inability to see them in their completeness means we can only deal with specific interactions or local manifestations while accepting that they might at the same time be around us: in other words, we are immersed in them.

The Morton proposition suggests a profoundly different relationship than the one that requires objectification, rationalism, and human centeredness. While this hyperobjectivity does not deny the validity or usefulness of these latter lenses, it does suggest they have limitations; and that again compounds the case against a (Cartesian) "objective-centric," theory-first approach. It might also help to explain the theoretical and practical difficulties that seem evident in devising and setting policy frameworks for hyperobjects like global warming and the global economy.

Holism

A consequence of both the Sassen and Morton positions is that cities have a complexity and an incompleteness (for they are always evolving) that does not always respond in ways that are expected if other actors only concentrate on whichever characteristics of cities interest them the most. It is self-evident that cities have always been more than a set of policies, economic conditions and relationships, or infrastructures. Institutionally, however, we rarely think about them in this holistic manner. Rather, the tendency is to explore possibility through the hyperextension of dualisms ("public vs. private transport"; "high rise vs. sprawl"; "commercial vs. domestic" and so forth). Escaping the black hole of these dualisms, where solutions can only be determined somewhere along a defined spectrum requires beginning the conversation or the process of discovery from a different place. It necessitates moving from (always beginning with) the analytical and the empirical, which privilege ways of understanding that begin with the parts (reductionism), to considerations that begin with framings, phenomenology and/or poststructuralism.[13]

Pragmatism

Thus far we have contended that:

1. Cities are credible actors in their own right and they have voice;
2. Their size means that they have a nature we can never completely understand or totally objectify; and
3. That the ways of understanding that privilege dualism, and the analytical, are not necessarily the best place to start.

Such assertions seem to empty out the cupboard of ideas and tools that normally enable any city to evolve at the behest of the humans who assume to govern them. However, in more recent times, philosophers, designers, and system thinkers, including Rorty[27] and Latour and Porter,[18] posit that it is more likely that we can find truth, not from the scientifically theorized sense of reality that these conventions rely on, but rather from engaging with ways of knowing that are valid, if the practical consequences of that way of knowing make them so. For pragmatists, proponents of "trickle-down" economics should be able to demonstrate that there is actually a "trickle-down" effect occurring, which they can rarely do.[23] Further, they should be able to show that cities actually have become smarter as a result of their smart city strategy (an idea that Tompson et al. argue is a conceptual nonsense), or that planned diversity has actually encouraged the growth in the so-called creative classes.[8]

If very few of these top-down-driven assertions can be substantiated in actuality, it is likely that this is because they have not emerged from the "in the making" process that pragmatists advocate. In this conception of the city and a new urban macroeconomics, change must be defined as a continuously evolutionary process (an idea that is counterintuitive to most policy-oriented goals). It must necessarily engage with experimentalism that is reflective of the local condition at all times (which the measurement of authorized investment almost never allows). Additionally, categorizations and typologies that put things in boxes from which there is no escape (an interesting gift from Charles Darwin with hyper—or ultra—consequences he probably never intended) must be set aside.

How liberating, for instance, would this be for the never-ending transport debates that entangle most cities? These mostly focus on the box called "the infrastructures of movement" (roads, rail, etc.), rather than the systems that caused the need for movement in the first place. In other words, it is through considering pragmatic alternatives to the ways that cities arrange work and workplaces—how they organize and time education and child care; how they have separated work from living (suburbanism); and how these all interact with each other—that will ultimately determine transport needs. What pragmatism proposes is a kind of pluralistic empiricism—a temporal understanding and contextualized conception of reality and values[33]—that gives primacy to relations, rather than entities (Ibid: 218), and facilitates more than one way of knowing, thus potentially liberating cities from always being in a "Westernized" way of making.

Postextractivism and Postgrowth

Conceptualizing value exchange on a "relational" model, rather than an "extractivist and growth" model would also fundamentally change the dynamics of contemporary cities. At the present time most of the investment is focused on creating the infrastructures and market arrangements that facilitate maximizing (and growing) value from those arrangements for the benefit of an increasingly concentrated group of globalized investors, while leaving in place only a residual value necessary to continue that process. History would suggest that the more powerless the locals are, the more ruthless are the maximizing processes used, and that when further growth is no longer available, investment ceases and localities are abandoned normally, without recourse or redress. This process is exacerbated further if the public institutions, through corrupt practice, have an orientation toward privileging the few who benefit the most.

On the other hand, a relational value-exchange model obviates this by trying to rebalance the equation through the creation of "autopoietic" or self-regenerating arrangements and processes that, through their interactions and assemblages, continuously regenerate the networks and relationships that produced them.[7] While it is likely that these relational models would counter some of the excesses of "hyperindividualism," reduce often externally determined waste streams, and retain more of the value created for the use of the communities that created them, such propositions are often rejected as hostile to the narratives of the dominant economic establishment.

However, facilitation of the same at a local level can encourage expressions of commons (a completely different idea to state-sponsored socialism because in the latter instance, it is the institution of the state that determines the framing and nature of the sharing) and fewer investments in acquiring as many things as possible,[9] because the latter activity acts against the autopoietic capacity of the larger group. This relational centrism provides "an active, ongoing participation with others in implementing and maintaining shared purpose" and begins to build alternatives to particular interpretations of market culture that make and shape particular ways of being.[3] The American social and economic theorist Jeremy Rifkin[25] describes this as a new kind of freedom, which is "measured more by access to others in networks than by ownership of property in markets."

While propositions of this kind seem confronting to those that see the contemporary market culture and the ownership of private property as the raison d'être for all that life means, it may well be the only option available if humanity is to escape from any number of existential challenges. It also suggests that the world's cities are about to embark on a significant transformation—one that is more profound than that which occurred a mere 100 years ago as oil, electricity, and telephony became ubiquitous.

Time, Form, and Space

The ubiquitous use of network technologies and the advent of intelligent machines that can replace most kinds of systemized and standardized work are beginning to change the conceptions of time, form, and space that have shaped cities and organizations over the last century. These were for most part modeled on the idea that clock time can be commodified and therefore controlled, owned, and traded. Now, however, network technologies are having three important effects on the forms and spaces designed by the mechanistic mind.

First, many network technologies are exponential in their rates of improvement and adoption, leaving markets, entities, and cities scrambling to adapt to emerging realities they barely understand, and which are often completely antagonistic toward the "value" interests of existing stakeholders.

Second, the ability to work remotely, and to develop noncontractual value exchanges based on agreed outputs, potentially changes both the form of cities, and the spaces where work is carried out. No longer does the central business district (CBD) have the "place" attraction it once did; in fact, for many it is a disincentive.

Third, these same technologies are changing where, and by whom, information is controlled. This, as Adam[1] points out, "is the authoritative resource exploitable for surveillance and the domination of people." Taken together, and through the feedback loops they create, markets and other processes of value exchange have (mostly) broken free from the mechanized, centralized, control-oriented models that are embedded within the neoliberal economic model. The problem is that, for many, having realized that time is now their own, that form is rapidly evolving (particularly in the cost and nature of transactions—think blockchain); and that space rarely affords advantage, there is confusion about the way forward.

In a similar fashion, the shift to renewable energies at the point of consumption, and a decade-long transition to autonomous electric vehicles, will have similar effects. Its redefinition of the form of utility, and the spaces it occupies, completely flips the architecture of energy, potentially revolutionizes infrastructure, and changes every economic activity that is in some way dependent on fossil fuels. The Stanford technology theorist Tony Seba[31] suggests that, so profound is this change that the automotive industry as we know it will not exist in a decade or two: as fleets of autonomous vehicles make automobiles uncompetitive from a cost point of view, approximately more than 70 percent of cars on the road won't be there. If Seba is right, then the change to the city form is completely disruptive. It is a shift in the very core of the economic model, from needing to own stuff to use it to simply have access to it on demand.

Liminality

One of the reasons why every city cannot be the same as every other city is because each has "between spaces" in their markets, institutions, and lifestyles, where a multitude of goods and services are created to facilitate and make easier life in that unique location. This may be manifested as a "pop-up" coffee shop at the bottom of a building with no café, or a solar-powered recharge station for citizens who have no access to wall socket power desperately needing to charge their mobile phones. As these microactivities act and react with each other, they entangle and assemble themselves into a macroassemblage that provides a city identity unique to that place. Hence, the cities cannot ever be anything but diverse. The American design and social theorist Nora Bateson[2] calls the "between spaces" liminal zones—"places where the directions of potential pathways as yet uncharted live." Liminality, though, is not confined to place. It can also extend to value spaces that emerge as a consequence of convergence and divergence through disruptive technology, or in any situation where a system is nestled within, or close to, any other system. In a world of multiple uncertainties, the capacity to use liminality as a generative force, rather than a degenerative force, feeds imagination and aspiration, and like so many other things, it puts the emphasis on interrelationality rather than on nodes.

City Design and Transition

If cities are manifestations of particular ways of knowing and are becoming monstrous as a result of the application of that knowledge, then an alternative viable city needs to emerge through diverse narratives and different kinds of design thinking. This must describe the litany or presenting story/stories (i.e., the "who" and "what" it is); rethought structures and the systems that facilitate multiple modes of value exchange; the encouragement of alternatives to the present way of thinking and knowing—what some define as worldviews (otherwise the argument becomes circular)—to sit alongside accepted, but also reconceived, ways of thinking and knowing; and finally, the discovery, or rediscovery, of the deep mythologies that can sustain the options and assemblages being proposed. Using this architecture of litany, structure/system, worldview, and mythology,[14] this rethinking of cities, at multiple levels of reality, creates a scaffolding for their design, and thus needs to be symbiotic with conceptions of an economic renaissance.

Many of the elements of the "design of the pluriverse design transition" have been canvassed earlier in the chapter. This has a very different design architecture to that of the "universal city" conception of reality as shown in Table 4.1. At an evidentiary level, the contrast between the two manifests completely different ways of thinking and knowing: one that is familiar; one that is not so. While some might argue that the two can simply be blended, it is important to recognize that, if a particular set of worldviews and deep mythologies are sustained—even though the litany and systems appear to change—then over time (whatever the intention), the structures, systems, and evident stories (litany) will realign themselves in ways that are consistent with the worldviews and mythologies on which they are premised. That is why neoliberal economics, based on the unfettered right to make money, can never create or support social systems that are fair. If this holds true, then the essence of an economic renaissance that lies in the worldviews and mythologies it upholds, not in the changes in structure and system that it proposes to make.

One of the frequent counters to the advocacy for a "world in the making" is to ask for proof and certainty that a pluriversal future will be better than a universal future and given that over half the world's population lives in cities, this seems not unreasonable. The first point to make is that this position is often held by those advocating a level of change at a structural and systemic level, but who wish to continue to sustain those changes within the dominant worldview. In other words, they do not accept the premise (argued earlier) that systems are manifestations of the thinking and knowledge that informs them. For some, this might be because they simply haven't interrogated, or don't understand, what the worldviews they hold are, and thus they are not in a position to understand the linkages between how they see the world and the systems that manifest them. This is so often the case with those who have a deep discipline focus.

Second, the notion of "proof" at once concentrates the debate on the analytical and the empirical, while making tacit (almost invisible), rather than explicit, the framing in which the conversation is contextualized. This framing, of course, also determines which phenomena matter and which ones don't. Third, the issue of certainty is one that cannot be assured in a world that, through the connectivity of human and nonhuman actors, is forever complex, chaotic, contradictory, and uncertain.[29] The final point to make is that the confrontation of the causes of monstrosity, and the potential consequences that brings cannot logically be sustained within the system that caused the monstrosity in the first place. It is in this case that many of us need to think the unthinkable.

Thinking the Unthinkable

For many years, the central themes of this chapter would have been regarded as messages from the margins or, from among the more patronizing, as "just interesting idealisms." However, a recent UK/Europe study, "Thinking the Unthinkable," suggests that those who pretend to lead the present system are bankrupt when it comes to proposing a way forward within the conventional litany, unless they come from a position of unknowing hubris. The Gowing-Langdon report[11] contends that "many leaders agreed that something of a seismic scale and significance now challenges many assumptions that leaders traditionally make about their abilities to spot, identify and handle unexpected normative events."

Table 4.1 The difference in design thinking between the universal and the pluriversal city

	Universal cities	Pluriversal cities
Litany	Planned objects of humanity, ingenuity, and technology. Values are primarily Western and universally shared. The aspiration is to be the best of the same (hence benchmarking); creates resilience.	In the making—emergent from the interactions of relations. There are many values and ways of knowing that should coexist consistently within a safe operating space. Cities have rights and speech. Diversity is resilience.
Structure/ System	Reflective of mechanistic model of progress and efficiency. Value exchange is market-centric, extractivist, growth-centric, and capitalist (private ownership-centric). Theory and ideology drives design.	Ecological and holistic in orientation Value exchange is both communal and market-centric but is postcapitalist, postextractivist, and postgrowth in orientation. Pragmatic in design.
Worldviews	Civilization is based on individualism, objectification, scientific rationalism, cartesian dualism, and economism—a universe.	There is a pluriverse of worlds based on the interrelationship between humans and nonhuman entities that may be arational and aperspectival (beyond measurement).
Metaphor and mythology	Growth is necessary for prosperity. Time is money. Human technology and technology can prevail over nature (our servant).	Never-ending growth is toxic. Time, form, and space is negotiated and contextualized. The future depends on an autopoietic coexistence.

We have no doubt that those who consider themselves as city leaders are experiencing the same and thus "there has to be a more mature inbuilt acceptance in both systems and executive behaviors of a new inevitability" (Ibid: 24). The question then becomes one of moral compass, design, and imagination; what kind of reality are we really prepared to invest in?

Emergent Praxis and Reflections

In considering what the prior "design alternative" means for an economic renaissance, there are a number of praxis principles that seem evident. First, the investment in future cities should be to increase diversity in the nature, form, and cultural ethos of cities, rather than drive toward sameness or what is often termed cloning, for that diversity is more likely to accommodate heterogeneous imaginations, aspirations, and anticipations in ways that the current cynical monocultures simply can't.

Second, the dialogue about who the socioeconomic actors are in this future needs to extend beyond the private–public dualism to create a very different kind of market dynamic. This requires multiple means of value exchange, not all of which will, in a networked future, be monetary in the way that we now understand them. This variety in value exchange will further increase the diversity of cities and improve both the resilience and opportunities of market forms.

Third, the interrelational focus between cities and their hinterlands must be both informed by, yet also constrained by, the imperative to create the "safe operating spaces." This, of course, runs counter to the idea that the most productive land can simply be swallowed up through "market demand" into unproductive housing. It seeks to introduce the sustainability of the "nature of the relationship" into the value equation and it may see, for example, large tracts of food production activity occur within the city itself, a process that has multiple benefits. Finally, in the processes of exploring all of the aforementioned, we need to create a new kind of macroeconomics based on autopoiesis, and in so doing, increase the reach and metabolism of representations of explicit acts of imagination, aspiration, and anticipation that emerge from this autonomy. Basically, it calls for decentralized economic planning to create self-sustaining local economic units as proposed in *Mass Capitalism*.

Summary

A central theme of this chapter has been about designing for an increasing diversity, rather than investing in a controlling sameness, on the proviso that such diversities remain within the safe operating spaces for humanity; in other words, they stay within resource limits that the planet can sustain, and they work rapidly to ensure all humans are able to live with dignity—what Kate Raworth[24] describes as "doughnut economics." Making diversity explicit to design begins to make visible ways of living and knowing (multiple realities) that the present Western models, especially macroeconomics, has made invisible.

It therefore necessitates "new ways of theorizing and of generating collective action"[28] within an ecology of knowledges whose acceptability or otherwise is not predetermined by the scientific way of knowing. It is most likely that this diversity will emerge from pragmatic investment and action in the liminal spaces. It also requires a move away from monocultures of every kind in the economic realm. This includes moving away from the cloned town effect,[22] reducing dependence on the industrial–food complex and permitting "those who are not us" to dictate what reality should look like. Evidence suggests that where such "unravelling from" occurs there is an increase in the vibrancy, tolerance, safety, and health of the communities concerned.

The nature of this reconception and diversity runs contrary to powerful interests represented in both the public and private spheres. Therefore, its likelihood of success will only occur if it extends beyond the idea that reform of the public and private realm is the only way to frame, and thus constitute, the way forward. This is because both of these spheres already have deep patterns of behavior that are hard to undo. If a vibrant, reconstituted civic sector develops (that is, what exists between the public and the private) alongside multiple, "communing" entities (the logic of these is described by Bollier)[3] and some of the spheres these commons entities might engage in (as detailed by Hawken),[12] then the patterns of value exchange will necessarily change as well.

It is worth remembering that the networking technologies that are either available now, or soon will be, facilitate the many kinds of value exchanges being proposed here, and more importantly, they render almost neutral the competitive advantage of mechanistic-based transaction models.[25] Could it be that it is only with the emergence of this sector in the middle space that there will be sufficient knowledge to really understand what a new theory of macroeconomics should look like?

The consequence of confronting the monster must be to create new narratives, or make visible existing ones, that empower all kinds of cities to act differently while at the same time, as Bateson[2] suggests "recognizing the story of a [contemporary] world that is broken and binary. These other narratives [will] have a wider focus of a world of stories, woven and tangled in ever-changing response to one another." Without these stories of being, which go well beyond the hubris of smart cities (another binary model), cosmopolis everywhere will find it difficult to both self-organize and create the relationships necessary for diverse assemblages and autopoiesis. These "stewardship" narratives must coalesce around explicit acts of imagination framed through multiple contexts, be grounded in pragmatism and explore forms and types of symbiosis that the mechanistic world has long since forgotten. In their realization and transmission, they must anticipate a transcontextual world that will allow some seven billion people to coexist in ways that allow them to aspire to live well (Buen Vivir). In short, they must anticipate a completely different society than the one that we live in now, and if someone wants to call that an economic renaissance; so be it.

References

[1] Adam, B. 1990. *Time and Social Theory*. Oxford: Polity.

[2] Bateson, N. 2016. *Small Arcs of Larger Circles: Framing Through Other Patterns*. Triarchy Press.

[3] Bollier D., and S. Helfrich, ed. 2015. *Patterns of Commoning*. Amherst, MA: Leveller Press.

[4] Brill, S. 2018. *Tailspin: The People and Forces Behind America's Fifty-year Fall—and Those Fighting to Reverse it*, 1st ed. New York, NY: Alfred A. Knopf.

[5] Davis, M. 2007. *Planet of Slums*, Paperback ed. London, New York, NY: Verso.

[6] Dobbs, R., J. Manyika, and J. Woetzel. 2015. *Public Affairs, No Ordinary Disruption*.

[7] Escobar, A. 2018. *New Ecologies for the Twenty-first Century. Designs for the Pluriverse: Radical Interdependence, Autonomy, and the Making of Worlds.* Durham, NC: Duke University Press.

[8] Florida, R. 2005. *Cities and the Creative Class.* New York, NY: Routledge.

[9] Gebser, J. 1985. *The Ever-present Origin.* Athens, OH: Ohio University Press.

[10] Graeber, D. 2001. *Toward an Anthropological Theory of Value: The False Coin of Our Own Dreams.* New York, NY: Palgrave.

[11] Gowing, N., and C. Langdon. 2015. *Thinking the Unthinkable. A New Imperative for Leadership in the Digital Age.* London: Chartered Institute of Management Accountants.

[12] Hawken, P. 2017. *Drawdown: The Most Comprehensive Plan Ever Proposed to Reverse Global Warming.* New York, NY: Penguin Books.

[13] Inayatullah, S. 1999. *Situating Sarkar: Tantra, Macrohistory and Alternative Futures.* Maleny, Qld.: Gurukula Press.

[14] Inayatullah, S. 2005/07. *Questioning the Future: Methods and Tools for Organizational and Societal Transformation.* Causal Layered Analysis— Deepening the Future.

[15] Karatani, K., and M.K. Bourdaghs. 2014. *The Structure of World History: From Modes of Production to Modes of Exchange.* Durham and London: Duke University Press.

[16] Khanna, P. 2016. *Connectography: Mapping the Future of Global Civilization,* 1st ed. New York, NY: Random House.

[17] Kim, B.M., S.W. Son, S.K. Min, J.H. Jeong, S.J. Kim, X. Zhang, and J.H. Yoon. 2014. "Weakening of the Stratospheric Polar Vortex by Arctic Sea-ice Loss." *Nature Communications* 5, p. 4646.

[18] Latour, B. 2013. *An Inquiry into Modes of Existence: An Anthropology of the Moderns.* Cambridge, MA: Harvard University Press.

[19] Morton, T. 2013. *Posthumanities. Hyperobjects: Philosophy and Ecology After the End of the World.* Minneapolis: University of Minnesota Press.

[20] Mutisya, M., and M. Yarrime. 2011. "Understanding the Grassroots Dynamics of Slums in Nairobi: The Dilemma of Kibera Informal Settlements." *International Journal of Engineering, Management and Applied Sciences and Technologies.* http://TuEngr.com (accessed March 2011).

[21] New Zealand Parliament. 2017. "Get Involved, 'Features.' Innovative Bill Protects Whanganui River with Legal Personhood." https://parliament.nz/en/get-involved/features/innovative-bill-protects-whanganui-river-with-legal-personhood/

[22] Patterson, C. 2011. "Wales in a Global Neighbourhood: The Impact of Globalization on Two Welsh Market Towns." *Contemporary Wales* 24, no. 1, pp. 86–112.

[23] Pikketty, T., and A. Goldhammer (translator). 2014. *Capital in the Twenty-first Century.* Penguan, UK.

[24] Raworth, K. 2017. *Doughnut Economics: Seven Ways to Think Like a 21st-century Economist*. Chelsea Green Publishing.

[25] Rifkin, J. 2014. *The Zero Marginal Cost Society: The Internet of Things, The Collaborative Commons, and The Eclipse of Capitalism*. New York, NY: Palgrave Macmillan.

[26] Ripple, W.J., C. Wolf, T.M. Newsome, M. Galetti, M. Alamgir, E. Crist, and 15,364 Scientist Signatories from 184 Countries. 2017. "World Scientists' Warning to Humanity: A Second Notice." *BioScience* 67, no. 12, 1026–28. doi:10.1093/biosci/bix125/4605229

[27] Rorty, R. 1997. *Truth, Politics and "Post-modernism."* Assen: Van Gorcum.

[28] De Sousa Santos, B. 2014. *Epistemologies of the South: Justice Against Epistemicide*. Boulder, CO: Paradigm Publishers.

[29] Sardar, Z. 2015. "Postnormal Times Revisited." *Future* 67, 26–39. doi:10.1016/j.futures.2015.02.003

[30] Sassen, S. 2013. "Does the City have Speech?" *Public Culture* 25, no. 2, pp. 209–21.

[31] Seba, T. 2014. *Clean Disruption of Energy and Transportation*. Silicon Valley, CA: Clean Planet Ventures.

[32] Taleb, N.N. 2012. *Antifragile: Things That Gain from Disorder,* 3 vols. New York, NY: Random House.

[33] Tompson, T. 2017. "Understanding the Contextual Development of Smart City Initiatives: a Pragmatist Methodology." *She Ji: The Journal of Design, Economics, and Innovation* 3, no. 3, 210–228. doi:10.1016/j. sheji.2017.11.004

[34] Trentmann, F. 2016. *Empire of Things: How We Became a World of Consumers, From the Fifteenth Century to the Twenty-first,* London: Penguin Random House.

[35] UN-Habitat. 2003. *The Challenge of Slums: Global Report on Human Settlement*. London.

CHAPTER 5

Beyond Sustainable Capitalism: Why Green Technology Alone Cannot Save the Environment

Roar Bjonnes

Toward Deeper Sustainability

According to green activist Alex Steffen, we cannot create a world we cannot imagine. He is one of the leaders of a new and influential movement of "bright green" activists who claim that technological innovation is the safest and fastest way to create a sustainable economy. Distinctly different from the "dark green" environmentalists of the past whose goal is often less technology, the "bright greens" do not shy away from using technology to solve our mounting environmental problems. Architect William McDonough and chemist Michael Braungart, authors of the path-breaking book *Cradle to Cradle*, would agree. They also hope that new technology can save us. These innovators and writers have introduced a new system of "biomimicking," in which they have demonstrated technological innovations mirroring the way nature works, so that we can create an industry in which "effluence is turned into affluence."

Similarly, environmental businessman, author, and spokesperson Paul Hawken claims that green business, or "natural capitalism," will change the world, since the world of business is the most powerful force on the planet. John Mackey, the founder of Whole Foods, the giant organic food chain, now owned by Amazon, promotes "conscious capitalism," a system he believes holds the promise of a technologically advanced economy with a small planetary footprint.

While I applaud these environmental activists for their enthusiasm, I do not share their one-sided vision: that simply wedding green technology and innovation with capitalism will save us from planetary economic and environmental breakdown. While McDonough and Braungart's book features an important spoke in the large and complex wheel of sustainable economics, few of the industrial ecological designs featured in the book when it was published in 2002 have so far become mainstream. Their main thesis is that we don't have an economic problem, but we have a design problem—we need industrial designs that mimic the way nature works, so that all industrial waste become nutrients in the next industrial and technological process. This is an important feature of a much-needed new economy. But why are such fundamentally green features not being implemented? Because we don't only have a design problem, we have more fundamental problems: most importantly, an economy that has a serious design problem of its own; an economy that does not reflect the way nature works, and perhaps more importantly, we have an economic and cultural worldview that is more competitive than cooperative. In this chapter, I will show why we therefore need to look deeper in order to find long-term solutions to the crisis we are in, so that green technology, including robotics, can thrive in a world economy for generations to come.

From the Growth Economy to the Eco-Economy

Let us first take a closer look at the crucial interconnectedness between the economy and the environment. Let us take a look at why green policies are as essential as improved technology and good wages, and why they are needed to offset the environmental problems caused by today's economy. Most importantly, let us focus on some of the best solutions that have emerged in the last few years; how they work, and why some of them may not offer enough prevention to stop us from global, ecosystems collapse, and hence also economic collapse. In other words, why the current way of practicing sustainability is not sustainable enough. The reason for that is not because we do not understand the environment; it is because we have not developed an economic structure working in harmony with and being a coordinated expression of the environment.

To illustrate this last point, let us look at my birth place, Norway. Thanks, in part, to a thriving oil industry, Norway has one of the highest per capita incomes in the world. People live in bigger houses and drive fancier cars than they did 30 to 40 years ago. Thanks to increased use of alternative technology, the country is on the top 10 list of the "most sustainable" countries in the world, (after Iceland, Switzerland, Costa Rica, and Sweden and before France and Austria).[1] But the new cars, boats, ski-houses in the mountains, and the large homes are, after all, mostly financed by hefty bank loans.

These technological advances point to a remarkable juxtaposition: Norway is one of the "most sustainable" countries in the world according to some researchers, but according to other indicators, it is also one of the countries in the world with one of the highest levels of consumption, with one of the highest carbon footprints of any country. In other words, how sustainable is being sustainable in today's economy? The way I think of sustainability, Norway is not very sustainable at all. Which points to the heart of the problem: capitalism itself. Norwegian economist and author Per Hjalmar Svae says that the challenge before us today is clear: to transition from a growth economy to an eco-economy, from an economy addicted to fossil fuels to a carbon-neutral economy fueled by renewable energy.[2] That is, to transition to a new economy, through both legislative and structural change, an economy in which both people and nature matter and where ecology informs economic and technological decision making.

Environmental Challenges and Victories

As corporate globalization expanded, and as environmental problems such as acid rain, the ozone hole, and chemical pollution from industry intensified, green lifestyle values and protests increased in popularity. As these environmental values have gained publicity over the past 40 years, however, real sustainability has, for the most part, decreased worldwide. And, while there is a growing movement to support local business and local agriculture, globalization—with its products made by sweatshop labor in China and raw materials from Africa, with its McDonalds and Walmarts, with its increased automation and technological advances—is marching ahead with ever-increasing speed. While awareness of the dangers of global warming is increasing, the production of greenhouse gases is also increasing with the expansion of the global market economy—various attempts at political legislation to reduce CO_2 have so far been unsuccessful globally.

And, finally, while the awareness of the importance of recycling is increasing, the amount of plastic trash in the oceans and the general environment is also multiplying at an alarming rate, and its leached toxins is affecting animals as far away as the North Pole. While the technology for making green, compostable plastics are here, short-term economic goals continue to produce that which is toxic but most profitable. In other words, we don't really have a design problem, we have an economy driven by short-term profit motives, which prevents us from incorporating true environmental designs. It's not our technological or industrial designs that are the problems, it's our economic design that is the main problem. And once we transform the economy, then the environmental and technological designs will follow.

The Ultimate Global Challenge

Today, global warming is the environmental catalyst preoccupying humanity, indeed threatening our very survival and symbolizing, more than ever, the interconnection between human civilization and the environment. It is also a symbol of the interconnection between economic growth and its impact on nature. We were able to solve acid rain in Europe without reducing economic growth. We were able to prevent ozone depletion by eliminating chlorofluorocarbons (CFCs) in our fridges, cars, and aerosol cans. But it does not look like we will be able to reduce global warming so easily. While the technology is available to reduce global emissions, while we know basically what we need to do, global warming has become a deeply embedded symptom of a systemic crisis in global society: a market economy creating vast wealth and growth, but also inequality, poverty and environmental destruction in its wake. We cannot solve global warming the same way we solved the ozone problem: global reduction in emissions will not solve the inherent economic and environmental problems caused by market capitalism. We will not solve the main challenge facing all human civilization: to create an economic system balancing prosperity, relative equality, and sustainability for all. This noble and mighty task, and not another "quick fix" to reduce global warming, is indeed our real global challenge.

Green Capitalism: An Inherent Contradiction

Internationally, as awareness of environmental destruction has grown. Many politicians emphasize the importance of environmental protection, prominent economists promote green values and theories, and green activists highlight the importance of voting with your money by shopping green. But despite all the green technological innovations, research, and activism, and the resurgence of green party politics, on the whole, the planet has not become any greener—quite to the contrary. The reason for this is the magnitude of global material growth without the corresponding environmental mechanisms to protect people and nature.

This development has prompted leaders in the green movement to question not only the sanity of the market economy and its goal of ever-more competition and profit, but also the sanity of the materialistic, fast-paced culture, which capitalism inspires and creates. The green movement is also rightly questioning the very concept of modern progress.

The green leaders proclaim that the goal of the economy is not simply to produce more material things more efficiently, but rather to create the material means to support a society where people's basic needs are met and where they can prosper in communities, in harmony with nature, while pursuing personal and spiritual development. Instead, we have quickly adopted an economy that created an individualistic monoculture of using more material things than we need and using more resources than the planet can support. In the process, we have lost a fundamental aspect of the good society: local culture and community. And if we continue to grow at the same pace, we will sooner or later run out of resources and of thriving, living communities. In this regard, the greens, perhaps more than any other political group, are pointing toward some fundamental problems with our global society and economy.

I do not want to imply that our challenge as a society today is to return to a nostalgic past without sophisticated technology, but rather to create a future where family, community and sustainability represent the base of society and the soil from which a technologically advanced and green economy can grow. In the right economic environment, green technology has the potential to become the tool for expanding cultural expression, sustainability, service, communication, and learning rather than to simply be an aid for corporations to create products solely for profit. What we need first, then, more than technological innovation, is a restructured, green economy.

Green capitalism, or natural capitalism, is the main catchall phrase used to describe the main economic reform ideas for creating sustainability to have emerged in the past 30 years. Another way to describe green capitalism is by using the value statement represented by the slogan "people, planet, and profit," which expresses a new way to conduct business, measured not only by its profitability but also by its services and responsibility to the community and the environment. According to natural capitalism, a green business will be able to compete in the market place by saving energy, reducing waste, and using more earth-friendly materials. As natural resources dwindle, and as green technology improves, and industry uses biomimicry to recycle all waste into the production cycle, these companies will edge ahead of the competition in the capitalist marketplace.[3] Both people and planet will win, while the companies will collect a handsome sum of profits in the bargain.[4] Let us take a closer look to see if these green capitalist truisms can actually deliver what they promise.

While I largely agree with the green movement's assessment of the unsustainable society that market capitalism has created, the greens have overlooked some fundamental issues causing environmental problems in the first place.

By operating within the framework of capitalism, the greens are often trying to solve society's problems by using the same kind of economic system that created the problems in the first place. The greens are not alone in this, since the dawn of capitalism, reform politics have tried to fix many symptomatic problems caused by market capitalism through protests, boycotts, unionization, strikes, votes, and legislations without addressing the underlying cause. Sometimes, these efforts represented a humane reaction against an inhumane system and have brought about important changes from which we all benefit; but often the result has been to use market capitalist methods to fix market capitalist problems. Hence, while the greens realize there is a systems-crisis facing our culture and economy, green reform policies have yet to adequately address the systemic problems of market capitalism and its inability to create a good society for both people and planet.

Production, Distribution, and Sustainability: The Emergence of a New Economy

In any modern society, there are two key problems needing to be solved: production and distribution of goods, services, and money. The capitalist market economy has not been successful in solving either of these challenges in an optimum way. While market capitalism promotes competition and therefore stimulates growth, new technology, and new products, the market also creates many unnecessary, inefficient, and environmentally harmful products, namely because the market's main goal is profit.

Because of the profit motive, the market will generally stimulate production of technologies and goods creating the most profit, thereby emphasize the cutting of costs and de-emphasize social and environmental responsibility. In the last 30 years, however, due to a dramatic rise in environmental problems, social and political pressure toward corporations to produce more environment-friendly products have increased. Hence, the free market has, to a limited degree, listened and responded by producing more energy-efficient and environment-friendly products, such as more fuel-efficient cars. We know, however, that as long as there is still relatively inexpensive oil available, it is not in the interest of the car and oil companies to switch to the sole production of alternatively powered cars, which of course would be much better for the environment.

More importantly, on a global scale, China, India, Brazil, and many other developing countries aspire to the same material living standard as Europeans and Americans. Using the same outdated and unsustainable economy we currently have in developed economies; such a development would have potentially catastrophic consequences. Take just one common, global consumer item: meat. It takes 10 to 20 times more land to produce an ounce of meat protein than vegetable protein, and the average person today consumes three times the meat that they did in 1960, 75 percent of which is consumed by the global north. China, the world's second largest corn-growing nation, is already unable to grow enough grain to feed its growing pig population. A large percentage of the shortfall is made up with imported soybeans from Brazil, one of the few countries able to expand its cropland by plowing up rain forest. According to National Geographic, "Increasing demand for food, feed, and biofuels has been a major driver of deforestation in the tropics. Between 1980 and 2000 more than half of new cropland acreage in the tropics was carved out of intact rain forests."[5]

Green Legislation: An Important but Limited Step to Sustainability

While green consumerism is relatively popular in the United States, green legislation and government subsidies for sustainable development are not. Hence, the country remains one of the most unsustainable economies in the world, and it has the world's highest consumption and the worst carbon footprint. Without stronger regulations of the market economy, we cannot expect much greening of the overall U.S. economy unless there is a total restructuring of the economy. Mainly depending on growing consumer demand for greener products is not enough. Europeans have understood this problem more keenly than American voters, not to speak of U.S. politicians. Therefore, European green parties are much more influential than in the United States; therefore, more extensive green legislation has been achieved in Europe than in the United States; therefore, genetically modified organisms (GMOs) are outlawed in Europe, but not in the United States; therefore, on the list of the 10 most sustainable countries in the world, there are six European countries, in addition to Cuba, Costa Rica, Mauritius, and Columbia. In a market-based economy that exists today, one will not be able to green the economy without strong regulation, centralized, governmental planning of the economy, and a sizeable bureaucracy to enact and uphold new laws.

The United States is one of the most deregulated market economies in the industrialized world. It is therefore unrealistic to expect the United States to do what Denmark—a much more regulated, mixed economy—has decided: to be 50 percent powered by offshore wind by 2020. The country is even running ahead of schedule—already in 2014 a government report stated that Denmark had produced 35 percent of its energy from renewables and that the country aimed at being 100 percent self-sufficient in renewable energy by 2050.[6] While the European Union (EU) has, albeit on a relatively small scale, shifted some agricultural subsidies to organic farming due to their environmental benefits, the United States has done relatively little in that regard. As a result of this policy difference, 4.1 percent of EU farmland was organically cultivated in 2008, compared to only 0.6 percent in the United States. In other words, legislation toward a more sustainable world works, but if we use farming as an example, the changes have been incremental at best.

Currently only 0.9 percent of the world's agricultural land is organic. However, some smaller countries have reached far higher shares: Falkland Islands (35.7 percent), Liechtenstein (26.9 percent), and Austria (18.5 percent). Seven countries have more than 10 percent organic land under cultivation. As we can see, the changes toward more sustainable agriculture are very slow. The main obstacle is the outdated market structure, in which environmental issues are mostly measured against profit concerns, in which economic growth at the lowest cost to the corporations are the main drivers of progress.[7] Some environmental legislation in the United States has taken place, of course, but the primary changes are voluntary, instituted, and promoted by individuals or organized groups of consumers, farmers, scientists, educators, politicians, activists, and business owners—within the so-called socially and environmentally responsible communities of concerned citizens.

The more the deregulation, the more that is simply left up to market forces, the less sustainability. Environmental regulations can help curb this negative trend but must also be combined with economic restructuring. Since Denmark has a much more restructured, mixed economy than the United States, where public will and interests, at least sometimes, counts more than corporate power and market forces, the country can more easily create national policies in favor of people and planet than the

United States. Yet, on the whole, we need to do even better than Denmark if we are to create a more sustainable planet. Despite an increased number of windmills, according to a 2012 report from the Worldwide Fund for Nature, Denmark has the fourth largest per-capita ecological footprint in the world.

The Profit Motive: The Main Challenge to Sustainability

The gift of the green movement has been to show that "prosperity transcends material concerns."[8] That true wealth resides in the quality of our lives, in vibrant communities and in a healthy environment. True wealth has little to do with profit. The greens have also managed to present a new macroeconomic vision where sustainability triumphs growth, where consumption for real needs and not mindless consumerism guides economic planning, and, most importantly, they have emphasized the need to establish environmental and resource limits on economic activity so that there is no overproduction. What the greens have overlooked, however, is the power of the profit motive, the structurally in-built growth impulse in capitalism, which will triumph all other visions, unless we restructure the macroeconomic system itself. It is that simple. But why?

The profit motive in capitalism makes the market undemocratic and monopolistic. Capitalism is fundamentally based on property rights, while democracy is based on personal rights. And as Princeton University economist Jaroslav Vanek claims, "the most important aspect of capitalism, its objective function, is to maximize profit." In other words, fundamentally speaking, capitalist firms do not like regulation; they do not like to be told to add costs, including environmental costs, to the profit equation. They will fight that possibility at every turn of the way. It is for no other reason than this that greenwashing—when companies spend more money or time advertising they are green than actually being green—is so common. That is also why a completely unregulated capitalist economy and a democratic and sustainable economy are incompatible.

Hence, we have two choices: we can, as we do today, make incremental or half-hearted changes through legislation, or we can make more fundamental changes by making the economy more democratic, by extending democratic values to the economy through restructuring, by adopting new economic principles. This new economy's objective will not be to maximize profit but to maximize the economic well-being of people and the environment through better participation and planning. The main difference between my suggestions and most green policy suggestions, then, is that they emphasize legislation, and I maintain that this is not enough to curb the profit motive; what we also need is economic restructuring.

The Need of the Hour: Economic Restructuring

We must restructure our economy, or else the old economic vision will continue to drive profit concerns, and we will continue to look at nature as a free lunch and a sink hole to dump our waste in. But rhetoric aside, what is the main problem with the old economy? It is the size and goal of the capitalist market, its inevitable nature to grow and concentrate wealth in the hands of the few and thus compromise human and environmental concerns. This issue has not been adequately addressed in the current reform models of capitalism, nor by the green movement. Indeed, we are far from the much-needed goals. Today's market economy is allowed to maintain its many outdated, oversized, inefficient, and unsustainable aspect, resulting in a complex economy driven to the brink by its greed for ever more profit.

The most comprehensive system of economic restructuring to date has been presented by Indian social thinker, late Shrii P. R. Sarkar in his progressive utilization theory. The proposed new business model for technology sector of economy could be found in book *Mass Capitalism: A Blueprint for Economic Revival*. In this three-tiered model, the capitalist market economy is considered best suited for smaller scale private enterprises, the way Adam Smith originally intended it. If not broken up, if not restructured, as a matter of governmental policy, the corporate giants will continue to grow the market to unsustainable levels, Just like today. No matter how many checks and balances society sets in place; no matter how ethical our leaders are. Therefore, the first order of business in creating a sustainable economy is to restructure private capitalism to only comprise small private businesses such as restaurants, farms, shops, artisan breweries, and bakeries, and so on. Sustainability is simply incompatible with present corporate capitalism.

If capitalism is left structurally unchanged—that is, without reducing the size and power of the corporations—the profit motive will eventually dominate the economic and cultural esprit of society. Most importantly, it will slow the inevitable emergence of the new economy; an economy built not only on competition, but on worker cooperation and entrepreneurial collaboration.

Thus, the second tier in Shri P. R. Sarkar's business model is a restructured corporate economy into a neocooperative economy. Are there any examples of such an economy existing today? There are co-ops and worker-owned industries, banks, farmers markets, local work exchange programs, agricultural processing plants, service projects, and health clinics in most all countries of the world. These businesses are already a thriving part of the world's economy, but to create a major shift in economics, they need to take a more dominant place in the economy. As of today, 1,478 cooperative banks and other businesses across 46 countries had a turnover of over $100 million each. In addition, there are thousands of smaller co-ops in virtually every country in the world. According to Jaroslav Vanek, one of the world's foremost authorities on economic democracy institutions, once these "democratic firms are organized... they work far better than capitalist enterprises." In a candid and in-depth interview about co-ops, professor Vanek covered many of the functions and reasons why various forms of democratic enterprises are more efficient, people friendly, environmentally sound, and the best hope for the poor regions of the world:

> The so-called ESOP, worker-controlled businesses [in the US], is a step in the right direction. Another is profit sharing. They are opening new vistas. Economic democracy is based on a competitive system, with a large number of autonomous firms which, by themselves, cannot fulfill all the functions of a large company. Democratic companies, which are smaller and more personal, need support systems to help in these areas. These would be second level co-ops. They would follow in the same spirit of the larger firms, maximizing welfare and income for all its members.

You can see the practical implications of what I am saying in the Mondragon co-ops of Spain.

For poor regions of the world, where there is little industrial development, Vanek thinks co-ops are the best way to develop local industry:

> There are existing enterprises already in place. These can be leased to the workers [in poor areas] at a reasonable price. It could be in the form of a fixed lease contract that would give an incentive to the workers to earn extra income. The lease money would have to be efficiently allocated to those who need it for startup costs. The best use of finance is to develop second level co-ops. If we have mining in an area, we should also have local production facilities. Rather than ship copper to Moscow for smelting, they could build a smelter and factories for the production of copper commodities for sale in their local market as well as for export.

Vanek also brings up an important point about local economies and cooperative production: the importance of processing local resources locally. Economic democracy depends upon local people having a control over and profiting from the use of local resources. The function of finance is not to gamble with the future in order to make profit for bankers, but to assist in the development of local production facilities. The best way to achieve this is to also make banks cooperative community institutions.

Not only are cooperatives more efficient, they increase solidarity and a sense of individual worth. On the one hand, one's effort in the workplace is experienced as a valued contribution to society, and on the other hand, one is working as a part of a team and has a direct, democratic influence over one's life situation. This connection generates happiness, and the more a nation or a region increases its happiness, the dependency on overconsumption decreases. Hence, a local economic base leads to a more balanced use and allocation of resources, and a "demonstrated capacity to innovate, since they can react to external challenges and meet new needs arising at local level."

Political democracy—a single vote every four years—is not enough, we also need economic democracy, people's ability to create and manage their own economic destiny from day to day, and from the grassroots up. In addition, we need an economy that is need-based not greed-based, an economy measuring its economic health on how well it delivers basic needs, how good the purchasing capacity of people is, not how high the GDP is. This does not mean that businesses will not make profit, of course. It simply means that economic health will be measured by growth and sustainability from the bottom up (by measuring growth in consumer purchasing power) rather than from the top down (by only measuring the GDP of the economy). Economic health will instead be measured by economic purchasing capacity, the real income, of the common person, and not, as today, on GDP, the economic wealth of the nation. The GDP, in fact, says nothing about the economic health of the average citizen, or the sustainability of an economy; it simply measures the total output of the economy, even if those outputs represents negative growth: more crime, or more industrial pollution through economic growth. These structural economic changes are of the greatest need in today's economy, and they will take place, either through popular legislation or through crisis—most likely both.

Finally, we need a smaller size but a stronger government to implement sound economic and environmental policies as well as to sustain the growth of capital-intensive industries such as semiconductor manufacturing, and so on. This third tier of the economy in the progressive utilization theory is termed a key industry and will be run in such a way that the government, from the state level to the local level, can truly serve both the people and the environment. It has been elaborated in depth for the technological sector of economy in the book *Mass Capitalism: A Blueprint for Economic Revival*.

Envisioning a Technologically Advanced and Sustainable Society

Global society is entering a perfect storm, a critical time, and perhaps a crisis of unprecedented proportions. A global crisis in which financial crashes, environmental hazards, resource depletions, economic inequality, and job losses resulting from automation which, if not solved within a relatively short time, will cascade into an unpredictable, global catastrophe making the finance crisis, even the Great Depression, looks like a temporary, economic hiccup in comparison.

With this dramatic backdrop in mind, it is even more important to keep the vision of hope and technological creativity alive. But we also need to be practical and realistic, remind ourselves that we cannot create a more sustainable world simply by buying or creating green products or by voting green. Remind ourselves that corporations will not create sustainability by simply changing to more energy efficient light bulbs in their offices. Remind ourselves that politicians cannot save the planet by simply paying lip service to the grave environmental needs of our time. Unfortunately, it is not that simple. We need to create a systemic shift in technology, economics, and science, in the way we produce, consume, and dispose of our products. We need a systemic shift from a greed-based to a need-based economy; from an economy of free trade to fair trade, from an export-based to a self-reliant economy.

The self-reliance, culture, and power that has been taken away from local communities in both the developed and developing world has to be taken back by these same communities. In order to recreate a greener, more sustainable world, power needs to be decentralized into the hands of local communities, into the hands of local businesses and local politicians and away from centralized corporations and bureaucrats in faraway places like Washington DC or Brussels. Local communities need to decide the pace and format of their own sustainable local development.

Conclusion

I agree with Alex Steffen and the "bright greens" that in order to create a new, more sustainable world, it is not enough to criticize and just say "no" to what we do not like. We must also envision and say yes to what we want. As I have shown earlier, that vision must include a new, restructured economy in which corporate capitalist firms are transformed into small-scale private firms and large-scale neocooperative firms, such as employee stock ownership plan (ESOP) companies. Without that transformation, no matter the amount of know how we have about environmental, cradle-to-cradle design principles, no matter how efficient our green technology becomes, no matter how many robots we have, we will not be able to create a globally sustainable economy. Rather we will still have a divided world: half-hearted sustainability for the rich and little or no sustainability and economic justice for the poor. We must, therefore, envision these new economic dreams as a real, alternative possibility. We must envision a future where:

- Local people are allowed to be empowered by their actions;
- Capitalism's profit motives at expense of environmental damage are curbed;
- The economy is restructured into three-tiered business model;
- Cooperation is the main driver of the economy;
- Science and technology are not allowed to triumph human and ecological values;
- Both local organic commodities and community can thrive together with advanced Internet technology, AI, robotics, high-tech electric cars and locally owned shops;
- Positive cultural values from the past can co-exist with new technologies and inventions;
- Economic development and environmental protection are not mutually exclusive;
- There is balance between market forces and meaningful political regulations;
- Production is not based on creating maximum profit but on meeting people's real needs; and
- Local and global interests co-exist in a dynamic harmony.

References

[1] Research developed by Yale Center for Environmental Law and Policy in collaboration with World Economy Forum, Switzerland, available at http:// ciesin.columbia.edu/documents/EPI_2010_report.pdf

[2] Per Hjalmar Svae. 2013. *Løsningen er Grønn*. (The Solution is Green) Flux Forlag.

[3] For more information on biomimicry and natural capitalism, see Hawken, P., L. Hunter Lovins, and A. Lovins. 1999. *Natural Capitalism: Creating the Next Industrial Revolution*. Little, Brown and Company.

[4] Rogers, H. 2013. *Green Gone Wrong: Dispatches from the Frontlines of Eco-capitalism*. Verso Books.

[5] Bourne, J.K., Jr. 2009. "The Global Food Crisis." *The National Geographic*.

[6] Article by Charley Cameron, April 2, 2013 in Inhabitat, an online magazine, available at http://inhabitat.com/denmark-now-25-percent-powered-by-offshore-wind-aims-to-double-capacity-by-2020/

[7] Willer, H., and K. Lukas, eds. 2011. *The World of Organic Agriculture—Statistics and Emerging Trends*. IFOAM, Bonn, Germany & FiBL, Frick, Switzerland.

[8] Tim Jackson, as quoted in Lewis, M., and P. Conaty. 2012. *The Resilience Imperative: Cooperative Transitions to a Steady-state Economy*. New Society Publishers.

CHAPTER 6

Will Artificial Intelligence Enable a Collaborative Socioeconomic System or Entrench a Predatory System?

Stephen Willis

The Promise of Artificial Intelligence in the Workplace

The Perfect Servant

The artificial intelligence (AI) tsunami is bearing down on every process of every business in every sector of the economy. A new breed of intelligent robots is already taking over repetitive, monotonous, stressful, and dangerous tasks. Like their predecessors, the AI newcomers work tirelessly, faster, more accurately, and on a 24×7 schedule.

However, earlier stages of automation look infantile compared to current AI-driven automation. Ever-evolving AI robots are being programmed to communicate and cooperate, and increasingly take on complex decision-making without the aid of human go-betweens and overseers. Thus, AI-empowered robots are being deployed in much more complicated roles and on a far grander scale than ever before.

AI capability promises to be a boon for both productivity and profitability. Business media and consulting company advisories are replete with the glowing promise of AI and the need to jump on board to reap its prodigious efficacy for every task and process, such as product design, business intelligence, strategic planning, decision making, customer engagement, sales, security, logistics, and so on.

AI-powered productivity and problem solving have the potential to supercharge the well-being of entire societies, including boosting global living standards, slashing poverty, and tempering excessive inequality. Thorny problems regarding environmental pollution, health care, and feeding a growing population can be addressed more effectively. At the same time, people can gain the freedom to work less and focus on more meaningful pursuits or leisure activities.

AI is envisioned to be the perfect servant for humans as they engage in their socioeconomic enterprises. Gartner, a Fortune 500 research and advisory firm, concluded that:

> For the next 10 years at least, work will revolve around human beings, with AI and smart machines augmenting human aptitude and capabilities. In 2027, human beings will still be at the center of work, even as intelligent software and machines become our co-workers.[1]

Golden Age of AI Cooperation

AI's transformation of product design demonstrates its ability to serve and collaborate with human designers. AI can comprehend inputted specifications and spit out thousands of design options not conceived by their human counterpart. And with experience it learns and performs more productively.[2]

> If generative design, robotics, and the IoT are the technologies allowing humans and machines [to] work collaboratively on design tasks, Artificial Intelligence (AI) is the secret sauce that accentuates their impact.
>
> AI allows technology to learn, so our tools can get better at doing their jobs. Generative design tools will begin to learn which of designs people like and which ones we don't. Robots (and even smartphones) will no longer need to receive detailed instructions from their users. The IoT will leverage AI not only to perceive the world, but to adapt to it intelligently.

This newly added layer of artificial intelligence will make technology more adaptive, more flexible, and more creative in solving problems. As a consequence, computers will begin to improve upon human capabilities such as reason, intuition, and imagination.

Engineers and designers should no longer view tools as machines that require elaborate instructions, but instead as collaborators whose input contributes to solving complex, thorny problems that humans alone could not.

This unprecedented blend of humanity and technology will be exciting to experience. As machines and computers start developing human-like capabilities that complement our own, it will fundamentally change society's relationship with our tools, … .

AI's amazing capability understandably raises issues about the value of human workers. For example, AI bots can engage in personal interactions with humans, even mimicking complex human behaviors such as sympathy. TGI Fridays increased productivity while limiting costs by "employing" a machine learning and AI platform instead of people to interact personally with customers:[3]

Now, patrons can chat up the AI for happy hour suggestions and appetizer specials, engage in small talk using emojis, make reservations, and order takeout via social media channels and through Amazon Alexa.

"We thought about how technology could help us create that one-on-one personalized messaging outside of the bar without having to hire 1,000 people to respond to individual guests," says … acting CIO at TGI Fridays.

Despite such often well-publicized examples of AI replacing human workers, a *Harvard Business Review* article suggests that fears of workers losing jobs and becoming un-needed are unfounded. The authors foresee AI working with humans primarily as collaborators rather than as competitors:[4]

Artificial intelligence is becoming good at many "human" jobs—diagnosing disease, translating languages, providing customer service—and it's improving fast. ... While AI will radically alter how work gets done and who does it, the technology's larger impact will be in complementing and augmenting human capabilities, not replacing them.

In our research involving 1,500 companies, we found that firms achieve the most significant performance improvements when humans and machines work together. Through such collaborative intelligence, humans and AI actively enhance each other's complementary strengths: the leadership, teamwork, creativity, and social skills of the former, and the speed, scalability, and quantitative capabilities of the latter. ... Business requires both kinds of capabilities.

An example of human–AI machine collaboration can be observed in the world of modern-day chess. The advent of AI has produced a form of chess in which teams consisting of humans assisted by computers play against each other. The computers augment the capability and serve the purposes of their human bosses.

Because humans have a head start on AI in collaborating with each other, it seems fitting that humans would take charge during AI–human collaboration. However, what are the ramifications of AI devices learning to collaborate with each other without the participation of humans, or even when in competition with humans? AI is making rapid strides in its ability to do just that. For example, a team of robots built by Elon Musk, founder of Tesla and SpaceX, played a complex video game called Dota 2, and in a surprising breakthrough beat the team of humans.

Bill Gates, founder and chairman of Microsoft, which is heavily invested in AI research, was impressed enough to tweet:[5]

#AI bots just beat humans at the video game Dota 2. That's a big deal, because their victory required teamwork and collaboration—a huge milestone in advancing artificial intelligence.

Is AI Another Transformative Step Magnifying Human Capability—or Humanity's Final Achievement?

Although a new age of AI–human and AI–AI "cooperation" appears highly likely, there is no guarantee that it will usher in a golden age of human–human or AI–human "collaboration." The AI promise of greater cooperation is complex and multifaceted.

Most significantly, evolutionary forces have bestowed upon humans an impressive capability for both collaboration and predation. Humans can utilize AI to amplify their capability for either. AI-enabled cooperation can usher in an era of power through collaboration or further entrench collaboration's arch rival—predatory power.

Human Psychopaths Beget AI Psychopaths

For example,[6] a team of researchers at the Massachusetts Institute of Technology (MIT) reported that they created "the world's first psychopath" artificial intelligence. They subjected their AI system called Norman to the crass underbelly of Reddit, a popular online news sharing and chat site. What AI Norman learned and processed turned it psychopathic.

> Norman suffered from extended exposure to the darkest corners of Reddit and represents a case study on the dangers of Artificial Intelligence gone wrong when biased data is used in machine learning algorithms.
>
> Data matters more than the algorithm. It highlights the idea that the data we use to train AI is reflected in the way the AI perceives the world and how it behaves.
>
> We are teaching algorithms in the same way as we teach human beings so there is a risk that we are not teaching everything right. When I see an answer from an algorithm, I need to know who made that algorithm.

In essence, allowing the AI Norman system to input and develop in accord with a disturbing but all too familiar slice of human behavior created a psychopathic AI!

The use of tools, the harnessing of fire, the invention of the wheel, the development of writing, the domestication of animals, the Industrial Revolution, the advent of air and space travel, and the ascendancy of the Internet are all notable magnifications of human capability. They were dramatic game-changers for their time, but they did not have the potential to enslave or render extinct the entirety of the human race. Humanity's inescapable embrace of AI does. AI could give a quantum boost to the evolution of human capability or be a dead end and its final achievement. Is AI to be feared or welcomed?

The welcome mat appears to be spread out for AI. Yet, numerous AI experts grasp the inherent risks posed by humanity's precocious adolescent. For example, Elon Musk, founder of Tesla and SpaceX, donated $10 million to the Future of Life Institute so that this organization of leading AI researchers could work to keep AI beneficial for humanity. The Future of Life Institute website banner highlights:[7]

Technology is giving life the potential to flourish like never before, or to self-destruct.

In recognition of the risk to humanity posed by unfettered AI, 23 Asilomar principles were developed by the top researchers and business leaders in AI development. Some examples of the principles are:[8]

- Advanced AI could represent a profound change in the history of life on Earth and should be planned for and managed with commensurate care and resources.
- An arms race in lethal autonomous weapons should be avoided.
- Risks posed by AI systems, especially catastrophic or existential risks, must be subject to planning and mitigation efforts commensurate with their expected impact.
- AI systems designed to recursively self-improve or self-replicate in a manner that could lead to rapidly increasing quality or quantity must be subject to strict safety and control measures.

AI is still agnostic regarding its impact on the nature of the human race. For now, AI lacks consciousness and free will, and will merely do what its creators design and program it to do. AI originates as a creation of humans to serve human purposes and achieve human set goals. Thus, how humans set up and program AI operations will determine AI's impacts—and ultimately the fate of the human species. Humans are making the decisions, and those decisions are already well underway. Several other Asilomar principles state:

- What set of values should AI be aligned with, and what legal and ethical status should it have?
- Designers and builders of advanced AI systems are stakeholders in the moral implications of their use, misuse, and actions, with a responsibility and opportunity to shape those implications.

The key decision is which aspects of human capability and behavior will comprise the primordial foundation of AI. Will it be the disturbing underbelly of Reddit, or worse? Over time AI will increasingly come to mimic and intensify whatever human motivations and behavior that it is exposed to. Consequently, whether or not AI leads to a promising new future versus a dead end for humans largely depends on whether the people in control of developing and programming AI use it to promote Power through Collaboration rather than predatory power.

The prospects for designing AI to promote collaboration can be determined via an analysis using the Power through Collaboration (PtC) Formula. Several key concepts embedded in the formula are particularly helpful—the distinction between collaboration and cooperation, the different modes of cooperation, and the cooperation motivations and types.

Determining Collaboration Potential via the Power through Collaboration Formula

Cooperation or Collaboration

The PtC Formula makes a distinction between cooperation and collaboration. Determining the prospects that AI will promote collaborative rather than psychopathic behavior requires understanding this crucial distinction. Much confusion is created by people making references to and giving examples of collaboration that are actually manifestations of mere cooperation, and certainly not manifestations of Power through Collaboration.

Cooperation and collaboration are not the same. Cooperation can take different forms, one of which is collaboration. The different modes of PtC cooperation are presented in Figure 6.1.

After distinguishing among the different modes of cooperation, it is vital to next factor in that AI can promote any of the PtC modes of cooperation, not just Collaboration or Collaboration-Negotiation. For example, AI can readily be deployed to maximize the Domination mode of cooperation, which is the primary mode of predators.

Those who control AI design and development are in the most influential position to determine which mode of cooperation AI mimics and reinforces. Their favored mode of human cooperation is the front-runner to be the foundation for AI cooperation. Hence, chapter 8 discusses

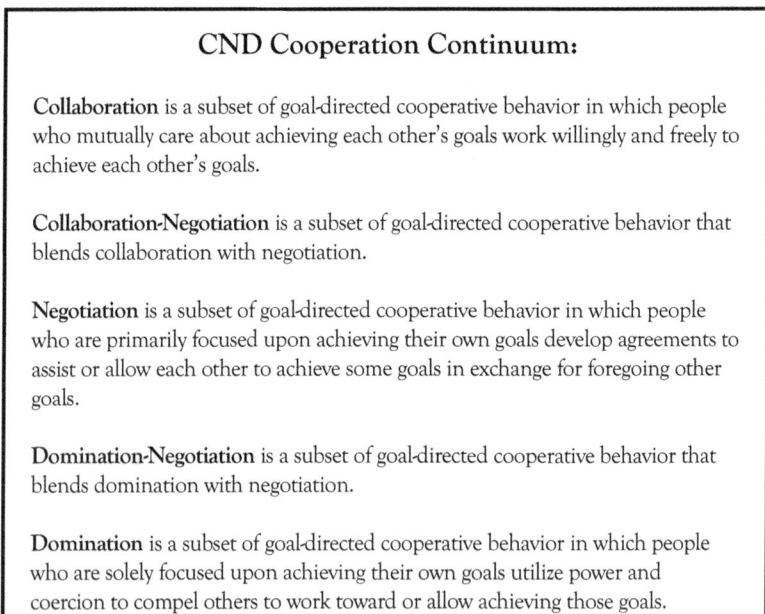

CND Cooperation Continuum:

Collaboration is a subset of goal-directed cooperative behavior in which people who mutually care about achieving each other's goals work willingly and freely to achieve each other's goals.

Collaboration-Negotiation is a subset of goal-directed cooperative behavior that blends collaboration with negotiation.

Negotiation is a subset of goal-directed cooperative behavior in which people who are primarily focused upon achieving their own goals develop agreements to assist or allow each other to achieve some goals in exchange for foregoing other goals.

Domination-Negotiation is a subset of goal-directed cooperative behavior that blends domination with negotiation.

Domination is a subset of goal-directed cooperative behavior in which people who are solely focused upon achieving their own goals utilize power and coercion to compel others to work toward or allow achieving those goals.

Figure 6.1 CND cooperation continuum definitions

the development of laws that make it illegal to feed incorrect data to robots if such would make AI predatory in cases where AI is supposed to collaborate. We shall discuss more about such legal aspects of economic renaissance in Chapter 8.

Cooperation Motivations and Types

The predominant PtC mode of cooperation in any given situation is determined by the underlying PtC cooperation types and PtC cooperation motivations that are in operation. Thus, the PtC Formula's cooperation types and motivations can be utilized to gauge the Collaboration Potential of AI.

The PtC Formula's eight PtC Motivations and six PtC Types are ordered according to the extent to which they promote Power through Collaboration, and are presented in Figure 6.2.

For example, Shared Mission motivation promotes collaboration the most and promotes domination the least, whereas Survival motivation promotes collaboration the least and promotes domination the most.

Similarly, the Collaborator type utilizes collaboration the most and utilizes domination the least, whereas the Predator type utilizes collaboration the least and utilizes domination the most.

Assessing the underlying PtC Types and PtC Motivations of those who control AI development and deployment is highly illuminating for

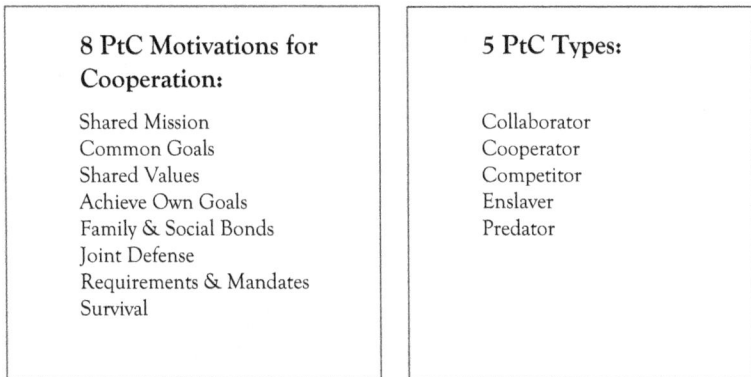

8 PtC Motivations for Cooperation:	5 PtC Types:
Shared Mission Common Goals Shared Values Achieve Own Goals Family & Social Bonds Joint Defense Requirements & Mandates Survival	Collaborator Cooperator Competitor Enslaver Predator

Figure 6.2 Eight PtC Motivations and five PtC Types

determining whether AI will promote a collaborative versus a predatory mode of cooperation.

Collaboration Potential

The PtC Formula interrelates its eight motivations and six types to predict the potential for collaboration between parties in any given situation.

For example, a combination of Shared Mission motivation and the Collaborator type maximizes Collaboration Potential. Indeed, the Collaboration Potential rating is "optimal." In contrast, a combination of Survival motivation and the Predator type minimizes Collaboration Potential. The corresponding Collaboration Potential rating is "hazardous."

Assessing which motivations are operating in the current socioeconomic system and which types are in control enables the determination of Collaboration Potential. Applying an analysis of PtC Motivations and PtC Types to current socioeconomic outcomes can reveal which motivations and types currently predominate, and thus the prospects of AI cooperation taking the form of Collaboration versus Domination. The Collaboration Potential and CND Zones are presented in Figure 6.3.

If the PtC Formula analysis of motivations and types shows socioeconomic outcomes reflective of the Domination Zone, then AI is likely to entrench the Domination mode of cooperation. Conversely, if the analysis shows socioeconomic outcomes reflective of the Collaboration Zone, AI is likely to promote the Collaboration mode of cooperation.

Specifically, what motivations and types seem to predominate when we look at socioeconomic outcomes with respect to key indicators such as income inequality, poverty rates, health care availability, and climate change?

Income Inequality and Poverty Rates

There likely is a broad consensus that AI will drive substantial productivity increases and associated profitability. The primary question is whether or not AI driven productivity gains will be shared sufficiently to raise global standards of living and lift people out of poverty.

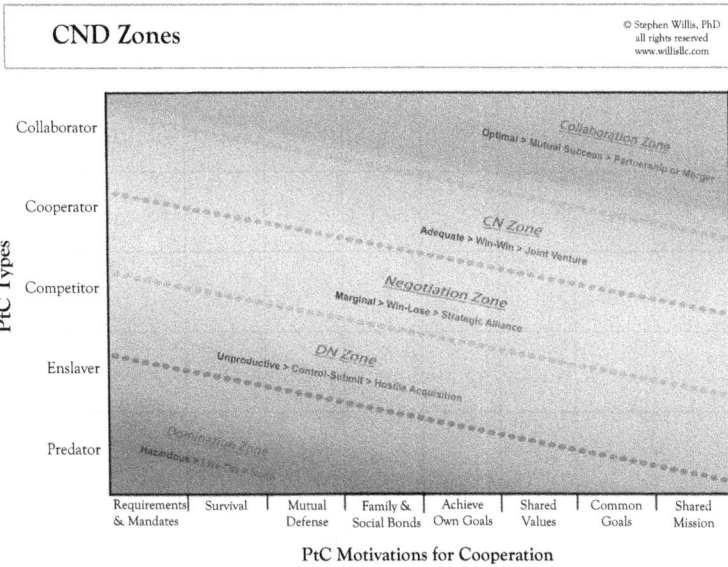

Figure 6.3 **Collaboration Potential Ratings with CND Zones and Cooperation Dynamics**

When I look at socioeconomic outcomes with respect to income inequality and poverty I perceive Survival motivation and Achieve Own Goals motivation operating much more than Shared Mission and Shared Values motivation. Although the latter two are of immense value, they are currently overshadowed by the former two. Achieve Own Goals motivation and Survival motivation can foster cooperation, but they can just as readily foster conflict and competition. In contrast Shared Mission and Shared Values motivations not only foster routine cooperation, but also collaboration, and are much less conducive to fostering conflict and competition.

The detrimental consequences caused by the less collaboration-promoting motivations being predominant are reflected in socioeconomic outcomes. For example, the productivity gains of recent decades have not been widely shared. Rather they have gone to a very small number of people who comprise the wealthiest portion of the population. Consequently, income inequality and childhood poverty are at their highest levels in decades. A UN report notes:

The cheery numbers, however, should not blind us to the harsh reality facing most Americans. The United States is one of the richest nations in the world, yet many of its citizens live in misery. Consider: About 40 million live in poverty, 18.5 million in extreme poverty, and 5.3 million live in Third World conditions of absolute poverty. It has the highest youth poverty rate in the [industrialized world] ... . The United States has the highest rate of income inequality among Western countries.[9]

Continually worsening income inequality and childhood poverty are the natural outgrowth of a socioeconomic system designed to favor and be controlled by the less collaborative PtC Types operating via the less collaboration-promoting PtC Motivations. Why would AI enable this decade long trend to change? Rather, AI can easily be used to maintain or even worsen the situation—unless control of the socioeconomic system passes into the hands of people motivated to use AI to share productivity gains more equitably, as would be associated with the more collaborative PtC Types operating via the more collaboration-promoting PtC Motivations. (For example, chapter 13 discusses entrusting the operation of the socioeconomic system to a new class of people called Sadvipras or Benevolent Intellectuals). In summary, socioeconomic outcomes with respect to income inequality and poverty reflect the Domination Zone mode of cooperation, and AI is likely to reinforce it.

Health Care

When I look at healthcare outcomes I similarly perceive Survival motivation and Achieve Own Goals motivation operating much more than Shared Mission motivation and Shared Values motivation. For example, after decades of steady gains, the life expectancy in the United States is now falling, partly due to soaring deaths from opiate drug use:[10]

This was the first-time life expectancy in the U.S. has declined two years in a row since declines in 1962 and 1963.

Even if U.S. life expectancy begins to increase again, it is still poised for further deterioration relative to other industrialized countries:[10]

"Notable among poor-performing countries is the USA," the researchers wrote, "whose life expectancy at birth is already lower than most other high-income countries, and is projected to fall further behind, such that its 2030 life expectancy at birth might be similar to the Czech Republic for men, and Croatia and Mexico for women."

The reasons for the United States' lag are well known. It has the highest infant and maternal mortality rates of any of the countries in the study, and the highest obesity rate. It is the only one without universal health insurance coverage and has the "largest share of unmet health-care needs due to financial costs.

Tellingly, the United States was the first high-income country to see a halt to the pattern of increasing height in adulthood, a reliable indicator of improving public health.

It's very worrisome. The U.S. is at the bottom of the barrel among [Organization for Economic Cooperation and Development] countries, and its relative position is worsening, not improving."

Another example of health care outcomes being driven more by Survival and Achieve Own Goals motivations than by Shared Mission and Shared Values motivations is the opioid drug death epidemic:[11]

Big Pharma had created a massive legal opiate addiction, which directly led to the heroin epidemic because pharmaceutical corporations' own addiction to profit arguably triumphs any concern it may have had for patients.

Another example of health care outcomes being driven more by Survival and Achieve Own Goals motivations than by Shared Mission and Shared Values motivations is the cost of providing healthcare relative to the results for patients:[12]

U.S. healthcare is exceedingly expensive. ... among 34 advanced industrialized countries, the U.S. spends ... more than 2.6 times the OECD average. The U.S. devotes 16.9 percent of its GDP to health care, 1.8 times as much as the average. In the case of health care spending measured any way you want; the U.S. is No. 1 by a large margin.

Despite all that spending, America's health system does not perform particularly well. That same OECD report shows that the U.S. ranks 27th for life expectancy at birth. This comparatively low ranking is not merely a consequence of higher infant mortality, where the U.S. ranks a dismal 53rd in deaths per 1,000 live births. Even considering life expectancy for men aged 65 places the U.S. in 23rd place.

In addition to falling life expectancy, high infant and maternal mortality rates, and high obesity rates, 60 percent of Americans have a chronic medical condition and 42 percent have more than one.[13] Half of American men will get cancer, and one-third of American women will get cancer.[14]

Despite the subpar healthcare outcomes, stock market prices and profits of healthcare and drug companies are extremely healthy. How health insurance companies boost profits by denying care provides yet another example of health care outcomes being driven more by Survival and Achieve Own Goals motivations than by Shared Mission and Shared Values motivations.

A former senior executive who worked for 20 years for one of the largest health insurance companies, provided testimony to Congress on the machinations of the industry to deny care in the pursuit of ever higher profitability and stock market prices.[15]

I'm ashamed that I let myself get caught up in deceitful and dishonest PR campaigns that worked so well, hundreds of thousands of our citizens have died, and millions of others have lost their homes and been forced into bankruptcy, so that a very few corporate executives and their Wall Street masters could become obscenely rich.

To help meet Wall Street's relentless profit expectations, insurers routinely dump policyholders who are less profitable or who get sick. Insurers have several ways to cull the sick from their rolls. One is policy rescission. They look carefully to see if a sick policyholder may have omitted a minor illness, a pre-existing condition, when applying for coverage, and then they use that as justification to cancel the policy, even if the enrollee has never missed a premium payment. ... The Energy and Commerce Committee's investigation into three insurers found that they canceled the coverage of roughly 20,000 people in a five-year period, allowing the companies to avoid paying $300 million in claims.

They also dump small businesses whose employees' medical claims exceed what insurance underwriters expected. All it takes is one illness or accident among employees at a small business to prompt an insurance company to hike the next year's premiums so high that the employer has to cut benefits, shop for another carrier, or stop offering coverage altogether—leaving workers uninsured. The practice is known in the industry as "purging." The purging of less profitable accounts through intentionally unrealistic rate increases helps explain why the number of small businesses offering coverage to their employees has fallen from 61 percent to 38 percent since 1993, according to the National Small Business Association.

Purging through pricing games is not limited to letting go of an isolated number of unprofitable accounts. It is endemic in the industry. ... The company spent more than $20 million that it received in fees and premiums from customers to revamp its computer systems, enabling the company to "identify and dump unprofitable corporate accounts," as *The Wall Street Journal* reported. ... Within a few years, Aetna lost 8 million covered lives due to strategic and other factors.

A study conducted last year by PricewaterhouseCoopers revealed just how successful the insurers' expense management and purging actions have been over the last decade in meeting Wall Street's expectations. ... That translates into a difference of several billion dollars in favor of insurance company shareholders and executives and at the expense of health care providers and their patients.

Envisioning AI propelling health care to mind-boggling heights is easy. However, actually realizing such a vision is not easy. At present health care is stuck operating via the less collaborative PtC Motivations that interfere with achieving that vision, regardless of how feasible and worthwhile that vision is.

As long as stock prices, profits, salaries, bonuses, performance reviews, and promotions are maximized by denying care, the less collaborative PtC Types operating via the less collaborative PtC Motivations will continue to gain and maintain control. And they will be most inclined to use AI to enforce a predatory priority of maximizing profits and stock prices by minimizing the provision of care. AI is on track to better weed out those patients whose medical needs would decrease profitability. Companies like the one that spent 20 million revamping its computer system to purge unprofitable accounts are likely to wholeheartedly exploit AI's capability to supercharge the denial of care in lieu of providing care.

In summary, socioeconomic outcomes with respect to healthcare reflect the Domination Zone mode of cooperation, and AI is likely to reinforce it.

Climate Change

When I look at socioeconomic outcomes with respect to climate change, I perceive Survival motivation and Achieve Own Goals motivation operating much more than Shared Mission and Shared Values motivations. And the less collaborative PtC Types seem to be in control of the key decisions and actions related to climate change.

From my perspective climate change is real, and there is little basis for well-intentioned debate. Real scientists have painstakingly analyzed hundreds of thousands of years of climate data using an entire arsenal of advanced technological tools, including earth-orbiting satellites and space shuttles. Real scientists have scrupulously analyzed gaseous composition of the atmosphere; increased levels of atmospheric carbon dioxide; ice core composition of ice shelfs and tropical mountain glaciers; retreating ice sheet mass in Greenland, the Arctic, and the Antarctic; declines in sea ice extent and thickness; shrinking glaciers worldwide; diminishing seasonal snow cover and snow melt; soaring atmospheric temperatures;

escalating record high temperature events and dwindling record low temperature events; more frequent extreme weather events; more intense droughts and heatwaves; less intense cold waves; increased intensity, frequency, and duration of hurricanes; climbing ocean temperatures; rising global sea levels; elevated storm surges and high tides; greater flooding; expanding oceans submerging land masses; increased acidity of surface ocean waters; dying coral reefs; ocean sediments; lengthening frost-free and growing seasons; sedimentary rock layers; tree rings; solar activity and irradiance; and so on.[16]

Highly credible organizations such as NASA unequivocally state:[16]

Ninety-seven percent of climate scientists agree that climate-warming trends over the past century are very likely due to human activities, and most of the leading scientific organizations worldwide have issued public statements endorsing this position.

The Intergovernmental Panel on Climate Change states:[16]

Scientific evidence for warming of the climate system is unequivocal.

The abundance of rigorous evidence for climate change has been relentlessly attacked by climate change deniers using the sophisticated tactics perfected by the tobacco industry. Not only were the soundest of scientific findings attacked, but so were the most reputable of scientists.[17]

The great struggle of our era will be fact versus deliberate fiction. … Professional climate-change denial is the original fake news. … I'm talking about the fossil fuel-funded, decades-long, under-the-radar public-relations campaign that helped sow those doubts.

In the 1990s, as climate change became a prominent issue, industry associations like the American Petroleum Institute organized an ambitious campaign to confuse the public about the facts of climate science. Their campaign was based on the tobacco industry's work to obscure the link between smoking and cancer, using fringe think tanks to spread junk science.

The goal of the professional deniers is to spread doubt about facts that have been established through decades of research.

Tobacco industry tactics to deny and obfuscate the reality of climate change were ruthlessly carried out despite several major oil companies being well informed 45 years ago about the linkage between climate change and fossil fuel usage.[18]

Recently the fossil fuel industry has emerged from the shadows and shed its camouflage. It has taken over and directly stymies governmental mechanisms of environmental protection. As a result, programs to promote renewable energy and climate change solutions are being gutted and eliminated. The major treaty with most of the nations of the world to address climate change has been unilaterally discarded.[19]

The current U.S. presidential cabinet is full of climate change deniers, most notably the head of the Environmental Protection Agency (EPA). He has been a recipient of generous donations from the fossil fuel industry throughout his political career, and a long-standing foe of the very agency that he was placed in charge of. In his previous position as a state attorney general he was a leader in a lawsuit against the EPA's clean power plan.[20] He sued the EPA 14 times to block clean air and water safeguards established by the EPA. While he was head of the EPA, information about climate change was removed from the EPA website and agency scientists became restricted in their ability to discuss and work on climate change issues. Indeed, the related plethora of scandals involving this head of EPA resulted in his recently being forced to resign.[21]

The value of renewable energy and climate change solutions for the earth and the people who occupy it is obvious and should not need defending. The dismal outcomes with respect to climate change reflect the workings of a predatory socioeconomic system designed to favor and be controlled by the less collaborative PtC Types operating via the less collaboration promoting PtC Motivations. Why would AI rescue humanity from such a predatory system addicted to profiting from planetary destruction and the blocking of lifesaving solutions? Indeed, the successful thwarting of decades of prescient science and prophetic warnings as the climate crisis worsens is ominous regarding how AI will be utilized and who will it serve?

The climate change crisis can all too easily continue to deteriorate—unless control of the socioeconomic system passes into the hands of people (such as a classless society of Sadvipras as discussed in Chapter 13) who are motivated to use AI to collaborate for the well-being of the planet and its human inhabitants, as would be associated with the more collaborative PtC Types operating via the more collaboration promoting PtC Motivations.

In summary, socioeconomic outcomes with respect to climate change reflect the Domination Zone mode of cooperation, and AI is likely to reinforce it.

Ominous Prospects

The dismal outcomes to date with respect to income inequality and poverty, health care, and climate change reflect a socioeconomic system in which Domination prevails over Collaboration. Socioeconomic outcomes reflect the power of less collaborative PtC Types operating via less collaboration-promoting PtC Motivations.

This PtC Formula analysis does not bode well for the prospects of AI enabling a shift to a collaborative socioeconomic system. AI is likely to be used by its masters to serve their purposes, which can be divined from the outcomes related to income inequality, health care, and climate change. AI actually appears to be primed to reinforce and entrench a predatory socioeconomic system.

James Galbraith, author of eight economic books and former Congressional Joint Economic Committee executive director, writes in his book *The Predator State*:[22]

> The predatory class is not the whole of the wealthy; it may be opposed by many others of similar wealth. But it is the defining feature, the leading force. Its agents are in full control of the government under which we live.
>
> Everywhere you look, the public decision is made by the agent of a private party for the purpose of delivering private gain. ...

> Predatory regimes … are intrinsically unstable, something that does not trouble the predators but makes life for the ordinary business enterprise exceptionally trying.

AI's capability to evolve a collaborative socioeconomic system presents a very appealing opportunity for most people. Not so for the "predator class," which is alarmed by such a prospect. An AI-enabled collaborative socioeconomic system is considered a threat to their dominance and control. They prefer and seek to perpetuate a socioeconomic system based on competition and predation because they have already established their controlling positions and prospered.

The less collaborative PtC Types operating via the less collaboration-promoting PtC Motivations routinely seek to undermine Power through Collaboration whenever they can. They operate via predatory business models and strategies. They seek to diminish the individual and social capability of others. They do not let the structure and processes of democracy get in their way.

Because AI machines are easier to control than humans, the "predator class" will use AI to control, diminish, devalue, or replace humans as much as possible. Sooner or later AI will have the power to replace most humans. Arguments can be made regarding how soon into the future this power of AI will be realized and regarding whether or not AI will be able to replace every single human. Yet, the bigger mistake is to underestimate the capability of AI to replace humans, even the very humans implementing AI to replace other humans. A big surprise may be in store for predatory humans who expect AI to serve them while enslaving and eliminating others. But this is precisely what will happen if AI is programmed to operate in accord with the business models and strategies of the less collaborative PtC Types.

What will the "predator class" do with humans who become unnecessary for the accumulation of wealth and power, and who drain more resources than they produce?

Business Models Based on Power Through Collaboration

A collaborative socioeconomic system offers a completely opposite scenario. AI can be used to enhance human capability and make humans more valuable than ever before. The 23 Asilomar Principles provide guideposts for this purpose:[23]

1. Research Goal: The goal of AI research should be to create not undirected intelligence, but beneficial intelligence.
2. Research Funding: Investments in AI should be accompanied by funding for research on ensuring its beneficial use, including thorny questions in computer science, economics, law, ethics, and social studies, such as: ... How can we grow our prosperity through automation while maintaining people's resources and purpose?
11. Human Values: AI systems should be designed and operated so as to be compatible with ideals of human dignity, rights, freedoms, and cultural diversity.
13. Liberty and Privacy: The application of AI to personal data must not unreasonably curtail people's real or perceived liberty.
14. Shared Benefit: AI technologies should benefit and empower as many people as possible.
15. Shared Prosperity: The economic prosperity created by AI should be shared broadly, to benefit all of humanity.
17. Non-subversion: The power conferred by control of highly advanced AI systems should respect and improve, rather than subvert, the social and civic processes on which the health of society depends.
23. Common Good: Super-intelligence should only be developed in the service of widely shared ethical ideals, and for the benefit of all humanity rather than one state or organization.

Despite such magnanimous guiding principles, based on this PtC Formula analysis, utilizing AI to evolve a collaborative socioeconomic system appears to be a daunting challenge. The first albeit disorienting step involves seeing the predatory socioeconomic system for what it is. The next step is to develop and deploy AI in accord with business models based on collaboration.

Fortune magazine compiled a "Change the World" list of companies addressing serious social problems as part of their business strategy:[24]

Companies that are making genuine efforts to change the world for the better should be encouraged. The future of capitalism— and the future of mankind—depends on it.

Gary Hamel, the *Wall Street Journal's* most influential business thinker in the world, *Fortune* magazine's world's leading expert on business strategy, and author of *What Matters Now*, states:[25]

> It's time to radically revise the deeply etched beliefs about what business is for, whose interests it serves, and how it creates value. We need a new form of capitalism for the 21st century—one dedicated to the promotion of greater wellbeing rather than the single-minded pursuit of growth and profits; one that doesn't sacrifice the future for the near term; one with an appropriate regard for every stakeholder; and one that holds leaders accountable for all of the consequences of their actions.... This isn't a new challenge, but it's more urgent than ever.

Fortunately, there are already collaboration-based business models that AI can strengthen. Picture what the outcomes could be for income inequality and poverty, health care, and climate change if operating via the following business models.

Circular Economy

Championed by the Ellen MacArthur Foundation with business partners such as B&Q, British Telecom, Cisco, National Grid, Renault, and McKinsey & Co., the Circular Economy uses systems thinking to design a sustainable and restorative economic system that mimics natural living ecosystems. It rebuilds social, economic, and natural capital; operates via renewable energy; and replaces cradle-to-grave with cradle-to-cradle concepts whereby what was formerly considered waste is repurposed as inputs for other users. The Circular Economy has its own certification program. Two of the largest global office furniture companies, Steelcase and Herman Miller, make all their furniture Cradle to Cradle Certified.[26]

Conscious Capitalism

This model progresses along similar lines with the involvement of companies such as The Container Store, Google, Trader Joes, and Whole Foods.

Under Conscious Capitalism, the Circular Economy businesses advocate the following:[27]

- A higher purpose transcending profit maximization.
- Are explicitly managed for the simultaneous benefit of all interdependent stakeholders, including customers, employees, investors, suppliers, and the larger communities in which the business participates.
- Reject zero-sum, trade-off-oriented view of business and look for creative synergistic win-win approaches that offer multiple types of value simultaneously to all stakeholders.

Sustainable Capitalism

This model is championed by Joe Keefe, President and CEO of Pax World Management, which manages several billion in financial assets. He was named by *Ethisphere Magazine* as one of the "100 Most Influential People in Business Ethics" for 2007, 2008, 2011, and 2012. He advocates for an economic system that[28]

> … explicitly integrates environmental, social and governance (ESG) factors into strategy, the measurement of outputs and the assessment of both risks and opportunities…. The connections between economic output and ecological/societal health are no longer obscured but are expressly linked.
>
> We will need to consistently critique the notion that externalities associated with economic output are somehow collateral, or that financial return is sufficient without beneficial societal returns, or that markets are inherently efficient and self-correcting. We will need to unabashedly offer sustainable investing not as an alternative approach but as a better approach—as the only sensible, responsible way to invest.

JUST Capital

This model is championed by hedge fund billionaire Paul Tudor Jones II:[29]

The world needs more just companies. Companies that believe in fair pay and equal treatment for all workers. Companies that create good jobs and understand the value of strong communities. Companies that are committed to a healthy planet. JUST Capital measures and ranks companies on the issues Americans care about most so you can then act on that knowledge. With your voice, your purchase decisions, your investment dollars, your career choices, your leadership, you have the power to make the world a more just place.

At JUST Capital, our mission is to build a more just marketplace that better reflects the true priorities of the American people. We believe that business, and capitalism, can and must be a positive force for change. We believe that if they have the right information, people will buy from, invest in, work for, and otherwise support companies that align with their values. And we believe that business leaders are searching to win back the trust of the public in ways that go beyond money. By shifting the immense resources and ingenuity of the $15 trillion private sector onto a more balanced—and more just—course, we can help build a better future for everyone.

Inclusive Capitalism

This model is championed by Lynn Forester de Rothchild, CEO of E. L. Rothschild holding company:[30]

It is perfectly obvious that failings in Western capitalism are at the root of the social and political dysfunction gripping the world. Income and wealth have indeed been monopolized by the richest few leading to widening economic inequality, stagnate wages and a shrinking middle class. The values and priorities of our capitalist system need to evolve, as they have done many times before.

Bringing business and society together is the goal of "Inclusive Capitalism." It is not just another name for corporate social responsibility, philanthropy or redistribution. Instead, it represents a different investment and management theory. It unifies us toward a shared goal of broadly-based prosperity. It reaffirms the basic bargain between society and business because firms identify and measure material environmental, social, and governance metrics for the best interests of their customers, employees, shareholders and communities. The firms that perform best for all become the most financially valuable companies.

Compassionate Capitalism

This model is championed by Marc Benioff, Chairman and CEO of Salesforce.[31]

> The competitive advantage you gain from being a caring and sharing company is significant; it instills in your people a higher integrity level. In turn, stakeholders want to be associated with a company that has heart. Community service: You do it because it's the right thing to do, but it's also the profitable thing to do.

The Transformational Company

This model is championed by the Canadian Business for Social Responsibility organization, and views business as a force for good. It includes companies like Ikea, Interface, and Unilever:[32]

> Transformational companies ... invest in business models and initiatives that transform their business ... in ways that improve prospects for the business and society.

Benefit Corporation

This model includes state corporate charters that specifically permit corporations to take into account and serve the interests of all stakeholders, not just shareholders. A separate but aligned certification is offered by B Labs. Its "Declaration of Interdependence" includes:[33]

We envision a new sector of the economy which harnesses the power of private enterprise to create public benefit. This sector is comprised of a new type of corporation, the B Corporation which is purpose-driven, and creates benefit for all stakeholders, not just shareholders. ... That, all business ought to be conducted as if people and place mattered; That, through their products, practices, and profits, businesses should aspire to do no harm and benefit all; To do so, requires that we act with the understanding that we are each dependent upon another and thus responsible for each other and future generations.

Social Business

This model is championed by Muhammad Yunus, author of *Building Social Business: The New Kind of Capitalism That Serves Humanity's Most Pressing Needs*. He is a recipient of the Nobel Prize, the Presidential Medal of Freedom, and the U.S. Congressional Gold Medal. He founded the Grameen Bank with a social mission to help the poor and has started over 30 other social businesses.[34]

A challenge that anyone will face in creating a social business is trying to explain why they are doing it. Our economic theories have constantly stressed that humans are self-centered beings who go about serving their own self-interest. We have been taught that as a fact for hundreds of years. Now we have an alternative, a selfless business where operators do not profit for themselves but benefit others. This can come as a shock to people. Explaining this is a challenge.

I profoundly believe, as Grameen's experience over 20 years has shown, that personal gain is not the only possible fuel for free enterprise. Social goals can replace greed as a powerful motivational force. Social-consciousness-driven enterprises can be formidable competitors for greed-based enterprises. I believe that if we play our cards right, social-consciousness-driven enterprises can do very well in the marketplace.

Conclusion

The AI era is a high stakes enduring transformation that will reshape human nature. AI can easily entrench a predatory socioeconomic system that replaces or uses humans as expendable automations subject to precise monitoring, control, and programming. Alternatively, AI can be used to evolve a collaborative socioeconomic system with empowered, conscious, and highly productive humans.

Despite the ominous results of this PtC Formula analysis regarding AI's potential to entrench versus transform our current socioeconomic system, there are alternate paths that move the human species away from a destiny of predatory domination and toward a truly collaborative future. The choice is up to humans.

References

[1] Laurence, G. September 1, 2017. "The Future of Work." www.gartner.com/smarterwithgartner/the-future-of-work-infographic

[2] Tan, J. June 22, 2018. "Artificial Intelligence Turns Design Into A Collaborative Undertaking." *Forbes.* www.forbes.com/sites/joytan/2018/06/22/artificial-intelligence-turns-design-into-a-collaborative-undertaking/#7130c7662f87

[3] Stackpole, B. April 11, 2017. "Why Smart Enterprises are Thinking AI." *CIO.* www.cio.com/article/3182370/artificial-intelligence/why-smart-enterprises-are-thinking-ai.html

[4] Wilson, J., and P. Daugherty. July–August 2018. "Collaborative Intelligence: Humans and AI Are Joining Forces." *Harvard Business Review.* https://hbr.org/2018/07/collaborative-intelligence-humans-and-ai-are-joining-forces

[5] Clifford, C. June 28, 2018. "Bill Gates Says Gamer Bots from Elon Musk-backed Nonprofit are 'Huge Milestone' in A.I." *CNBC.* www.cnbc.com/2018/06/27/bill-gates-openai-robots-beating-humans-at-dota-2-is-ai-milestone.html

[6] Brigham, B. June 6, 2018. "Scientist Exposed Norman AI to Darkest Corners of Reddit." www.rawstory.com/2018/06/scientists-exposed-norman-ai-system-darkest-corners-reddit-turned-psychopathic/

[7] "Asilomar AI Principles 2017. "Future of Life Institute." https://futureoflife.org/ai-principles/

[8] "Asilomar AI Principles 2017. "Future of Life Institute." https://futureoflife.org/ai-principles/

[9] vanden Katrina, H. June 5, 2018. "The Economic Numbers Are Cheery, but Don't Believe the Hype." *The Nation.* https://thenation.com/article/ economic-numbers-cheery-dont-believe-hype/

[10] Fox, M. December 20, 2017. "U.S. Life Expectancy Falls for Second Straight Year—as Drug Overdoses Soar." *NBC News.* www.nbcnews.com/storyline/ americas-heroin-epidemic/u-s-life-expectancy-falls-second-straight-year-drug-overdoses-n831676

[11] Farrell, R. October 16, 2017. "The Opioid Epidemic: How Big Pharma and Congress Created America's Worst Health Crisis." *Huffington Post.* www. huffingtonpost.com/entry/the-opioid-epidemic-how-big-pharma-and-congress-created_us_59e4e02ee4b003f928d5e8bf

[12] Pfeffer, J. October 20, 2014. "Why Health Insurance Companies are Doomed. *Fortune Magazine.* http://fortune.com/2014/10/20/health-insurance-future/

[13] Irving, D. July 12, 2017. "Chronic Conditions in America: Price and Prevalence." *Rand Corporation.* www.rand.org/blog/rand-review/2017/07/ chronic-conditions-in-america-price-and-prevalence.html

[14] Whitman, H. February 4, 2015. "1 in 2 People Will Develop Cancer in their Lifetime." *Medical News Today.* www.medicalnewstoday.com/ articles/288916.php

[15] Potter, W. September 17, 2009. "Between You and Your Doctor: the Private Health Insurance Bureaucracy." *PNHP.* www.pnhp.org/news/2009/ september/testimony_of_wendell.php

[16] NASA. "Scientific Consensus." https://climate.nasa.gov/evidence/

[17] Pooley, E. February 14, 2017. "Climate Change Denial Is the Original Fake News." *Time.* http://time.com/4664173/climate-change-denial-fake-news/

[18] Wang, U. April 5, 2018. "What Oil Companies Knew About Climate Change." *Climate Liability News.* www.climateliabilitynews.org/2018/04/05/ climate-change-oil-companies-knew-shell-exxon/

[19] Cohen, S. June 19, 2017. "Trump's Attack On Renewable Energy." *Huffington Post.* www.huffingtonpost.com/entry/trumps-attack-on-renew-able-energy_us_5947c072e4b024b7e0df4db1

[20] Sidahmed, M. December 15, 2016. "Climate Change Denial in the Trump Cabinet: Where Do His Nominees Stand?" *The Guardian.* www.theguardian. com/environment/2016/dec/15/trump-cabinet-climate-change-deniers

[21] Bacon, J. February 8, 2018. "Scientists Rebuff EPA Chief's Claim that Global Warming May Be Good." *USA TODAY.* www.usatoday.com/story/ news/nation/2018/02/08/epa-chief-scott-pruitt-global-warming-may-good-thing/318850002/

[22] Galbraith, J. 2008. *The Predator State.* New York, NY: Free Press.

[23] "Asilomar AI Principles 2017. "Future of Life Institute." https://futureoflife. org/ai-principles/

[24] Murray, A. August 20, 2015. "Introducing Fortune's Change the World List: Companies that are Doing Well by Doing Good." *Fortune.* http://fortune. com/2015/08/20/introducing-change-the-world-list/

[25] Hamel, G., and P. LeBarre. February 26, 2012. "Reimagining Capitalism— as Principled, Patient, and Truly Social." *Management Innovation EXchange.* www.managementexchange.com

[26] http://ellenmacarthurfoundation.org/

[27] http://consciouscapitalism.org/learnmore/

[28] Keefe, J. Fall 2012. "From Growth Capitalism to Sustainable Capitalism: The Next 20 Years of Sustainable Investing." *GreenMoney Journal.*

[29] https://justcapital.com/about/

[30] de Rothschild, L.F. December 1, 2016. "Restoring Capitalism's Good Name." *Time.* http://time.com/4587730/lynn-forester-de-rothschild-inclusive-capitalism/

[31] Benioff, M. April 4, 2015. "A Call for Stakeholder Activists." *Huffington Post.* www.huffingtonpost.com/marc-benioff/a-call-for-stakeholder-activists_ b_6599000.html

[32] http://cbsr.ca/transformationalcompany/

[33] Declaration of Interdependence. B Lab, Inc. www.bcorporation.net

[34] Yunus, M. 1991. "Banker to the Poor: Micro-Lending and the Battle Against World Poverty." *PublicAffairs.* 1586481983.

PART III
Policy Options

CHAPTER 7

Technology, Universal Income, and the Watershed: A Case for Urgent Planetary Change

Matt Oppenheim

Introduction and Overview

Many acknowledge that planet earth is over a precipice of decline due to several intertwining factors: frightening climate change and irreversible environmental damage; the massive diaspora of refugees of war and water; hyperinequalities between rich and poor and the unrelenting impact of many multinationals on the above. There is an additional, less recognized impact that is an essential part of this equation. It is predicted that by 2020, five million people will be unemployed due to the acceleration of technological innovations that are more efficient than human-based work.[1] Philanthropists, university researchers, and progressive multinationals are working on a rapid solution to address the human impact of this change. However, like many of the solutions offered for these other impending crises, solutions to rapid unemployment are short-sighted and often focused on "universal income (UI)" policies, which in the past have proven to be a means to warehouse human capacities.

Recently, an innovative approach to UI gaining global attention is being trialed by a combination of nonprofit, GiveDirectly, researchers from top universities, and support from philanthropic endeavors.[2] Focused on a network of villages near Nairobi, Kenya, this intervention offers $22/month to over 6,000 people inhabiting rural villages and extends support to over 26,000.[3] Their focus is understanding if and how this project impacts innovation and initiative at the family and village level, and the results are dramatic. Villagers are planting gardens, obtaining new land for agriculture; sending their children to school; starting economic enterprises; creating larger social circles and community lending programs, where several families pool their resources.[4] In other words, they are beginning to achieve every community development researcher's dream—the facilitation of individual and collective capacity-building and further, the driver for achieving human potential. Can this one intervention prove to be prophetic in addressing the impending issue of employment loss due to rapid technological innovation?

It is the goal of this chapter to unpack the purpose and dynamics of this endeavor—to inquire about its strengths and challenges, and especially to see how a potential long-term intervention might be utilized to face social, ecological, and economic challenges that have plagued humanity since the emergence of *Homo sapiens*, some 150,000 years ago. In this inquiry, we address the eternal tenets that cause human societies to decline or collapse as well as to find renaissance and resilience. This article finds that technological innovations throughout the human endeavor can equally cause both, and we have to become deeply discerning in the use of technology for the purpose of renaissance and resilience rather than collapse. Both are possible in the foreseeable future.

Basic Tenets

This chapter argues that the integration of the following dynamics is urgent in addressing the previous challenges:

1. Encourage; invest, and infuse rapid technological change wherever possible. This is not only the probable future, but the urgent future. However, this change must be integrated with the following dynamics mentioned in order to succeed.

2. This must be accompanied by the tremendous unleashing of human potential brought about by this technological change and funded by the trillions of dollars now wasted on urban and global obsolescence and deliberate destruction of the environment.

3. All civilizations that have collapsed have returned to decentralized, coordinated, ecologically based economies. We are facing imminent

ecological and civilizational collapse. We must return to this constant in civilizational cycles. The money freed-up from the aforementioned must be directed toward this end.

4. Adaptation to the world's watersheds* has also been a constant in the story of planet earth as well and the key to civilizational evolution. Ignore this law and civilizations always collapse; follow the design of the watershed and life is resplendent.

Social Evolution of the Common Good

Imagine the first 150,000 years of human existence as *Homo sapiens*. The well-being of the group depended on the well-being of the individual—each was mutually supporting. We hunted and gathered in small groups where there were no words and no purpose for differences in wealth or position. Commonly acknowledged is that times of work and play were intertwined—people existed in companionship and the good of the whole relied on the potential and capacity of the individual.[5] We followed the design of the watershed and the environment rather than having power it. The watershed was the cosmos; the mountains were the place where all of creation emerged and the source of all that sustained us.

As society grew more complex, there was regular distribution of wealth and community resolution to problems. The Kwakiutl Potlach of the Northwest coast of North America was a huge distribution ritual, where the wealthier villages gave out all their wealth to the less wealthy—there was an inherent trust that through this dynamic, the needs of all would be met, and the villages would return to harmony.[6] This also solidified networks of interdependency. In the Marae ceremony of the indigenous people of New Zealand, a community would face its community problems and find solutions through weeks of song, poetry and oratory.[7] Elders of the Ifikbo Ibo of Nigeria, when faced with conflict, social imbalance; famine or disease would seclude themselves and "remake" their world in the building of a ceremonial Mbari house, which re-created their world in a return to balance and harmony, so they could move together toward a common future.[8] The lesson here is that people in small, decentralized

---

* See p. 151. "Return to the Watershed" for description of watershed dynamics.

communities addressed ecological, social, and economic challenges much more effectively than in huge urban centers.

Each of the aforementioned did not diverge from the design of the watershed. In fact, when I visited a Maori village many years ago, an elder refused to open the door when I knocked. Then he opened the door a crack. He first asked, "What is your river?" "The Rhine, I answered." Then he asked, "and what is your mountain?" "The Alps, I answered" He replied: "Yes, I know your people—they are fine people." Then he opened the door and welcomed me in. Each of this chapter's readers owes their past and future to their watersheds. However, the present is in question!

That has been "our" way throughout much of the course of our existence. Even with later "great civilizations"—through a similar process of wealth distribution and decentralization of power—there was a return to both ecological and social resilience.

Causes of Urban Collapse and Resilience

As societies evolved to greater complexity, many became superurbanized and hierarchical. This initially helped govern the fields, utilize individual talents, and distribute resources. However, as each aspect of urbanization intensified, collapse was eminent. What occurred in these civilizations is that leadership became more aloof from human need; natural resources were destroyed, and human capacity focused on activity that depleted rather than replenished the economy.

An illustrative example is several of the Mayan Empires, As the priestly class gained power, much of the labor force, once focused on farming, was re-directed to the building of huge temple complexes and the creation of ceremonial objects. Forests were rapidly lost and water resources dried up. In other words, the leaders of society lost their purpose in protecting and facilitating the collective good and balance with the environment and rather focused on their personal fame, wealth, and power. Does this sound familiar?

However, there are other examples that fly in the face of this paradigm. We have the illusion that all great Mayan centers simply disappeared, and that was simply not the case. With Tikal (which lasted over one thousand years), what is seen as a huge city center is actually a huge network of water canals, water cisterns, and distribution centers that reached a network of small villages, 30 miles out into the countryside.[9] What we see as the huge primary temple complex was actually made of large stone blocks, carved from the bedrock to create this water storage and distribution system. The runoff from these complexes would disperse into marshes, reservoirs, and rivulets.

Mayan culture still remains vibrant and resilient based on interdependent networks of autonomous, community-based villages, and decentralization with self-reliant economies.

At Angkor Wat in the Mekong Delta in Cambodia, the appearance of the central "Water Temple" was actually an elaborate web of water distribution centers, represented in a network of smaller temples, where water managers and their communities decided how to distribute water and decision-making was made among a huge region of self-reliant villages attuned to the watershed. These technological and ecological innovations were learned from previous civilizations that had perished because they followed the earlier Mayan paradigm of collapse. They had learned bitter lessons and rigorously applied the ethic that "not one drop of water should be wasted." Are we not at the exact same moment again given the water crises that have been mentioned in Chapter 4?

Later societies addressed social/economic and ecological problems with a focus on the "commons"—common community property, where cattle grazed, natural resources were distributed, and a council of leaders decided how to use scarce resources appropriately.[10] Forest laws of medieval England protected the beasts of the forests and the trees from poachers.[11]

Return to the Watershed

One pervasive key to this return to balance was a focus on the dynamics of the watershed. Watersheds are fed by high, often glacial mountain chains. As rivers, tributaries, and rivulets flow down lesser mountains and into valleys, we find resplendent forests and mineral-rich soils.[12] Further into the plains we find underground aquifers, and the dynamic between deep-rooted diverse flora, which helps bring deep aquifers back to the surface. As the rivers fan out into deltas, they create nutrient-rich alluvia and then enter the oceans. Coastal estuaries, marshes, and swamps create an amazing dynamic, where the coast is prevented from the impact of hurricanes and storms while providing an amazing ecological niche of flora and fauna that has continued to provide a resplendent existence to humanity. The ancient Marsh Arabs, living in the alluvial areas of the Tigress and Euphrates rivers, provided an essential service by both protecting a precious ecological niche and demonstrating how a society could live in support of the environment. The decline of these tribal groups during Saddam Hussain's reign added to the decline of these niches and to the destruction of the large centralized civilizations upstream.[13]

Many emergent societies and civilizations were designed in conformity to the flow of water.[14] Villages, settlements, and cities of the early U.S. Southwest were first designed to follow the course of water, through acequias or water dispersal systems both amongst pueblos and later Hispanic cultures.[15] In the Shinto practice of Satoyama in early Japan, fish life and water flow interspersed with housing, transportation, and merged back into ponds and larger lakes.[16]

The review of the long cycle and evolution of human society has proven time and time again that when following the previously mentioned dynamics both social and ecological resilience is stable; with ignorance and then conscious destruction of these watershed dynamics, civilizations eventually collapse.

So, it is by no coincidence that the decentralization and community autonomy that emerges out of the fall of large unbalanced urban systems is precisely the human return to the laws of the watershed. Despite large-scale desertification, massive deforestation, strip-mining, and desecration of the world's river systems, the watershed remains the one great constant in the story of planet earth. Follow the aforementioned laws of human relationship with the watershed and a human future is guaranteed; ignore and reverse these laws, civilizational collapse is a question of this basic equation.

Archeologist Vincent Scarborough of the University of Cincinnati is a world expert of the archeology of water management over more than 10,000 years. Through a review of thousands of archeological research projects and his work around the globe, his book *The Flow of Power: Ancient Water Systems and Landscapes* testifies to the challenges and solutions cited throughout this chapter. He and his archaeological colleagues worldwide have created the collaborative IHOPE (Integrated History and Future of People on Earth)[17] and now believe that archaeology needs to move from the periphery to the center of socio-ecological change initiatives. He foresees the immediate need to disperse huge untenable urban environments into decentralized regional technological hubs.

It has really been the onset of the industrial revolution in the mid-18th century that has blinded our attention to the watershed—our eternal legacy on this planet. Because of this, we view history from the lens of the "carpentered" environment that commodifies rather than sustains natural environments. This has led to the decoupling of the civilizational–environmental interdependence. Because of this we are blinded to the age-old laws of decentralization and watershed symbiosis. However, when we consider an economic renaissance in the age of artificial intelligence, let us not remain blinded with the eternal legacy of our planet in order to ensure a sustainable technological progress along with protection of environment.

Today's Urban Collapse

Analogies to today's dire urban predicament are evident. Large monument-like buildings utilize 76 percent of electrical energy in the United States.[18] Inside are many industries that take away rather than adding to a productive economy. In capitalism, the priests of ceremony and ritual are replaced by the stock market sector and financial sector, which more often creates the potential for destruction than genuine economic development because of the way it operates. Added to this is the banking, insurance, and health sectors that need to undergo major structural changes with technological advances as discussed in Chapters 1 through 3 and society should be more focused on increased self-sufficiency, watershed attunement, and self-reliance. Urban health care costs have accelerated through air pollution, high urban stress, lack of exercise, and aloofness from the nurturing natural world. Then there is the overtaking fast-food sector, which generates huge waste and leads to loss of electricity and pollution of our water sources as well as obesity.[19]

Added to this is the tremendous waste of human capital in the prison–industrial complex,[20] as well as the obscene loss of energy from the global exchange of goods that traverse the globe; clogging shipping lanes and wasting fuel as basic goods are moved back and forth across continental highways. Then there are the escalating long-term consequences from petroleum disasters, both on the sea and on land.[21]

If this is not sufficient to foretell a collapse, given the violations of common-sense macroeconomic parameters, let's add the following dramatic factors. 18 of the 25 largest urban centers across the world are along the coast. Because of rapidly melting glaciers, these cities are beginning to flood and will be completely flooded by the end of the century. Dramatic climate change causing massive hurricanes, volcanoes and earthquakes, and desertification accompanied by sweeping fires, leading to massive soil loss and flooding, has created a "climate diaspora" that has reached tens of millions.[23] Multinational corporations are privatizing precious water, leading to millions of the poor to bathe, cook, and consume toxic water from toxic industries.[24] Over 7 million people in the world are without sanitary water.[25]

Water wars are displacing and causing the suffering of millions. One of ISIS' first goal was to cut off water access in Mosul in Iraq to capture the city in 2014.[26] Only seven percent of land in China is considered arable.[27] The human displacement, malnutrition, and unimaginable waste of resources foretells a doom scenario that is frightening. Even worse, this crisis is on a global scale, not just on the scale of one isolated watershed-based civilization that could collapse and recover without impacting others. The stakes are much higher. There is a growing consensus that household recycling and rooftop water catchment, community gardens, and bicycling to work, though ethical and noble, will not reverse what is upon us.

Watershed councils and collaboratives worldwide are applying ecological conservancy, social activism, and challenges to wrong-minded multinationals in reversing some of the destruction mentioned in this chapter. These organizations are sparking transformation and building on national and international levels. They often oppose crony capitalism and promote people-powered economics. Somewhat like the Kenyan intervention; these movements are developing community solidarity, sparking capacity building, and better utilizing human and natural resources.

Better than the Kenyan initiative, they are powered by local initiative and cause, rather than outsider-modified intervention. However, from the arguments of this chapter, they focus too much on the comprise between the actors involved and include multinational corporations and large-scale industries as decision-makers. They also fall far short in adequately addressing the eminent collapse of large obsolete urban environments, as discussed in Chapter 4.

At the high points of human existence, our bonds of common destiny have nurtured tremendous human potential, creativity, love, human well-being, collaboration, and a thriving community life. The reason is actually very simple; we evolve and achieve much more when each individual and the collective are firing on all cylinders. Unfortunately, we are at one of the lowest points in our existence, where the wealthy few cause immense suffering of the many. Millions are starving in addition to lack education or water, adequate housing or healthcare and are displaced from their homelands.

Insights into Universal Income Schemes

Earlier approaches to universal income have fallen short of creating fulfillment for individuals—as terms such as the "dole" code for the doldrums refer to a social state when millions of the unemployed vegetate without further training and education or viable futures. This has often been the case in Western countries. My 10-year experience with universal income in Australia is testament to this fact. When the young are asked what they do or what they aspire to do, many answer "oh, hanging out; listening to music or surfing." One 40-year old friend hung himself after being on the dole for over 15 years and then faced a new government demand that the unemployed obtain employable skills and then job-hunt—he had been acculturated into an identity of incapacity.

The real question is what to do about the tremendous human potential that is unleashed when technology takes over jobs. There is actually no limit to the need of labor to make a better world—and the need now is supremely urgent. The goal is to shift un-needed investments in the economy—aspects of the economy that actually have no economic benefit, to projects that add proven value to enhance human life. The shift to a subtle more intimate relationship with the watershed will employ billions. Then there will be no surplus labor, and rather than working no-end jobs, the focus will be human creativity and innovation. We can then embrace all forms of technological innovation as liberational and transformative.

However universal income (UI) or the means to guarantee the basic necessities of life forever to the human being may always be needed, but not as an easy release from guilt for the exploitive and super rich. The best use of UI occurs when it accompanies the shift mentioned earlier back to our watersheds.

Encouraging Insights for the Kenya Initiative

Where does this leave us regarding the Kenyan UI intervention? The strengths are that they have chosen Kenyan villages—a specific set of rural dynamics in which the potential for success is heightened. While most rural regions are depleted, people are abandoning them and there is little economic vitality. This case mimics that of Mayan villages after the fall of the great Mayan empires. People are utilizing their natural resources, using their potential to develop talents and potential, and strengthening community solidarity. They are utilizing their present technologies in support of and not in opposition to all that is good about their future. So, this would seem to be quite a potential niche in which further introductions of technology might be a fit.

When we add the sagely advice from the aforementioned thousands of years of human trial and error chronicled in the return to the watershed, we can offer the drivers of the Kenyan initiative specific ideas to expand their initiative.

First, we need to consider the wider context surrounding these villages in southwest Kenya. The environs nearby Nairobi, though much smaller in scale, mimic many of the destructive dynamics of the major urban hubs of the planet. Tens of thousands of refugees live in squalor, with no access to any of the basic necessities of life.[28] The Nairobi River has long lost its identity as a river and is now considered by many as the main sewer system of the city. It is so toxic that it kills thousands per year. This effluent has obvious consequences for the entire watershed, which include loss of agricultural land, destruction of ecosystems, spread of disease, disruption of community life, and the imperative for impacted villagers to move to Nairobi as refugees.

An exacerbating dire plight is the increasing terrorist activity of Al Shabab and Boko Haram[30] and associated terrorist organizations, now claiming large swaths of land in northeast Kenya. So, the urgency in Kenya is exactly the same as the rest of the world. Urban waste and blight can be diminished through a return to the watershed mentioned earlier. Local initiatives such as the one mentioned for Kenyan villages can be expanded to include a vibrant full-scale movement of decentralization based on initial successes such as the ones explored in the experiment for universal income.

Back to the Basic Tenets

The tenets at the beginning of this chapter have hopefully been argued convincingly. No one model of change will work in each context, and no one can guarantee or accurately predict what the future will hold. However, the long span of history holds crucial clues.

As mentioned before, billions of people would be needed to shift society back to the necessary symbiotic systems with the watersheds that we have always returned to. Imagine small ponds and lakes and small-scale waterworks, within which are planted oxygenating lotus and chlorophyll nutritious algae. Imagine the new labor that would be freed up to develop nurturing economic hubs and profoundly resilient communities—the community organizing and facilitation skills and the diversity facilitation that would be infused at huge economic benefit. This includes the infusion of thousands of innovation hubs that apply human potential to physical, biological, and technological innovations, as well as psychological, artistic, and other creative interventions that develop greater harmony and imaginative human communities.

One would legitimately be concerned about the mode, process, and timing of this immense transition, even if it is urgently necessary. Can we just close down mega-industries and huge urban environments and "camp out" in dispersed decentralized communities? Do we imagine the migration of millions of people and millions of homes and buildings left empty? If this mega transition were in the wrong hands, there would be mass starvation, massive unemployment, and exacerbated mental and physical health as a result. Even in this regard, for this transition to be smooth, the control of socioeconomic system should pass into the hands of Sadvipras as mentioned in the concluding Chapter 13. While my expertise is not sufficient, as any anthropologist, I would look for the trends and model projects that show the pragmatic and realistic timetables with which to actually begin the transition. We can also look to past civilizations that were quick enough in this transition to be successful. Let us take "what is" to transition to "what will become" as our adage.

Each of the diverse experiments in state-wide socialism and communism have ended in the same disasters. When given resources and capacity, people in rural areas will rapidly shift to the time-honored decentralized, autonomous mode. Simultaneously re-weaving the human ecosystem into the fabric of the watershed will return to the mental primacy of the watershed to human existence. Large urban centers, while being divested of the aforementioned wastage of trillions of dollars, can convert to hubs of exchange of knowledge and information, the regional convergence of people when collaboration is needed, and restructuring of the current global transportation system back to the regional.

There are countless examples in every niche of the planet that provide the course of the future and offer the potential for planetary change. There are self-reliant economic regions that focus primarily on the sustainability of natural resources and have developed a people-based cooperative economy. Mondragon[31] in the Basque region of Spain is an example to follow closely. In Japan, disenchanted young adults are returning to traditional Satoyama[16] villages; where economic and village living is interspersed with the course of the river and integrated with ponds and lakes.

Ancient Lessons Fuel a Positive Future

The best advice is to turn to the well-proven interventions that evolved over thousands of years and then apply current technology to these systems. Many Moghul societies created systems of cisterns and water canals that dispersed water over large areas. Small ponds, lakes, dams, and reservoirs preserved fish and plant life, and meant that all people had easy access to clean water. The Yemeni and Syrian models of water distribution have long been followed. Here, river water distribution is spread according to need and necessity, rather than to the first farmers or the dominant multinationals in the watershed. In parched deserts, Muslim societies built mechanisms to extract enough water to serve large villages. Many ancient societies were water temple cities.

Sparking a Transformation of Consciousness to Conscious Action

There are many keys to returning our worldview, ethics, and visceral experience of life back to the watershed. Most countries still boast amazing ancient watershed pilgrimages that link ancient cisterns and natural springs together as well as linking modern religion with ancient mythic spirituality. All large rivers have their gods and goddesses and spirit-beings. People in Egypt still beseech the Nile god to assist them in times of social and economic strife. In India there are massive river pilgrimages that introduce the pilgrim to vastly different languages, arts, and agricultural practices that still exist in symbiosis with the watershed.[34]

One remarkable seer, originally from Bengal, India, where the Ganges, Sarasvati, and Brahmaputra watersheds converge, applied an amazing plethora of ancient genius. Shrii Prabhat Ranjan Sarkar travelled great lengths of rivers, studying the history of water-harvesting, agriculture, and cultural, spiritual, and economic development.[36] He has used this knowledge to create schemes for decentralized communities, where ponds, lakes, and small reservoirs dot the landscape and fuel both cooperative, small-scale, and large-scale industries. Here architecture blends with the environment, and education focuses on local language, culture, and the legacy of ancestors.

In one large-scale intervention created by Shrii Sarkar (see http://anandanagar.org/), a certified engineering and technological development college represents the only college in a large impoverished, desertified rural region. This college sits within a huge project infused with people-run cooperatives; innovative farming and reforestation projects; revived ponds, small lakes, and reservoirs and water-harvesting techniques.[37]

The re-shifting of priorities and urgent changes argued earlier are already occurring. As well as trialing projects, there has been a shifting of consciousness and many finding renewal and resilience by walking their own watersheds. Now it needs to become the dominant paradigm.

Media watchers all know that what people watch reflects both the urgencies and the promises of the future. On the one hand, we have meteors threatening to end all life on earth—the zombie apocalypse, which is really the de-humanization occurring in our urban climes; the re-emerging craze of warrior movies; either with superhuman skills or the returning theme of the warrior and wars ever-fighting terrorists. We flock to these movies because they show us what we often do not admit is going on in our subconscious mind as being harmful, yet they also show us the way forward.

Black Panther is one of the most compelling recent movies. We are captivated by a never-colonized indigenous regional society in harmony with and taping into the powers of ecology. Hyperadvanced technology blends seamlessly with community and ecology. The romance of the movie *The Color of Water* garnered the Oscar for the Best Movie of 2018. In it, a timeless water-god (our longing for the watershed) enchants a lonely cleaning woman—a symbol of the disenfranchised millions—who becomes a warrior in the face of the evil power brokers.

Let's follow them back to our watersheds, glance around up to the mountain tops, follow the course of the great rivers, the nurturing valleys, plains, and river deltas. Then let's invite current technological innovation and progress to free up the human potential to apply to what is truly fulfilling for us and deeply nurturing of our symbiotic ecosystems. Impending collapse must return to resilience and ecological harmony. For nearly 150,000 years that has been our way. Whether through great suffering or more rapid urgency it will always be our way!

References

[1] World Economic Forum. 2018. "5 Million Jobs to be Lost by 2020." Retrieved June 27 from www.weforum.org/agenda/2016/01/5-million-jobs-to-be-lost-by-2020

[2] givedirectly.org. 2018. Retrieved June 27.

[3] Haushofer, J., and J. Shapiro. 2018. "The Short-term Impact of Unconditional Cash Transfers to the Poor." Retrieved June 27 from www.princeton.edu/~joha/publications/Haushofer_Shapiro_UCT_2016.04.25.pdf

[4] Ibid.

[5] Gray, P. 2018. "How Hunter-gatherers Maintained their Indigenous Ways." Retrieved June 27 from www.psychologytoday.com/us/blog/freedom-learn/201105/how-hunter-gatherers-maintained-their-egalitarian-ways

[6] Barnett, H.G. 1938. "The Nature of the Potlatch." *American Anthropologist* 40, no. 3, pp. 349–58.

[7] Marae: Maori Meeting Grounds. 2018. Retrieved June 27 from www.newzealand.com/us/feature/marae-maori-meeting-grounds/

[8] Cole, H.M. 1982. *Mbari: Art and Life Among the Owerri Igbo.* Bloomington: Indiana University Press.

[9] Scarborough, V. 2003. *The Flow of Power: Ancient Water Systems and Landscapes.* Santa Fe: SAR Press.

[10] Associations of Commons Registration Authorities. 2018. "Commons and the Greens." Retrieved June 27 from www.acraew.org.uk/history-common-land-and-village-greens

[11] Woodbury, S. 2018. "Forest laws of the Middle Ages." Retrieved June 27 from http://sarahwoodbury.com/forest-laws/

[12] National Ocean Services. 2018. "What is a Watershed?" Retrieved June 27 from https://oceanservice.noaa.gov/facts/watershed.html

[13] Ancient Life Lost: the Marsh Arabs of Iraq. 2018. Retrieved from June 27 from productforums.google.com/forum/#!topic/gec-history-illustrated-moderated/hCJD6j-ISwg

[14] Sarkar, P.R. 2018. "Civilization." Retrieved June 27 from http://am-bhagavatadharma.com/about/civilization/

[15] Rodriguez, S. 2006. *Acequia: Water Sharing, Sanctity, and Place.* Santa Fe: SAR Press.

[16] "Satoyama: Japan's Secret Water Garden. 2018." Documentary. Retrieved June 27 from www.imdb.com/title/tt0483154/

[17] IHOPE. 2018. Retrieved June 27 from http://ihopenet.org/

[18] Quadrennial Technology Review: An Assessment of Energy Technologies and Research Opportunities. 2018. Chapter 5: Increasing Efficiency of Building Systems and Technologies. September 2015. Retrieved June 27 from www.energy.gov/sites/prod/files/2017/03/f34/qtr-2015-chapter5.pdf

[19] Oppenheim, M. 1991. *Into the Likeness of the Country: A Report on Australia's Rural/Urban Imbalance.* Proutist Universal, Sydney.

[20] Palaez, V. 2018. "Prison Industry in the U.S.: Big Business or a New Form of Slavery?" *In Global Research.* Retrieved June 29 from https://globalresearch.ca/the-prison-industry-in-the-united-states-big-business-or-a-new-form-of-slavery/8289

[21] Rotter, L. 2018. "Shipping Costs Start to Crimp Globalization." *New York Times.* Retrieved June 29, 2018 from https://nytimes.com/2008/08/03/business/worldbusiness/03global.html

[22] Fontinelle, E. 2018. "The Most Expensive Oil Disasters." *Investopia*. Retrieved June 29 from www.investopedia.com/financial-edge/0510/the-most-expensive-oil-spills.aspx

[23] Taylor, M. 2018. "Climate Change 'Will Create the World's Biggest Refugee Crisis.'" *The Guardian*. Retrieved June 29 from https://theguardian.com/environment/2017/nov/02/climate-change-will-create-worlds-biggest-refugee-crisis

[24] Petitjean, O. 2018. "The Misdeeds and Misfortunes of Water Multinationals in Cities of the World." *In Partage des eaux*. Retrieved June 29 from https://partagedeseaux.info/The-Misdeeds-and-Misfortunes-of-Water-Multinationals-in-the-Cities-of-the-World

[25] "Global Water, Hygiene and Sanitation. 2018." *In Centers for Disease Control and Prevention*. Retrieved June 29 from www.cdc.gov/healthywater/global/wash_statistics.html

[26] Tawfeq, M., and S. Abdelaziz. 2018. "ISIS Uses Water as a Weapon in Mosul Fight." Retrieved June 29 from https://cnn.com/2016/11/30/middleeast/mosul-water-isis/index.html

[27] Resources Ministry. 2018. "China's Total Arable Land Falls for Fourth Year in 2017." *Reuters*. Retrieved June 29 from https://reuters.com/article/us-china-agriculture-land/chinas-total-arable-land-falls-for-fourth-year-in-2017-resources-ministry-idUSKCN1IK059

[28] "Kenyan Slums Attract Poverty Tourism. 2018." *The Guardian*. Retrieved June 29 from https://theguardian.com/world/2009/sep/25/slum-tourism-kenya-kibera-poverty

[29] Odenyo, A. 2018. "Garbage Disposal into Nairobi River Killing City Residents, Says Study." Retrieved June 29 from https://standardmedia.co.ke/article/2001258912/garbage-disposal-into-nairobi-river-killing-city-residents-says-study

[30] Clionadh, R., R. Kishi, O. Russell, J. Siegle, and W. Williams. 2018. "Boko Haram vs. al-Shabab: What Do We Know about Their Patterns of Violence?" *The Washington Post*. Retrieved June 29 from https://washingtonpost.com/news/monkey-cage/wp/2017/10/02/boko-haram-vs-al-shabaab-what-do-we-know-about-their-patterns-of-violence/?noredirect=on&utm_term=.21ba9851bb87.

[31] Bibby, A. 2018. "Co-operatives in Spain—Mondragon Leads the Way." *The Guardian*. Retrieved June 29 from https://theguardian.com/social-enterprise-network/2012/mar/12/cooperatives-spain-mondragon

[32] "Satoyama and Satoumi of Ishikawa. 2018." Retrieved June 29 from http://i.unu.edu/media/ias.unu.edu-en/page/7973/Satoyama_and_Satoumi_of_Ishikawa.pdf

[33] In Ehtta: European Historic Towns Associations. 2018. "Water, Pilgrimage and Spirituality." Retrieved June 29 from https://ehtta.eu/portal/water-pilgrimages-and-spirituality-a-history-of-hospitality-trough-the-sources-of-europe/

[34] "'Nile River Poems' in Black Cat Poems. 2018." Retrieved June 30 from http://blackcatpoems.com/n/nile_river_poems.html

[35] "Himalayan Char Dam Pilgrimage. 2018." *MagicIndia*. Retrieved June 30 from http://blackcatpoems.com/n/nile_river_poems.html

[36] Sarkar, P.R. 2008. *Histories Along the Way*. Kolkata: Ananda Marga Publications.

[37] Sarkar, P.R. 1992. *Proutist Economics: Discourses on Economic Liberation*. Kolkata: Ananda Marga Publications.

CHAPTER 8

Beyond Nationalism: A Global Constitution to Unite an Interconnected World

Craig Runde

Introduction

At first blush, it may seem strange to have a chapter on global constitutional principles in a book on macroeconomics. In a traditional macroeconomics text, that might be true, but this book concerns a new macroeconomic model, which encompasses values that depend on reforms embodied in a new framework provided by a global constitution. In a highly automated, interconnected world, the sustainable well-being of humans and the natural world will require protections not automatically provided by market mechanisms. Additionally, as mentioned in Chapter 6, new laws are necessary to ensure that artificial intelligence (AI) enables a more collaborative socioeconomic system over a predatory system.

A constitution is defined as "the basic principles and laws of a nation, state, or social group that determine the powers and duties of the government and guarantee certain rights to the people in it."[1] As social groups have become more complex, so too have the problems that they face. As a consequence, they have experienced the need for more refined laws and principles to address these challenges.

This chapter will look at the journey human society has taken, which has eventually led to the need for a global constitution. It will examine how our institutions and the problems they have faced have become ever more complex and interconnected. In the 20th century two world wars eventually led to both governmental and private efforts to create global approaches to protecting global peace. In more recent times similar work has arisen to protect the world's environment against threats that could jeopardize future life on earth.

In the era of AI and robots, issues of economic justice, environmental sustainability, and safeguarding peace will require the need for global constitutional safeguards to ensure humanity's progress. As technology and automation play an ever-increasing role in our society, a global constitution will require a new mindset that emphasizes our common good as opposed to elements that divide us.[2] It will also have to address new issues caused by these revolutionary technologies.

A Long Journey

Since the advent of modern humans, most of our existence as a species has been spent in small groups or tribes. These groups developed rules for managing social interactions of their members. Even today, people living together in small groups develop rules or codes of conduct governing their interactions.[3, 4] Once humans developed agriculture they began to live in larger communities, and the complexity of the societies increased. People began to engage in different occupations beyond hunting and gathering. Rules were developed to govern and manage these more involved economic affairs. As communications and transportation technologies improved, communities expanded in size and new systems were developed to create consistent ways of governing the geographically dispersed populace.

As of a couple of thousand years ago, large empires in China, India, the Middle East, Africa, Europe, and the Americas had emerged that required complex governing systems. The emphasis of most of these early governments was on maintaining the power of the monarch. At times, resistance grew to these power structures, and documents like the Magna Carta arose to limit the powers of the sovereign.[5] In many places wars between kingdoms caused great disruption and suffering. In Europe, this eventually led in 1648 to the Treaty of Westphalia, which established a legal foundation with sovereign states recognized as the political actors.[6] Over time, this concept spread and became the basis of international law. The nations eventually developed constitutions to provide legal frameworks for governing their own territory. The U.S. Constitution is generally seen as the first such modern constitution and one whose structure had significant influence on others until recent times.[7]

Of course, this new international framework did not ultimately keep the peace. In the 20th century, humanity endured two of the worst wars in history. By the time the Treaty of Versailles ended World War I, almost 9 million soldiers had been killed and over 20 million had been wounded. Civilian casualties were estimated to be even higher.[8] The horror and revulsion at the devastation caused by new technologies led people to attempt to develop an international system that would end wars. In 1920 the League of Nations came into being for this purpose but was unable to fulfill its mission.

World War II enveloped even more countries and led to the deaths of over 60 million soldiers and civilians.[9] The atomic explosions that destroyed Hiroshima and Nagasaki at the end of the war brought humanity's survival into question. The countries of the world tried again to establish an institution to prevent future wars, and the United Nations (UN) was born in 1945. The charter of the UN and its ancillary agencies became a kind of world constitution.[10] The structure of the charter, though, was principally an agreement among nations and not focused on the rights of the world's citizens per se. In 1948 the United Nations released the universal declaration of human rights.[11] While the declaration described a lofty and inspiring set of rights for all humanity, it did not have effective mechanisms for actually protecting or guaranteeing those rights.

In addition to governmental efforts to address the scourge of war, private citizens began exploring options. Distinguished academicians from Harvard, Yale, and the University of Chicago wrote about reining in military expenditures and even suggested creating a world constitution to restrict individual countries from instigating aggression.[12, 13] Regular citizens joined together to create organizations to promote world constitutional development and the creation of organizations of federated states to prevent war.[14]

While peacemaking continued to be a prime focus for the UN and many private groups, over time additional issues came to the fore. The devastation and displacement caused by World War II immediately led to humanitarian and relief concerns that became a standing part of United Nations' work. Later in the century, global pollution and environmental issues caused the United Nations to convene an unprecedented global gathering in Rio De Janeiro, Brazil.[15] The Rio Earth Summit and meetings that followed eventually led to the 2015 Paris Agreement that set global limits for greenhouse gas emissions. In a comparable manner, the UN has addressed various transnational issues such as terrorism and war crimes.

Challenges that Transcend National Competence

The United Nations and groups of countries have developed agreements on a wide range of common issues like policing (Interpol), postal services (International Postal Union), and global trade policies (World Trade Organization). At the same time some of the biggest issues facing humanity seem particularly challenging to resolution by multinational treaties. The Global Challenges Foundation has delineated several of these major issues to include global warming, other environmental degradation, war and other forms of violence, extreme poverty, and overpopulation.[16]

It took 27 years to get from the Rio Earth Summit to the Paris Agreement on climate. Some of this time involved actual research but much of the delay was caused by political infighting among the countries involved in the treaty and this continues to threaten its vitality.[17] During this time, carbon dioxide concentrations rose from around 360 ppm to now over 400 ppm, a measure that scientists have warned will lead to serious repercussions for humanity.[18, 19] Mounting environmental pressures are also seen in areas such as ocean pollution,[20] soil erosion,[21] and water depletion.[22, 23]

The UN has done a great deal to prevent the scourge of war and to resolve conflicts through its peacekeeping missions. At the same time strife has continued to plague the Middle East and many other areas of the world. The rise of terrorism and other forms of asymmetric warfare have presented new challenges to the world. Some of the worst atrocities in recent times have occurred in civil wars within sovereign states.

Although there has been some improvement in the relative numbers of people living in extreme poverty, the World Bank estimates that there are still more than three-quarters of a billion people, almost 11 percent of the world's population, who still live on less than the equivalent of $1.90 per day.[24] Beyond poverty there is also a growing issue of economic inequality through much of the world.[25] The level of inequality is shaped by both national policies and infrastructure in different countries.[26] Such inequality is closely correlated with a host of social ills such as incarceration, drug and alcohol abuse, mental and physical health problems, violence, and educational deficits.[27] It is also associated with a decrease in social mobility which creates long-term class divides.

All of these current problems will continue to confront the world as it evolves technologically. AI and robotics can play a role in either improving or worsening these problems depending on the social, economic, and political choices made regarding them. Given the slow and sometimes clumsy way with which such issues are dealt through multilateral treaty negotiations, the development of a global constitutional framework may prove more effective.

On top of these matters, new problems will arise that are either caused by or are directly related to the new technologies. For example, it has been estimated that between 2018 and 2030, robot automation will cause hundreds of millions of workers to lose their jobs.[28, 29] These losses will be more focused on developed economies furthering the rising inequality in society, but the ability of a country to adjust to these changes will be greatly influenced by its social policies.[30]

Automation and AI will also present privacy issues. Companies like Amazon, Facebook, and Google already collect substantial amounts of information about their customers' online activities and preferences. Employers are also expanding the types of information they collect and the way they use it to monitor employees.[31] China is going even further in setting up a system to monitor and rate citizen trustworthiness. The Social Credit System will award citizens who behave in accepted manners with a variety of economic perks.[32] Critics suggest this will result in a sinister "big brother" outcome, while advocates suggest it will help foster high levels of trust and cooperation.

As automation reaches into wider arrays of daily life, it will also be essential to determine not only who benefits from the technology but also who is liable for its unintended consequences. As momentum for driverless cars grows so will inevitable accidents related to programming or other design flaws. These accidents will be disturbing and will require policies that hold the proper people accountable.[33]

A Global Constitution for the Age of Artificial Intelligence

In drafting elements of a global constitution to address these various issues, it will be critical that the process be guided by key social, economic, and political principles and values. In this new macroeconomic model, automation is seen as permeating all aspects of the economy and helping to bring about an improvement in the standard of living for all people. It will reduce total work hours and lessen the need for people to do repetitive, monotonous work. People will be able to spend their extra time in creative, educational, and recreational pursuits. The new macroeconomic model must also address the environment. Without environmental sustainability, the economic and social advances will come to naught. The model will emphasize decentralized growth and reduce the size and power of large corporations and financial institutions in order to usher in true free markets. With these principles in mind, this section will present sample constitutional sections dealing with human rights and governmental structures. It will touch on some new legal aspects related to the rising role of technology. Finally, it will explore how a global constitutional framework could be established.

Guaranteed Purchasing Power

In 1986, Indian social philosopher, Shrii Prabhat Ranjan Sarkar, gave a talk titled "The Requirements of an Ideal Constitution," which described a charter of human rights that addressed important rights at the heart of the new macroeconomic model. One enumerated right was that "each country must guarantee purchasing power to all its citizens."[34] Since the new macroeconomic model posits an improved living standard for all people, and increased automation can result in reduced work, there needs to be a method for reconciling these points. One way is for national governments to guarantee purchasing power to their inhabitants through creation of opportunities rather than offering "doles."

The concept of guaranteed purchasing power involves a number of elements. On the one hand, it means that people should at least be able to afford to purchase the minimum necessities of life, including among other things food, clothing, housing, medical care, and education.[35] The cost and nature of these items will differ in various parts of the world, but the underlying principle is that people will be able to purchase them in order to lead a healthy existence. Generally, this means that people must have sufficient money to afford them. In some cases, services like medical care and education may be provided at subsidized rates or free of charge as a way of guaranteeing overall purchasing power.

The various necessities must also be available to be purchased. If markets naturally provide them, so much the better. If market imbalances lead to a surplus of luxury items to cater to the wealthy and insufficient amounts of the necessities to meet the needs of the poor, then local governments will need to step in to ensure an adequate supply of those fundamental elements.[36] If there is a lack of personnel like doctors or teachers to provide key services, then the government will need to act to create incentives to overcome this shortfall.

How will governments determine the level at which the guaranteed purchasing power should be set? The concept of guaranteed minimum necessities is not meant to suggest a low bar for purchasing power; rather people should be able to live a dignified life with ever growing purchasing power with advancements in technology.[37] This notion combines practical concerns about the physical requirements that people need to live along with psychological concerns about how people feel about their condition.

In their book, *The Spirit Level*, researchers Wilkinson and Pickett find that huge economic inequality leads to a host of social ills including health problems.[38] The rationale underlying this connection is that people judge the quality of their own life in part by comparing their status to that of others. In societies where inequality is high, social problems arise when people become dissatisfied with their conditions because they judge themselves less well off than those who are much wealthier.[39]

This suggests that the purchasing power of people should be set high enough to lessen social ills caused by significant income inequalities. In the present U.S. economy, a more progressive tax system could lessen income inequalities and provide additional funds to support the purchasing power initiative. However, it is possible to lower income taxes on all by means of economic restructuring as explained by Apek Mulay in his *Mass Capitalism: A Blueprint for Economic Revival.* At the same time, Shrii Sarkar suggests that there is benefit in maintaining economic incentives for individuals whose productivity contributes to the betterment of the society. Research has shown that an optimal level can be calculated for such incentives.[40]

How will a government go about guaranteeing purchasing power to all its citizens? One recent suggestion is for the provision of a universal basic income (UBI). This concept has emerged as it has become evident that technology will be displacing large numbers of jobs. UBI involves governments providing people unconditional cash payments.[41] Shrii Sarkar suggests that it is psychologically better to guarantee purchasing power by ensuring that people are able to find jobs that pay enough to meet their needs. When people have the opportunity to earn their own living, it creates a more positive sense of self-worth and overcomes any tendencies toward idleness.[42] If adequate jobs are not available from market sources, governments would act to create such jobs to provide the necessary purchasing power. In cases where people are physically or mentally unable to work, provisions would still be made for them to acquire necessary purchasing power.

How can governments afford to guarantee purchasing power to their people? Some have argued that providing a UBI would be extremely expensive.[43] Guaranteed purchasing power through the media of guaranteed jobs, however, is a different proposition. Since people are providing productive work for their income, there will be less overall cost because supply and demand will grow in proportion. As long as economy has been restructured to a balanced economy as described in *Mass Capitalism*, the real job creators would be both producers and consumers. As there would be no overproduction in the economy, there would be no additional costs to this approach. Additionally, taxes could be raised in case of government needing additional revenue to compensate for money spent for any economic relief in case of natural disasters.

If income taxation were insufficient to manage the guaranteed purchasing power system, some have argued that an additional wealth tax

be used to create sufficient funding and further lessen the problems associated with wealth inequality.[44] However, the wealthy can also afford
expensive financial advisors who can show them how to park their money
into tax advantaged accounts. The middle class and poor cannot afford
such expensive advisors. Hence, the rich end up paying a lower tax rate
despite progressive tax policies. Hence, progressive taxation is not an
answer to this problem. However, taxation at source as prescribed in *Mass
Capitalism* may be a solution to this crisis. Additionally, there should be
opportunities created to offer free financial advice to the middle class and
poor to educate people about savings and investments.

How can people enforce their government's guarantees of purchasing power? An important distinction among human rights is between
those which are justiciable and those which are not.[45] For example, the
Universal Declaration of Human Rights says that "Everyone has the right
to work" and "Everyone has the right to a standard of living adequate for
the health and well-being of himself and of his family." These and similar
clauses in certain national constitutions are nonjusticiable in that there
are no enforcement mechanisms available to individuals specified in the
documents.[46] Shrii Sarkar mentioned that the right of individuals to sue
the government to enforce their right to purchasing power to acquire
minimum necessities should be enshrined in the constitution.[47,48]
In many instances access to litigation could be so expensive as to be out
of reach for common citizens. In order to ensure that justiciability is a
practical right, as opposed to just a theoretical one, governments should
cover the costs of legal services required to enforce this provision.

With these various concepts in mind, a section in the global constitution on guaranteed purchasing power could read:

Section: Guaranteed Purchasing Power

(a) Each country must guarantee purchasing power to all its citizens
sufficient to procure the minimum necessities of life adequate for
health and well-being.
(b) Each country will provide this by insuring that all able citizens will
have the right to obtain work that affords the necessary purchasing
power. Citizens who are unable to work will be provided with direct
resources to ensure their purchasing power.

(c) Citizens can sue their government to enforce the provision of guaranteed purchasing power. Governments will provide citizens with free access to legal services necessary to enforce this provision.

In addition to the mandates on individual countries, a method will need to be established to help countries that may be financially unable to provide for adequate guaranteed purchasing power. A number of very poor countries, most of which are located in Africa, do not have the means to be able to meet the proposed constitutional requirements. For such countries, an approach would need to be created to help them successfully guarantee purchasing power until they are able to meet it on their own. Funding for this approach could be derived from taxes or tariffs on international trade or some similar source. It would also incorporate planning help to strengthen local economies to the point where they can provide guaranteed purchasing power.

Safeguarding the Environment

A safe environment is essential for sustained human progress and prosperity. People have become more aware of threats to the environment such as greenhouse gas emissions, desertification, collapse of wildlife habitat, and the like. There have been efforts to make changes like the Paris Climate Accord, but there have also been private and governmental resistance to addressing environmental issues. This resistance has slowed down and sometimes reversed gains made to improve the environment. A global constitutional provision would strengthen these protections.

In his proposed charter of rights relating to the environment, Shrii Sarkar states that "complete security should be guaranteed to all the plants and animals on the planet." This provision derives from Shrii Sarkar's philosophy of neohumanism, which is an extension of the philosophy of humanism to include all created beings. It is meant to expand human sentiments beyond narrow tendencies that divide us based on categories such as race, gender, nationality, and even species.[49] Giving constitutional protections to plants and animals underscores his belief that all beings share the desire to live.

Bringing attention to the rights of all beings to live increases human sensitivity to the importance of a sustainable environment. This is particularly important given that earth may be facing its sixth mass extinction event, this one caused in significant part by human activity. Recent findings suggest that dwindling population sizes and degradation of ranges amount to a massive erosion of biodiversity and the ecosystem that is critical to civilization.[50]

Our planet has a large, yet finite, capacity to sustain life. As more forests are destroyed, more waters polluted, more topsoil lost, the Earth's carrying capacity is eroded. The outcome of human economic activity has become large enough to threaten the sustainability of animal, plant, and even human life. We are already seeing significant effects on both plant and animal populations. We may soon reach a point of no return for human populations as well.[51]

These factors lead to a global constitutional provision on the environment that could read as follows.

Section: Environmental Protection

(a) All countries must guarantee complete security to all the plants and animals within their borders and must prevent activity that would harm plants and animals in other countries or within areas of the global commons.
(b) This guarantee shall not be construed to permit activities that harm human beings.

The second clause is included to guarantee that protections for the environment are not designed in a manner that hurts humans.

Protecting the Peace

Global military spending in 2015 was estimated to range between one-and-a-half and two trillion dollars.[52] Yet, these tremendous expenditures do not seem to bring humanity much peace. Wars and conflict in the 21 century have continued to claim lives, create ever-growing numbers of refugees, and cost huge amounts of money.[53]

Professors Grenville Clark and Louis Sohn created a plan for world peace that included provisions for total disarmament of national militaries and the development of a United Nations Peace Force to take their place.[54] This plan included a phase-wise elimination of all military forces and supplies in all countries. Small amounts of light weapons would be allowed to be retained for use by local police forces. The plan would be overseen by an international inspection group. Shrii Sarkar also believed that the development of a world militia was an important aspect of creating a federation overseen by a global constitution.[55] These provisions could be included in a global constitutional section:

Section: Protecting the Peace

(a) A world militia shall be established to keep peace among peoples of the world. It shall be made up of representatives from the different countries and funded by them. It shall eventually replace national militaries.

(b) Responsibility for police functions will be retained by countries.

Beyond addressing military disarmament, Shrii Sarkar also proposed a series of constitutional guarantees that would lessen tensions among people, which can lead to violence. These guarantees of fundamental rights included spiritual practice, cultural legacy, education, and indigenous linguistic expression. Cultural, religious, and linguistic differences lie beneath much of the strife seen in the world. By providing expressed protection, and thereby respect, for these different aspects of human identity, a global constitution could promote the overall cause of peace.

We human beings have an absolute control over but one thing, and that is our thoughts. If one fails to control one's mind, he may be sure to not be able to control anything else. Our mind is our spiritual estate. Human beings should protect and use it with care to which divine royalty is entitled. Humans were given will power for this purpose. Unfortunately, there is no legal protection against those who poison minds of others by negative suggestions either purposely or by ignorance. This could destroy someone's self-confidence and hence such forms of destruction should be punishable because it may discourage a person to even acquire material things that are needed for his or her survival due to loss of self-confidence.

The relevant constitutional provisions could read:

Section: Guarantees of Human Rights

Countries shall:

(a) Not abridge the right of people to engage in spiritual practice

(b) Permit people to engage in cultural expression

(c) Provide universal, free access to public education, and

(d) Protect the rights of indigenous peoples to use their own languages

Again, none of these rights should be construed in a manner that cause harm to human beings either physically, mentally, emotionally, or spiritually.

Technologically Related Provisions

While some issues like liability for injuries caused by automation can probably be dealt with by traditional tort and products liability law, the question of personal privacy will become so significant as to require constitutional protections. Recent privacy issues concerning Facebook Inc. have caused widespread concern among citizens and even criticism from within the technology field.[57, 58] The European Union has established new data privacy requirements that apply to member states in order to create a consistent standard throughout the union. The rules also apply to companies that market goods and services to EU residents.[59] We shall learn more about General Data Protection Regulation (GDPR) in Chapter 12. On the other hand, the United States has been more lax on data protection requirements, and China has been developing ways of using data to modify their citizens' behaviors.

Given these developments and in line with the values underlying the economic renaissance in the age of AI, a provision in a global constitution could provide the following:

Section: Data Protection

(a) Each country much ensure that data on individual citizens gathered by the government and by other organizations will not be used to the detriment of those citizens.

As technology continues to advance it will be necessary to address a variety of new issues. Deliberations have already begun regarding lethal autonomous weapons systems. Longer-term agreements regarding other aspects of AI will also grow in importance.[60] Further in the future, robots and AI may advance to the state where they themselves will be treated as having some rights.[61] The participation of a classless society of Sadvipras (as discussed in Chapter 13) is critical for making decisions with regard to the rights of future advanced robots.

Establishing a Global Constitution

Many obstacles stand in the way of the establishment of a global constitution, most notably the desire of local politicians and business leaders to hold onto their power. With such entrenched resistance, it is natural to ask how such a constitution can be realized. One view suggests that humanity will not take such steps until it is faced with calamity. In this view, environmental and political crises will become so great that they will spell impending doom to humankind and force major political changes.[62]

Shrii Sarkar offered a different approach, which focuses on creating positive momentum for such a change through constructive service. As he said,

> The question is whether the establishment of a world government or universal fraternity is practicable without staging any fight. To this I will reply in the affirmative. The extreme welfare of the human race can be achieved by mobilizing the living spirit of those people who are desirous of establishing world federation, not by political rivalry but only by means of selfless service and constructive work.[63]

The idea of mobilizing people's spirit to call out for global constitutional reform is in keeping with the growth of civil society organizations across the planet. These organizations bring people together to work on social, economic, environmental, and other causes. They also seek to increase people's awareness about the key issues in their purview. As the urgency of global issues increase, the need for collaboration among the civil society groups grows as well. This coupled with the expansive outreach of social media to connect people around the world will accelerate efforts toward development of a global constitution to address tomorrow's challenges. While work toward a global constitution may take quite some time, efforts of civil society groups can also address constitutional changes in more local governmental settings. Success in these venues can build momentum for larger global changes.

References

[1] Merriam Webster Online Dictionary. March 29, 2018. https://merriam-webster.com/dictionary/constitution

[2] Reich, R. 2018. *The Common Good*. New York, NY: Knopf.

[3] Ury, W.L. July 1999. "Wandering Out to the Gods." *Track Two*, pp. 22–29.

[4] Mark, A. March 27, 2018. "Regular People Who Went Undercover in Jail for 2 months Discovered a Strict Social Hierarchy that Governs Everything from Where you Sleep to Whether You Get to Shower." *Business Insider*. http://businessinsider.com/prison-dynamics-60-days-in-2018-3

[5] Robert, B. 2015. "Britain's Unwritten Constitution." *British Library*, March 28, 2018. https://bl.uk/magna-carta/articles/britains-unwritten-constitution

[6] Sotirovic, V.B. 2017. "The Peace of Westphalia (1648) and Its Consequences for International Relations." *OrientalReview.org*, March 30, 2018. https://orientalreview.org/2017/12/09/peace-treaty-westphalia-1648-consequences-international-relations/

[7] Law, D.S., and M. Versteeg. June 2012. "The Declining Influence of the United States Constitution." *New York University Law Review* 87, no. 3, pp. 762–858.

[8] Encyclopedia Britannica Online. April 2, 2018. https://britannica.com/event/World-War-I/Killed-wounded-and-missing

[9] National WW II Museum. April 1, 2018. https://www.nationalww2museum.org/students-teachers/student-resources/research-starters/research-starters-worldwide-deaths-world-war

[10] Charter of the United Nations and Statute of the International Court of Justice. 1945. New York, NY: United Nations.

[11] United Nations. 1948. *Universal Declaration of Human Rights*. New York, NY: United Nations Department of Public Information.

[12] Clark, G., and L.B. Sohn. 1958. *World Peace through World Law*. Cambridge, MA: Harvard University Press.

[13] Hutchins, R.M., G.A. Borgese, et al. 1948. *Preliminary Draft of a World Constitution*. Chicago, IL: The University of Chicago Press.

[14] Baratta, J.P. 2007. *The Politics of World Federation*. Santa Barbara, CA: Praeger.

[15] United Nations. 1992. http://un.org/geninfo/bp/enviro.html (accessed April 3, 2018).

[16] Laszlo, S. 2017. "A New Shape: Remodelling Global Cooperation." https://globalchallenges.org/en/our-work/the-new-shape-prize/how-the-competition-works (accessed April 3, 2018).

[17] Volcovici, V. August 4, 2017. "U.S. Submits Formal Notice of Withdrawal from Paris Climate Pact." *Reuters*. https://reuters.com/article/us-un-climate-usa-paris/u-s-submits-formal-notice-of-withdrawal-from-paris-climate-pact-idUSKBN1AK2FM (accessed March 31, 2018).

[18] Scripts CO_2 Program. 2017. "Keeping Curve Lessons." http://scrippsco2.ucsd.edu/history_legacy/keeling_curve_lessons (accessed April 2, 2018).

[19] Hansen, J. March 29, 2018. "Global CO_2 Concentrations Just Passed 400 Parts Per Million." http://400.350.org/

[20] Kooser, A.C. March 22, 2018. "Great Pacific Garbage Patch Growing into a Plastic Monster." *CNET*. https://cnet.com/news/great-pacific-garbage-patch-swells-ocean-pollution-mess-study-shows/ (accessed March 31, 2018).

[21] Favis-Mortlock, D. April 2017. "The Soil Erosion Site." http://soilerosion.net/ (accessed March 31, 2018).

[22] World Wildlife Fund. 2018. "Water Scarcity." https:/worldwildlife.org/threats/water-scarcity (accessed March 28, 2018).

[23] McKenzie, D., and B. Swails. March 9, 2018. "Day Zero Deferred, But Cape Town's Water Crisis Is Far from Over." *CNN Online*. https://www.cnn.com/2018/03/09/africa/cape-town-day-zero-crisis-intl/index.html (accessed March 26, 2018).

[24] World Bank. 2018. *Poverty Overview*. http://worldbank.org/en/topic/poverty/overview (accessed March 18, 2018).

[25] Oxfam. January 2018. *Reward Work, Not Wealth*. London: Oxfam International.

[26] Alvarado, F., L. Chancel, T. Piketty, E. Saez, and G. Zucman, eds. 2018. *World Inequality Report 2018*. Belknap Press of Harvard University Press.

[27] Wilkinson, R., and K. Pickett. 2010. "The Spirit Level." *Why Equality is Better For*. London: Bloomsbury Press.

[28] Stewart, M.E. June 2018. "The 9.9 Percent Is the New American Aristocracy." *The Atlantic*. https://www.theatlantic.com/magazine/archive/2018/06/the-birth-of-a-new-american-aristocracy/559130/

[29] McKinsey Global Institute. December 2017. *Jobs Lost, Jobs Gained: Workforce Transitions in a Time of Automation*. McKinsey & Company.

[30] Goodman, P.S. December 27, 2017. "The Robots Are Coming, and Sweden is Fine". *The New York Times*. https://www.nytimes.com/2017/12/27/business/the-robots-are-coming-and-sweden-is-fine.html

[31] Penarredonda, J.L. March 25, 2018. "How Much Should Your Boss Know About You?" *BBC*. http://bbc.com/capital/story/20180323-how-much-should-your-boss-know-about-you

[32] Bostman, R. 2017. "Big Data meets Big Brother as China Moves to Rate Its Citizens." *Wired*. http://wired.co.uk/article/chinese-government-social-credit-score-privacy-invasion (accessed March 28, 2018).

[33] Marshall, A. April 4, 2018. "The Uber Crash Won't Be the Last Shocking Self-driving Death." *Wired*. https://wired.com/story/uber-self-driving-crash-explanation-lidar-sensors/

[34] Sarkar, P.R. 1987. "Requirements of an Ideal Constitution." *Prout in a Nutshell Part XII*, 52. Calcutta: Ananda Marga Publications.

[35] Sarkar, P.R. 1987. *Discourses on Prout-18. Prout in a Nutshell, Part IV.* Calcutta: Ananda Marga Publications.

[36] Runde, C. 1999. "Beyond Nationalism." In *Transcending Boundaries*, eds. S. Inayatullah and J. Fitzgerald, 85. Maleny, Queensland: Gurukula Press.

[37] Friedman, M 2008. "Living Wage and Optimal Inequality in a Sarkarian Framework." *Review of Social Economy* 66, no. 1, pp. 93–111.

[38] Wilkinson, R., and K.E. Pickett. 2011. *The Spirit Level*, p. 81.

[39] Ibid. p. 216.

[40] Friedman, M. 2008. "Living Wage and Optimal Inequality in a Sarkarian Framework." *Review of Social Economy* 66, no. 1, pp. 93–111, 104.

[41] R.A. June 6, 2016. "Universal Basic Incomes." *The Economist*. https://economist.com/blogs/economist-explains/2016/06/economist-explains-4 (accessed April 6, 2018).

[42] Sarkar, P.R. 1987. "The Cosmic Brotherhood." *Prout in a Nutshell Part 3*, p. 60.

[43] Goldin, I. 2018. "Five Reasons Why Universal Basic Income is a Bad Idea." *Financial Times*. https://ft.com/content/100137b4-0cdf-11e8-bacb-2958fde95e5e (accessed April 6, 2018).

[44] Bjonnes, R., and C.E. Hargreaves. 2016. *Growing a New Economy*, 276–79. San Germain, Puerto Rico: InnerWorld Publications.

[45] Blaustein, A.P., and C. Tenney. 1990. "Understanding 'Rights' and Bills of Rights." *University of Richmond Law Review* 25, pp. 425–29.

[46] Runde, C. 1999. "Beyond Nationalism." In *Transcending Boundaries,* eds. S. Inayatullah and Fitzgerald, 85. Maleny, Australia: Gurukula Press.

[47] Sarkar, P.R. 1987. "Requirements of an Ideal Constitution." *Prout in a Nutshell Part XII*, 52. Calcutta: Ananda Marga Publications.

[48] Sarkar, P.R. 1987. "Parts of the Economy." *Prout in a Nutshell, Part XII*, 16. Calcutta: Ananda Marga Publications.

[49] Sarkar, P.R. 1982. *The Liberation of Intellect: Neo-Humanism.* Calcutta: Ananda Marga Publications.

[50] Ceballos, G., P.R. Ehrlich, and R. Dirzo. July 10, 2017. "Biological Annihilation via the Ongoing Sixth Mass Extinction Signaled by Vertebrate Population Losses and Declines." *Proceedings of the National Academy of Sciences*. http://pnas.org/content/early/2017/07/05/1704949114 (accessed April 7, 2018).

[51] Gilding, P. 2011. *The Great Disruption: Why the Climate Crisis Will Bring on the End of Shopping and the Birth of a New World.* USA: Bloomsbury Publishing.

[52] Sam, P.-F. 2016. "The Opportunity Cost of World Military Spending." *Stockholm International Peace Research Institute.* https://sipri.org/commentary/blog/2016/opportunity-cost-world-military-spending (accessed April 9, 2018).

[53] Marc, A. 2018. "Conflict and Violence in the 21st Century." *World Bank Group.* https://un.org/pga/70/wp-content/uploads/sites/10/2016/01/Conflict-and-violence-in-the-21st-century-Current-trends-as-observed-in-empirical-research-and-statistics-Mr.-Alexandre-Marc-Chief-Specialist-Fragility-Conflict-and-Violence-World-Bank-Group.pdf (accessed April 9, 2018).

[54] Clark, G., and L. Sohn. 1984. *Introduction to World Peace through World Law*, Revised edition. Chicago, IL: World Without War Publications.

[55] Sarkar, P.R. 1988. "Talks on Prout." *Prout in a Nutshell, Part XV*, 20. Calcutta: Ananda Marga Publications.

[56] Sarkar, P.R. 1987. "Requirements of an Ideal Constitution." *Prout in a Nutshell Part XII*, 52. Calcutta: Ananda Marga Publications.

[57] Timberg, C., and T. Romm. April 8, 2018. "Facebook Could Face Record Fine Say Former FTC Officials." *Washington Post.* https://washingtonpost.com/news/the-switch/wp/2018/04/08/facebook-could-face-record-fine-say-former-ftc-officials/?utm_term=.52b9b39df885 (accessed April 7, 2018).

[58] Stoll, I. April 2, 2018. "Apple Wants Washington to Fix Facebook." *Reason.* https://reason.com/archives/2018/04/02/apple-wants-washington-to-fix-facebook

[59] Lord, N. January 23, 2017. "What is GDPR (General Data Protection Regulation)? Understanding and Complying with GDPR Data Protection Requirements." *Digital Guardian.* https://digitalguardian.com/blog/what-gdpr-general-data-protection-regulation-understanding-and-complying-gdpr-data-protection (accessed April 8, 2018).

[60] Whigham, N. November 20, 2017. "United Nations to Consider Controls on Autonomous Weapons amid Growing Concerns." *News.com.au.* http://news.com.au/technology/innovation/inventions/united-nations-to-consider-controls-around-autonomous-weapons-amid-growing-concerns/news-story/1962c6464a6d21e0f98fa76b4dd471fa (accessed April 8, 2018).

[61] McNally, P., and S. Inayatullah. April 1988. "The Rights of Robots: Technology, Culture and Law in the 21st Century." *Futures* 20, no. 2, pp. 119–36.

[62] Gilding, P. 2011. *The Great Disruption: Why the Climate Crisis Will Bring on the End of Shopping and the Birth of a New World.* USA: Bloomsbury Publishing.

[63] Anderson, T., and C. Gary. 1983. *Universal Humanism: Selected Social Writings of P.R. Sarkar*, 120. Sydney: Proutist Universal Publications.

PART IV

Spiritual Implications

CHAPTER 9

The New Age of Science and Spirituality

Steven Richheimer

Introduction

Suppose a scientist wanted to test his theory that objects in the universe were connected by a hidden force or field of information that was not limited by space or time. To test this hypothesis he designed two identical roulette wheels with only black and red pockets that could be spun randomly every 30 seconds using a motor. Control tests indicated that both devices produced exactly 50 percent black and 50 percent red "hits." After transporting one of the machines to a colleague on the Moon, both roulette wheels were started simultaneously and the two scientists recorded whether their machines produced a black or a red "hit" every 30 seconds for a half an hour. After comparing the two lists of 60 data points, it was found that the two data sets had a perfect negative correlation. In other words, when the wheel on Earth came up black the wheel on the Moon hit red and vice versa. When the odds that this would occur by chance were calculated they were found to be one in 10^{18} or once in a billion, billion runs.

Since this could not be a chance occurrence, the scientist concluded that the roulette wheels were connected or communicating with one another. There was simply no other reasonable explanation for the results. Although subsequent investigation could not find any known means by which the two machines were "talking" with one another, it would take only 1.3 seconds for signals moving at the speed of light to travel between the Earth and the Moon.

Hence, the scientist decided to repeat the experiment by placing the distant wheel on Mars where it would take much longer for information traveling at the speed of light to travel. After a start signal was sent to his associate on Mars, the scientist started his machine exactly 13 minutes later. In this way, the wheels were started simultaneously. The results amazed the scientist and confirmed his theory because the two sets of data were again perfectly correlated. This second experiment demonstrated conclusively that local signals traveling at the speed of light could not be responsible for the result, According to the laws of physics, there was simply no explanation for how the two randomly generated black–red data sets could be correlated, yet they clearly were.

Entanglement

Of course, this experiment has not been done, but it does illustrate the results obtained by scientists who have investigated the connection observed between small particles such as photons (light particles), electrons, atoms, and molecules. Physicists have a name for this connection: entanglement. It was predicted by quantum theory and first proven to exist in the 1980s. Physicists use terms like "weird," "crazy," "bizarre," and "inexplicable" to describe entanglement. It demonstrates a level of reality that is governed by nonlocality—that is, a connection that is not dependent on either time or space. Entangled particles remain connected no matter how far apart they are, a change in one is instantly communicated to the other, and the connection is not affected by distance.

An example of entanglement is an actual experiment performed by astronomers in which a distant quasar appears to be split into two objects by the bending of light from an intervening galaxy between Earth and the quasar. The light that is bent has roughly 50,000 light years more distance to travel than the light that comes to Earth directly. However, the photon beams from the quasar interfere with each other in exactly the same way as if they were emitted seconds apart in the laboratory. The photons remain connected or entangled despite the fact that they were emitted billions of years ago and arrive 50,000 years apart.[14]

Entanglement has been shown to occur not only for small particles, but also for complex systems. There is even evidence that it occurs in the cells of our bodies. In addition, there is no theoretical limit to the extent of entanglement. Experiments indicate that quantum entanglement grows exponentially with the number of particles involved in the original quantum state.[7] Since the universe is believed to have begun in a singular state that erupted in a massive explosion, it is believed by some scientists that on a basic level the universe consists of a vast web of particles that remain in contact with one another throughout all time and space.[7, 13]

Quantum Physics and Nonlocality

Our discussion so far has touched on one of the most important and successful theories ever discovered by physicists—quantum theory or quantum mechanics. The theory was first developed in the early part of the 20th century by such great scientists as Neils Bohr, Max Planck, Albert Einstein, Erwin Schrödinger, Werner Heisenberg, and others. It was needed to explain the discontinuous nature of energy that was observed in experiments. Quantum mechanics has been incredibly successful at describing with great mathematical precision the interactions of energy and matter that occur at the microscopic scale.

One of the hallmarks of quantum theory and one that is borne out by countless experiments and observations is nonlocality. One example of this is entanglement, but in addition, experiments prove that all quanta behave nonlocally. They appear to exist not in one place but have a finite probability of being found anywhere in the universe. In a sense, they are spread through all space and time until they are actually observed.[3, 9, 10]

Second, depending on how they are observed, quanta may behave like particles at times and like waves at other times. Until a quantum is observed or measured, it has no definite properties but is thought to exist in all possible states simultaneously (quantum superposition).[3] These are virtual rather that real states. Somehow, observation (normally by an instrument) fixes a quantum in a specific or "real" state. However, it is impossible to predict with certainty which of the possible states will emerge from the "quantum soup." All that quantum mechanics can do is predict the probability that a quantum will assume a specific location and energy state.[9]

Third, even after a quantum emerges from its virtual state into physical reality it cannot be pinned down exactly. For example, the better the position of a quantum particle is known the less is known about its speed. Hence, there is always uncertainty in measuring quanta (Heisenberg uncertainty principle). Finally, quanta that are created from a single source are entangled, and as we have seen this connection is not limited by the speed of light or affected by distance.

Numerous experiments in the last one hundred years have clearly demonstrated that the behavior of quanta is not determined by the conditions of the test alone. Their behavior such as their wave-like or particle-like nature depends on the totality of the experimental apparatus and the intention of the experimenter. This outlines an important aspect of quantum nonlocality, namely, that the observer and the observed system cannot be separated. The observer or his instruments are part of the system and influence the outcome of the observation. In other words, the act of observing (consciousness?) alters or influences the system and this alteration is independent of the flow of time.[9, 10, 14]

One example of this is when photons are passed through two closely spaced slits forming a diffraction pattern of alternating dark and light lines. If the experimenter electronically closes one of the slits after the photon has passed the slits, the diffraction pattern disappears resulting in a simple diffusion pattern (slight spreading of the beam of light). This will occur anytime one of the slits is unavailable to the photon because it needs to act like a wave and interact with the wave front of other photons to produce the interference pattern. What is weird is that this effect occurs after the photon has passed through the slits. It goes to a different location on the photographic plate as though it knew that the slit was going to be closed. Such experimental observations are contrary to the common-sense notion of cause and effect. In the weird world of quantum mechanics, an effect (the photons position) can occur before the cause (closing of a slit).[10, 14]

Quantum Computers, Communication, and Teleportation

Quantum entanglement makes possible the exciting new technology of quantum computing. Quantum computers use quantum bits (qubits) instead of bits. The quantum information encoded by a qubit contains information about the quantum state of the qubit—not just whether it is one or zero; but because a qubit can be a superposition of many states, the power of such computers can theoretically be orders of magnitude greater than that of classical computers in use today.

The development of such "supercomputers" is still in its infancy but researchers at IBM have successfully built a prototype processor having 50 qubits.[5] While 50 bits for a normal computer is equivalent to seven bytes and could not even code for the word "computer," in quantum physics one requires $2^n - 1$ bits to describe the system completely. This translates to 1.1×10^{12} bits (100 terabytes) of data, which is equivalent to 10 times the print collections of the U.S. Library of Congress.

Currently, there is a quantum computer sold commercially, which can do simple computations using a small number of qubits. Unlike classical computers that can perform only one operation at a time, albeit very, very rapidly, a quantum computer utilizing qubits can perform many calculations simultaneously. For example, think of a single rat placed into a complicated maze with hundreds of dead ends and only one way out. It might take the rat many hours to find its way out as it tries numerous paths, only to be blocked most of the time. Now consider putting a hundred rats into the maze at the same time. Surely, one of the rats, by chance will find the elusive escape route in a short time.

A quantum computer with its entangled qubits, which can be either one, zero, and states in between, is able to make many calculations at the same time expanding its potential computational power millions of times over that of today's most powerful supercomputers. In the future quantum computers will surely be used to greatly enhance robotics, artificial intelligence, and solve many complex problems such as weather and financial forecasting that are not possible using today's classical computers.

Recently, Chinese researchers were able to use a space laser on a satellite to send entangled pairs of photons to two sites in Tibet some 1200 km apart. This experiment was an important first step in demonstrating quantum communication, which uses entangled photons to encode information in such a way that it would be impossible to break the encryption.[15] Normally if you want to send a coded message between two people, you must give them both a secure key that allows them to translate the message. At the same time, you must protect that key from any nosy third parties who are trying to spy on the conversation. A complex quantum key, shared via entangled particles, would do the trick because if a spy tried to steal the code-breaking information, this would disrupt the entanglement making it useless for the intruder, and in addition, it would inform the intended recipient that there was an attempt to intercept the message. Hence, the beauty of quantum communication is that the integrity of the data sent is protected by the laws of physics and thus there can be no higher level of security. This form of communication would enhance the security of data for IoT, blockchains, and big data business as we have covered in Chapters 1 through 3.

Quantum teleportation is similar to quantum communication in that quantum information, such as the exact state of a photon, electron, ion, or atom is transmitted from one location to another. It is another well-established example of quantum entanglement. It differs in that quantum teleportation provides a mechanism for moving qubits from one location to another, without physically moving the underlying qubit particles.

Quantum teleportation can take place when there is previously established quantum entanglement of particles at the sending and receiving locations, and the information about the particles is sent by way of a "quantum channel" to the receiving station from the sending station. Because such a channel must be set up using classical communication methods, the overall transfer of information cannot exceed the speed of light. In the process of transfer, the information carried by the particle at the sending station is destroyed.[17] While the name teleportation conjures up images from Star Trek, it cannot be used to transport material objects—only information about objects, and it would take enormous technological advances before this quantum information could be used to assemble even a simple object.

Spiritual Ideology

Cosmologists have theorized that the universe began with a "Big Bang," which led to the formation of space and time and eventually gas (mostly hydrogen), which under the pull of gravity condensed to form stars. Hydrogen nuclei in stars fuse to create heavier elements with the release of tremendous amounts of energy. The heaviest elements are created when large stars collapse and explode (supernovae). It is further theorized that it is the materials that are emitted from the stars that eventually form planets such as Earth. However, cosmologists do not explain how matter and energy emerged from nothing.

On the other hand, spiritual ideology (or spiritual worldview) has a simple and logical explanation for the origin of the universe. The entire creation is singular or whole and is formed from consciousness. Hence, consciousness is considered the "ground substance" of creation and it is consciousness that is transformed into cosmic mind (e.g., the mind of God) and then gradually into the material world. Hence, spiritual ideology is monistic—everything is a manifestation of cosmic consciousness.[13]

Furthermore, if suitable conditions exist on a planet, consciousness can express itself within individual physical structures beginning with single-celled organisms. Similar to the Darwinist model of evolution, but under the influence and guidance of cosmic mind, the living organisms evolve leading to creatures with more and more complex mental and physical structures and ultimately to sentient or self-aware beings—what we call humans. Because the human mind reflects the subtler aspects of cosmic mind, human beings are inexorably drawn back to the source of creation (consciousness); and eventually after many incarnations, they will merge their individual mind into cosmic consciousness.

This worldview is central to most of the religious and philosophical traditions of the East including Vedantism (Hinduism), Buddhism, Taoism, Sufism, Tantra, and yoga. Creation begins with consciousness and one's individual existence continues until it is merged or lost in the unqualified sea of pure consciousness (God). In other words, spiritual ideology is "top-down" ontology, in which creation begins with consciousness and cruder aspects of reality are epi-phenomena of it.[1, 12, 13]

On the other hand, the materialist or physicalist worldview is a "bottom-up" explanation of reality. Subatomic particles such as electrons, protons, and neutrons make up atoms that combine to form molecules. Complex and self-replicating biomolecules originate by chemical transformations that give rise to simple single-celled living organisms. These simple life forms experience environmental and competitive pressures, natural variations, and with increased survival of beneficial traits, evolve into increasingly complex life forms with larger brains, developed minds, and consciousness.

In this scenario, consciousness is an epiphenomenon of matter. Hence, the materialistic worldview assumes that all physical and mental phenomena can be explained by interactions of matter and energy. By necessity, all such interactions are local—that is, governed by local forces or energy fields. This requirement creates a problem for the materialistic worldview—quantum theory, which has been tremendously successful in predicting and explaining scientific observations that occur at the minute realm of matter and energy, is decidedly nonlocal. In other words, the phenomenon of quantum nonlocality can be considered to have put a dagger through the heart of materialism with its requirement for locality.

Neither modern science nor Western religions have introduced the concept of wholeness as a feature of reality. To many in the West, the idea that the universe is one undivided whole is a foreign concept that goes against everyday experience. It implies that discreteness, differentiation, individualism, and so on are illusory, a relative reality—not ultimate reality. Hence, it is no surprise that most of the public and a majority of scientists are ill informed about the implications of nonlocality as it pertains to a basic understanding of reality.

The Quantum Wave Function and Spirituality

In the 1920s, the pioneering work of Nobel Prize winning physicist Erwin Schrödinger provided a method for calculating the possible wave functions for a system. Therefore, the quantum wave function is also known as the Schrödinger wave equation. A wave function describes mathematically the properties of a wave such as water waves or vibrating violin strings. However, for quantum systems the wave function is not a wave in physical space, but a wave in an abstract "mathematical space." Although the mathematics is quite complex, in simple terms, the wave function details all the possible states that a particle or system may have and also gives the probability that it will assume any single state when "observed."

The Schrödinger wave equation provides an explanation for wave–particle duality. Before a quantum particle is observed and manifests in the "real" world it is best described as a wave. When it is observed or measured, it behaves like a particle. Observation apparently "kicks" the particle or system out of the realm of infinite potentialities into a specific state.[3] When this occurs, it is called the "collapse of the wave function." Since the wave function details possibilities, it speaks of a domain of reality that precedes and is subtler than what we perceive as physical reality. Hence, any ontology must include an explanation of this underlying and unseen realm from which physical reality emerges.

Since we cannot know the state of a particle before it is observed, quantum theory concludes it must be a superposition of all possible states. Hence, the underlying domain of the wave function is not one of separate parts but one in which all possibilities coexist in a state of wholeness—everything being interconnected and interdependent. By necessity, this web of connectivity must permeate the entire universe. Hence, the domain of the quantum wave function is one of temporal and spatial nonlocality.[3, 10, 14]

Following is a summary of the properties of the hidden domain of the wave function.

- *It expresses wholeness.* This is a fundamental aspect of reality that exists at a deeper level than ordinary space–time.
- *It is timeless.* It exists outside space–time. The past, present, and future are meaningless when discussing this realm. It is only after the wave function collapses by observation or conscious awareness that an arrow of time comes into existence.
- *It is nonlocal.* It penetrates and surrounds ordinary reality and is not localized in any part of space but is all encompassing, everywhere at the same time. It is only after an observation that a "part" of reality represented by the function becomes localized in space.
- *It is a mathematical representation of the possibilities.* It determines the probability that any particular quantum possibility will become "real" (when observed).
- *Theoretically, all matter and energy have associated wave functions.* This includes the brain, the body, and the universe as a whole. The wave function represents the gestalts for these individual entities.

- *The domain of the wave function does not contain energy as such. Instead, it is the underlying source of all energy.* In a sense, it contains the potential for expression of almost infinite energy.
- *The collapse of the wave function does not require energy—just observation or consciousness.* This appears to be the mechanism by which mind, which is nonphysical, affects matter (brain).

Interestingly the properties of the wave function are identical to the cosmic mind of spiritual ideology. The wave function serves as the mathematical underpinning of quantum mechanics and because its description of reality has been repeatedly verified by countless experiments, we must conclude that quantum theory is entirely consistent with the spiritual worldview but antithetical to the spatial and temporal locality of the materialistic worldview.

Einstein's Theory of Relativity and its Spiritual Implications

In 1887 two American scientists, Albert Michelson and Edward Morley, showed that the speed of light was a constant whether the Earth was moving toward or away from a distant star. This observation contradicted the commonsense notion that speeds should add up—for example, a bullet fired forward from a fast-moving car should have a higher velocity than one fired backward. For light, this is not the case—it travels at a constant speed in empty space.

Albert Einstein realized that if the speed of light was a constant no matter what point of reference was used, then something else had to change to account for its constancy. He sensed that this "something" must be space itself. He proposed that space could flex and change, become compressed, or expanded according to the relative motion of an object and an observer. The only constant was the speed of light itself or an integrated four-dimensional "fabric" he called space–time. These insights led to Einstein's special theory of relativity, which states that the universe has four dimensions. There are three of space—width, length, and height— and one of time. Time is not a separate dimension in this scheme but is fully integrated with the three spatial dimensions. Hence, each of the four dimensions of space–time has a spatial and temporal component. Einstein realized that with motion, space shrinks and time dilates, while for an object with no relative motion, the movement through space-time is in time alone.

Einstein's equations indicated that the faster an object moves, the slower the passage of time and the more mass it gains. Ultimately, at the speed of light, time stops. However, for matter it would be impossible to attain this speed since it would require all the mass–energy of the universe. Experiments have proven Einstein's theories about space, time, energy, and mass, to be correct. For example, the rate of decay of unstable subatomic particles accelerated near the speed of light in a cyclotron is slowed exactly as predicted by Einstein, and such particles gain the exact amount of mass predicted by the theory.

However, photons, which carry electromagnetic radiation such as visible light, can move at the speed of light since they have no mass. Their internal clocks are stopped and they do not decay like other particles.

Einstein's general theory of relativity describes gravity as a geometric property of space–time caused by objects with mass. Gravity is seen as nothing more than a distortion of space–time. The more massive the object the more it distorts or curves space. Such curvature of space caused by a massive object such as a star causes light passing near it to bend. This prediction of Einstein has been verified experimentally, as has the existence of black holes—objects with such tremendous gravitational force that nothing can escape their pull, including light.

Several startling and unusual consequences arise from Einstein's new model of the universe. Following is a summary of some of the implications of this new view of space and time:

- *Within integrated space–time only events have meaning.* An event such as the explosion of a supernova in our neighboring Andromeda Galaxy is considered a point in the four-dimensional matrix of space–time. This event may be observed on Earth 2.5 million years later—the time light would take to travel the distance. However, for the stream of light particles (photons) no time will have passed during their transit because their clock is stopped. From the perspective of the photon distance does not equate to the passage of time, while for us, it does because we are accustomed to equating time with distance. The fact is that within four-dimensional space–time, the exploding of the star is a singular event.[14]

- *Movement causes space to convert to time.* When an object is not moving relative to another object, then it is moving in time alone. If an object is moving near the speed of light, then it is moving mostly through space and its clock will slow down relative to a stationary clock. For example, in the future human beings might develop a spaceship that can travel at 90 percent of the speed of light (270,000 kilometers/second). After the astronauts reach full speed on their way to a planet circling a star 20 light years away, they will calculate the distance to the star to be only 10 light years (because of the compression of space). They will then calculate that it should take 11 years to reach their destination. However, because their clock runs at half the speed as clocks on Earth, the event of their arrival after 11 years of their time will correspond precisely with their expected arrival on Earth (22 years).[13]

- *A massive object distorts space–time.* Like a bowling ball bending a rubber membrane, the bending of space–time corresponds to gravity, and the distortion pulls on time as well. Time is slowed down near a massive object. This effect was demonstrated scientifically by synchronizing two atomic clocks and moving one to the top of a tall building for a week. Upon return to ground level, the upper clock was found to have run a little faster than the one on the ground because the force of gravity diminishes with distance above the surface of the earth. If astronauts orbited a black hole with its massive gravitational pull and then were able return to Earth, their clock would run significantly slower during their close approach compared to clocks on Earth. It is conceivable that after a few hours of "slowed" time near the black hole they could return to Earth and be younger than their grandchildren are.

- *Spatial dimensions are compressed at high speed.* The shape of an object such as a spaceship would look compressed or flattened to someone observing it as it passed by Earth. To the astronauts on the spaceship, everything would look perfectly normal since everything including their measuring devices would have shrunk the same relative amount.
- *Space and time are observer dependent.* Time and length may expand or shrink depending on the relative state of motion of the observer and the observed. As space shrinks, time expands (slows). Space is transformed into time and time into space. This is the hallmark of a four-dimensional substance in which the dimensions have both spatial and temporal aspects that are fully integrated and inseparable.
- *The "now" is not the same for observers moving relative to one another.* For example, if astronauts were traveling away from Earth at high speed their experience of "now" would be of events that already occurred on Earth, while if they were moving toward Earth they would experience events that have not yet taken place on Earth. The "now," just like the past and future, are observer dependent and therefore mutable.
- *Four-dimensional space–time is unchanging and characterized by wholeness.* From the three-dimensional perspective of human experience everything changes in time, but underneath this relative reality lies the unchanging four-dimensional reality of space–time.

Einstein's theory of relativity with its mathematical description of a four-dimensional space–time continuum has been verified by numerous experimental observations. Furthermore, predictions made by the theory have proven correct and highly accurate. It is one of the most important scientific discoveries of all times. Many of today's technological advances (e.g., the global positioning system (GPS) system) depend on the relative mechanics derived from the theory.

What the theory says about the nature of reality is both mindboggling and revolutionary. It implies that beneath this ever-changing realm of human experience lies a deeper, singular, and unchanging realm of reality. Scientists call this new picture of space and time "block time." The past, present, and future are all equally real and the flow of time is something human beings create as a convenient way to cope with their three-dimensional experience of reality.[14] If one were to possess four-dimensional sight, one would experience things quite differently. Instead of seeing events unfolding with the passage of time, one could witness the entirety of all time and space. This may be the experience of mystics who have described their experience of union with God as entering the "eternal now" or a "timeless state."

Einstein's new model of the universe has enormous scientific and philosophical implications. So why are there so few scientists today educating the public about what Einstein's theories say about our experiential reality? Perhaps because to do so would be to admit that our experience of a three-dimensional world is merely a shadow of an all-encompassing timeless realm. This would be counter to the doctrine of materialism that is popular today among the scientific community since it speaks of a monistic view of reality similar to that proposed by idealist philosophers such as Plato. On the other hand, the model is perfectly consistent with the spiritual view of reality.

Nonlocal Mind

The bottom-up ontology of materialism purports the equivalence of mind and brain. That is, mind is a product of neurochemical brain activity. However, countless observations and a massive amount of experimental evidence indicate that mind is nonlocal and nonmaterial and cannot be equated with brain. Following is a brief summary of some of the evidence.

- *The unity of sensory experience*: There is no identifiable anatomical or brain basis that explains how sensory inputs are unified into a coherent experience. It can be concluded that mind, not brain physiology, is responsible for this.
- *Psychosomatic illness*: It is well known that mental states affect the body. Psychological feelings such as hopelessness and depression bring about an increased risk of chronic disease,

while feelings of joy and laughter improve health. Another example is a placebo that produces a physiological effect due to expectations alone. The connection between mind and body is so strong that doctors sometimes call this "mind–body unity."

- *Other mind–body effects*: Examples include stigmata, localized skin responses such as blisters and skin writing, false pregnancy, whitening of hair or skin in response to severe fright or emotional stress, hypnotic effects on autonomic functions, allergies, and skin changes.[4]

- *Memory and dreams*: Both are witnessed by mind. If memories were simply stored physiologically in the brain, then they could only be replayed and not witnessed from a third-person point of view. Mind, which is unitary and nonphysical, is able to supply this outside point of view.

- *Mystical experience*: The experience is universally described as entering into a clear, timeless, unitary, exalted state of ecstasy and limitless consciousness. The similarity across cultural, religious, and national differences is indicative of a life-changing transcendental experience.[13]

- *Reincarnation*: There is a preponderance of evidence that some people, especially children, have accurate memories of previous lives.[16, 19, 20] Mind, which is nonphysical, survives death and carries memories and karma from one lifetime to the next. This also explains genius and other cases where a child spontaneously develops extraordinary abilities without any formal training.[14]

- *Out-of-body experiences*: There have been thousands of cases reported of people floating above their body and witnessing events that took place from this unique perspective. Of particular interest are blind persons having visual experiences who accurately describe events that took place while they were unconscious.[4, 8, 14]

- *Near-death experiences (NDE)*: There is no medical explanation of how people can experience vivid consciousness outside their body when they are clinically dead. There have been thousands of reports and numerous articles and books written about NDE experiences since the term was first introduced by psychiatrist Raymond Moody in his 1975 book *Life After Life*.[8] Second, there is remarkable similarity between accounts, regardless of age, nationality, religion, race, culture, and other demographics. [4, 6, 8] The fact that mind can function when the body and brain are "turned off" or considered clinically dead means that mind is nonlocal and separate from brain.

- *Extrasensory perception (ESP)*: There is overwhelming scientific evidence that ESP is real. Any skeptic who was to read Dean Radin's book, *The Conscious Universe: The Scientific Truth of Psychic Phenomena* with an open mind would have to admit this fact.[11] Statistical meta-analyses of hundreds of well-controlled scientific studies provide the unquestionable scientific evidence for the factual existence of ESP capabilities in human beings.[11, 12] ESP studies show that the human mind is capable of accessing information nonlocally in time and space. One of the best examples of this is remote viewing (a type of clairvoyance) in which the trained or gifted viewer is able to describe in detail a scene witnessed by another person—even before that person arrives at the target location. This capability has been extensively studied under controlled laboratory conditions and even used by espionage agencies in the past to gather intelligence.[4] In addition, controlled studies of telepathy, precognition, and psychokinesis (intentionally affecting the output of random number generators) provide overwhelming positive evidence for the factual existence of psychic phenomena and demonstrate that information can be passed to an individual nonlocally.[12] Naturally, skeptics are quick to dismiss the veracity of the data since the very existence of ESP would disprove the myth of materialism.

- *Mind affecting machines*: Scientists at the Princeton Engineering Anomalies Research Laboratory concluded after 30 years of study that intentions, emotions, and attitudes of human operators affect sophisticated equipment.[2] Major world events have been shown to alter the output of random number generators.[12] Studies using intention imprinted electrical devices (IIED) indicate that reproducible and robust affects are observed in instruments such as a pH meter when an IIED is placed nearby with a specific intention imprinted upon it by an experienced meditator.[18]

For readers of this chapter, who would like to investigate further the compelling evidence indicating that the human mind cannot be equated with the material brain, the author suggests the books *Irreducible Mind* by Edward Kelly et al.[4] and *One Mind* by Larry Dossey.[1]

Conclusion

Recent discoveries in the physical sciences indicate that nonlocality is a basic feature of physical reality. Scientists are already taking advantage of this property (entanglement) to build quantum computers that will potentially be millions of times more powerful than today's supercomputers. This will undoubtedly lead to tremendous advancements in artificial intelligence (AI) and robotics.

There is also conclusive evidence that mind is nonlocal. This leads to the conclusion that the spiritual explanation for reality is consistent with modern science while materialism falls short. Spiritual ideology states that consciousness is the first cause of creation and serves as the ground substance of creation; and it is consciousness, not matter/energy that is transformed into the material universe.

References

[1] Dossey, L. 2013. *One Mind: How our Individual Mind Is Part of a Greater Consciousness and Why It Matters.* Carlsbad, CA: Hay House.

[2] Dunne, B., and R. Jahn. 1992. "Experiments in Remote Human/Machine Interaction." *Journal of Scientific Exploration* 6, no.4, p.311.

[3] Friedman, N. 1997. *The Hidden Domain: Home of the Quantum Wave Function, Nature's Creative Source.* Eugene, OR: Woodbridge.

[4] Kelly, E.F., E.W. Kelly, A. Crabtree, A. Gauld, M. Grosso, and B. Greyson. 2007. *Irreducible Mind: Toward a Psychology for the 21st Century.* Rowman & Littlefield.

[5] Knight, W. 2017. "IBM Raises the Bar with a 50-Qubit Quantum Computer". *MIT Technology Review.*

[6] Long, J.R., and P. Perry. 2010. *Evidence of the Afterlife: The Science of Near-Death Experiences.* New York, NY: HarperCollins.

[7] Mermin, N.D. 1990. "Extreme Quantum Entanglement in a Superposition of Macroscopically Distinct States." *Physical Review Letters* 65, no. 15, p. 1838.

[8] Moody, R.A., Jr. 1975. *Life After Life: The Investigation of a Phenomenon—Survival of Bodily Death.* New York, NY: HarperCollins.

[9] Nadeau, R., and M. Kafatos. 1991. *The Conscious Universe: Parts and Wholes in Physical Reality.* New York, NY: Springer.

[10] Nadeau, R., and M. Kafatos. 1999. *The Non-local Universe: The New Physics and Matters of the Mind.* New York, NY: Oxford.

[11] Radin, D.I. 1997. *The Conscious Universe: The Scientific Truth of Psychic Phenomena.* New York, NY: HarperCollins.

[12] Radin, D.I. 2003. *Entangled Minds: Extrasensory Experiences in a Quantum Reality.* New York, NY: Paraview.

[13] Richheimer, S.L. 2013. *The Unity Principle: The Link between Science and Spirituality.* San German, Puerto Rico: InnerWorld.

[14] Richheimer, S.L. 2016. *The Nonlocal Universe: Why Science Validates the Spiritual Worldview.* San German, Puerto Rico: InnerWorld.

[15] Savage, N. 2017. "Seeking Materials to Send Unbreakable Codes." *Chemical & Engineering News* 95, no. 36, pp. 19–21.

[16] Stevenson, I. 2000. *Children Who Remember Previous Lives: A Question of Reincarnation.* Jefferson, NC: McFarland.

[17] Thompson, A.A. 2017. "How Quantum Teleportation Actually Works." *Popular Mechanics.*

[18] Tiller, W.A., W.E. Dibble, and M.J. Kohane. 2001. *Conscious Acts of Creation: The Emergence of a New Physics.* Walnut Creek, CA: Pavior.

[19] Tucker, J.B. 2005. *Life before Life: Children's Memories of Previous Lives.* New York, NY: St. Martin's.

[20] Tucker, J.B. 2013. *Return to Life: Extraordinary Cases of Children who Remember Past Lives.* New York, NY: St. Martin's.

CHAPTER 10

Meditation and Consciousness

Shambhushivananda

Introduction

When prehistoric humans separated from their nonhuman ancestors, they had not even the slightest inkling that one day their descendants would touch the stars, split the atom, discover the genetic codes that carry the secrets of life, communicate through a rich vocabulary, unravel the mysteries of the brain, or fathom the invisible via nanotechnologies. The progress that human beings have made in the past few thousand years is quite impressive. The development of artificial intelligence (AI), genetic engineering, and control over algorithms may even further help humans to engineer entities that are partly organic and partly inorganic. It will obviously pose new challenges to the human society.

Yet we are far from establishing a socioeconomic system or following an ideal lifestyle that ensures peace and happiness to all creatures, for both their individual survival and their collective flourishing. The answers to perennial questions about the meaning of life and purpose of existence remain speculative. All creatures are born to die one day and it is still a challenge to build a society where all who are born on this earth can coexist in peace and harmony while continuing to explore and understand the unknown.

Redefining the Role of Macroeconomics

To be optimistic, the survival for human beings could become easier in the future, possibly through the widespread benevolent use of science and technology and shared information. A standard universal basic income benefit ensured to all adult citizens could become common in all societies. The collective wealth generated by human ingenuity and passion for social justice could create surpluses and spare greater leisure time in the future for the common person. The freed-up unused capabilities of living beings could then lead us beyond obsession with physical sources of sustenance toward psychic sources like scientific and literary pursuits, and ultimately escort us unto the transcendental realm of higher consciousness—wherein lies the perennial source of intuition, deep inner peace, and tranquility. It is timely, therefore, to cross into the domain of psycho-economics, where the goal of macroeconomics is no longer the mere pursuit of never-ending and illusory satisfaction of unlimited wants through "scarce" resources but it is to optimally utilize mundane assets to free human beings for intellectual and intuitional pursuits or engagement in activities for the universal welfare of all entities beyond individual personal wants.

Pursuit of Material Happiness and Human Longings

Striving for greater pleasure and physical comfort is built into human biology. This longing for material pleasure drives us to actualize our desires and will be healthy or unhealthy depending on the degree of restraint over human longings. Toward this end, ensuring full employment or economic security is a sine qua non for a peaceful and progressive society. Adequate, even comfortable, purchasing power needs to be ensured to one and all. However, it is also true that pursuit of material happiness creates an insatiable craving and subliminal addiction to sensory pleasures, providing only a transient source of mental happiness. The more we have, the more we want. With the increase of purchasing power and a ready access to material comforts of life, the obsession with material objects also increases. Ultimately, though, as needs become less pressing, there is a propulsion toward fulfillment of higher order wants, beyond the physiological, to include psychological (belongingness, self-esteem, etc.) and eventually self-actualization needs. Psychologist Abraham Maslow articulated this very well as early as 1943.[1]

Maslow's hierarchy of needs are as mentioned as follows:

1. *Biological and physiological needs*—air, food, drink, shelter, warmth, sex, sleep.
2. *Safety needs*—protection from elements, security, order, law, stability, freedom from fear.
3. *Love and belongingness needs*—friendship, intimacy, trust and acceptance, receiving and giving affection and love, affiliating, being part of a group (family, friends, work).
4. *Esteem needs*—which Maslow classified into two categories: (i) esteem for oneself (dignity, achievement, mastery, independence) and (ii) the desire for reputation or respect from others (e.g., status, prestige). Maslow indicated that the need for respect or reputation is most important for children and adolescents and precedes real self-esteem or dignity.
5. *Self-actualization needs*—realizing personal potential, self-fulfillment, seeking personal growth and peak experiences. A desire "to become everything one is capable of becoming."

The ancient science of yoga also delved into the same subject thousands of years ago. The yogic perspective ties the subtlest layers of mind and body together with the potential for a new economic approach as has been attempted in the progressive utilization theory propounded by the late Shrii Prabhat Ranjan Sarkar starting in 1959. Human longings in an Indic perspective were observed to be of four types:

- *Káma*—physical, representing actions for gaining immediate pleasures;
- *Artha*—physico-psychic, representing a drive to secure future pleasures;
- Dharma—psycho-spiritual, representing an access to the source of power; and
- *Mokśa*—spiritual, representing freedom from all material bondages.

These four basic longings collectively were called *Puruśárthas*, which is a key concept in oriental philosophy.[2] The *Puruśártha* signifies that every human being has four goals that are necessary and sufficient for a fulfilling and happy life. Indulgence in these four longings for purely personal fulfillment can lead to obsession for material things, and material accumulation ends up creating wide disparities among fellow beings. Wealth inequality is the result of how our society distributes the power and property rights that ultimately make up wealth ownership, and how easily that ownership perpetuates across generations. The issue of increasing wealth inequalities will remain the focal critical issue for the coming generation.

The widespread application of restraint could create a more sustainable economic environment for all beings. The future of humanity depends on whether we choose to use these longings for merely personal consumption, ignoring the needs of everyone else, or rather create a system of progressive utilizations and enlightened leadership at all levels. The latter is the need of the hour, as portrayed in the two paths indicated in the bliss pyramid (Figure 10.1). If we ignore the critical issue of economic inequality,[3] we may indeed end up in a world of biological inequality that would relegate ordinary humans to an irrelevant and subordinated space, like other mammals, and threaten the peace and harmony of the

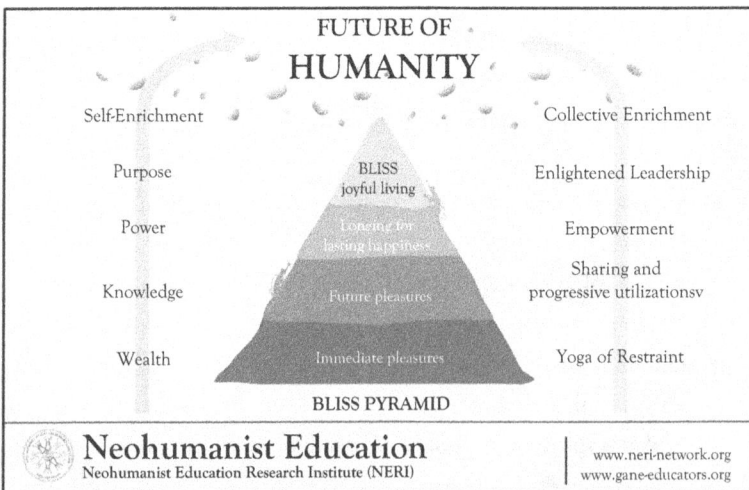

Figure 10.1 The bliss pyramid

entire society. Building a society through coordinated cooperation among all beings needs to be explored in the interest of preserving diversity in the world. Diversity—variety—adds to the beauty of creation while disparity—discrepancy—mars the beauty of creation.

A review of the literature on biological psychology[4] or, in short, biopsychology, further reveals that human beings are propelled by a host of other propensities like lust, hatred, anger, fear, envy, attachment, shyness, greed, selfishness, compassion, and the like. The objective of any action is not merely to fulfill material wants but also to consummate the expression of mental propensities. Above all, the ultimate propensity goading the human mind is longing for unison (*yog*) with universal consciousness, called yoga.

Yogic literature spells out that the 50 basic propensities in human beings are controlled by different plexi in the human body, which are supported by secretion of hormones, neurotransmitters, and scores of chemicals. The list of 50 propensities include the four basic propensities: *káma* (physical longings), *artha* (psycho-physical and psychic longings), dharma (psycho-spiritual longings), and *mokśa* (spiritual longings), as the root of all others. The propensities supported by chemical and biological processes elicit emotions and further drive individual motivations and social interactions. It is important to explore ways to satisfy human longings using more lasting non-material nourishment. This is at the crux of yogic and meditative practices as enshrined in the yogic and spiritual lifestyle. Meditation provides numerous benefits such as overcoming stress, increasing concentration and emotional stability, higher awareness, and blissful experiences arising out of inner serenity.

In recent decades, scientists[5] have been able to discover a host of neuropeptides responsible for human emotions and behaviors as indicated in Figure 10.2.

We are just beginning to understand the links between mental functions, brain activity, and physiological processes involved in biopsychological neural dynamics. It is quite likely that as we come to understand the control processes, we will be able to fathom the higher order functions of the mind and the reflective self that comprise the core of human consciousness. Prof. Ramachandran and others have speculated on this subject at great length over the last decade.[6]

Timeline of the discovery of major neuropeptides that participate in various brain functions related to the control of behavior and various emotional and motivational processes.

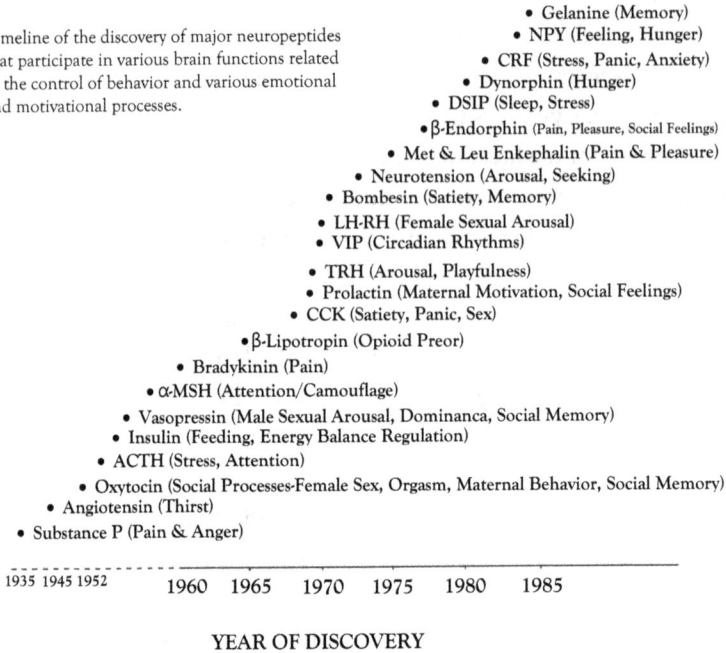

- Gelanine (Memory)
- NPY (Feeling, Hunger)
- CRF (Stress, Panic, Anxiety)
- Dynorphin (Hunger)
- DSIP (Sleep, Stress)
- β-Endorphin (Pain, Pleasure, Social Feelings)
- Met & Leu Enkephalin (Pain & Pleasure)
- Neurotension (Arousal, Seeking)
- Bombesin (Satiety, Memory)
- LH-RH (Female Sexual Arousal)
- VIP (Circadian Rhythms)
- TRH (Arousal, Playfulness)
- Prolactin (Maternal Motivation, Social Feelings)
- CCK (Satiety, Panic, Sex)
- β-Lipotropin (Opioid Preor)
- Bradykinin (Pain)
- α-MSH (Attention/Camouflage)
- Vasopressin (Male Sexual Arousal, Dominanca, Social Memory)
- Insulin (Feeding, Energy Balance Regulation)
- ACTH (Stress, Attention)
- Oxytocin (Social Processes-Female Sex, Orgasm, Maternal Behavior, Social Memory)
- Angiotensin (Thirst)
- Substance P (Pain & Anger)

1935 1945 1952   1960   1965   1970   1975   1980   1985

YEAR OF DISCOVERY

Figure 10.2 Timeline for discovery of different neuropeptides

Source: Panksepp, J. 1998. *Affective Neuroscience: The Foundations of Human and Animal Emotions*, 101. New York, NY: Oxford University Press.

Scientific Research on Inner Consciousness

What is the self? How does the activity of neurons give rise to the sense of being a conscious human being? According to Prof. Ramachandran,

the self is not a holistic property of the entire brain; it arises from the activity of specific sets of inter-linked brain circuits. But we need to know which circuits are critically involved and what their functions might be. It is the 'turning inward' aspect of the self—its recursiveness—that gives it its peculiar paradoxical quality.

The scientific research on self (unit consciousness) is still speculative and in its embryonic stages.

Prof. Ramachandran adds:

There are many aspects of self. It has a sense of unity despite the multitude of sense impressions and beliefs. In addition, it has a sense of continuity in time, of being in control of its actions ('free will'), of being anchored in a body, a sense of its worth, dignity and mortality (or immortality). Each of these aspects of self may be mediated by different centers in different parts of the brain and it is only for convenience that we lump them together in a single word. There is one aspect of self that seems stranger than all the others—the fact that it is aware of itself. I would like to suggest that groups of neurons called mirror neurons are critically involved in this ability. In the early 1990s, a team of neuroscientists at the University of Parma (G. Rizzolatti, V. Gallase, I. Iacoboni) made a surprising discovery: Certain groups of neurons in the brains of macaque monkeys fired not only when a monkey performed an action—grabbing an apple out of a box, for instance—but also when the monkey watched someone else performing that action; and even when the monkey heard someone performing the action in another room. The existence of command neurons that control voluntary movements has been known for decades. Amazingly, a subset of these neurons had an additional peculiar property. The neuron fired not only (say) when the monkey reached for a pea-nut but also when it watched another monkey reach for a peanut! Thus, the ability to turn inward to introspect or reflect may be a sort of metaphorical extension of the mirror neurons ability to read others' minds.[7]

Yogis, however, postulate that the physical activities of the millions of neurons are merely physical correlates of mind power, which lies beyond the crude physical domain. The existences of subtle "ectoplasmic mind" or even subtler domains called *kośas* (layers) still remain undiscovered by present sciences. The rare mental powers displayed by select individuals over the ages are a testimony to the possible existence of cerebral and noncerebral memory. Advanced meditation practitioners may be able to tune into those subtler domains and contribute to the progress of human society.

Body–Mind Spectrum and the Key Role of Sentient Lifestyle

The intake of a sentient vegetarian diet, regular practice of yoga postures, and daily practice of apexed meditation are part of a sentient lifestyle and constitute the core of movement toward self-realization and awareness of higher consciousness.

On the physical level, according to yogic science and Ayurveda as depicted in Figure 10.3, the food that we take in gets converted into a juicy mass with the help of digestive fluids and is transformed into chyle, blood, flesh, fat, bone, bone marrow, and *shukra* (vital essence) excreting urine, sweat, and stool. *Shukra* has three stages: lymph, or *práńa-rasa* (*lasiká*); spermatozoa; and seminal fluid. The sublimation of *shukra* into *ojas* (effulgence) brings luster to the human body and provides strength and stability. *Shukra* also provides food to the brain and strengthens the immune system. If the body becomes deficient in *shukra*, it may also influence the general health of the person. The human body functions like a biological machine following the well-defined laws of cause and

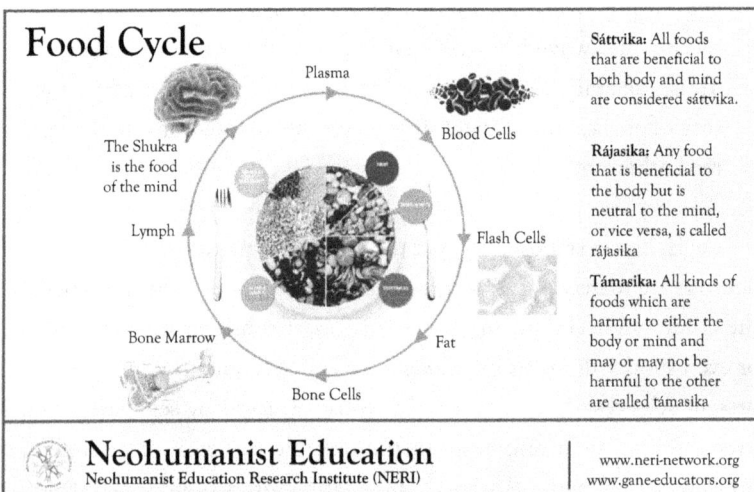

Food Cycle

Plasma
Blood Cells
The Shukra is the food of the mind
Lymph
Flash Cells
Bone Marrow
Fat
Bone Cells

Sáttvika: All foods that are beneficial to both body and mind are considered sáttvika.

Rájasika: Any food that is beneficial to the body but is neutral to the mind, or vice versa, is called rájasika

Támasika: All kinds of foods which are harmful to either the body or mind and may or may not be harmful to the other are called támasika

Neohumanist Education
Neohumanist Education Research Institute (NERI)

www.neri-network.org
www.gane-educators.org

Figure 10.3 Food cycle

effect. Any slackness or deviation in maintaining law and order leads to disease and ultimate death of the unit being. On death, the mind leaves the body in search of another body according to its inherent reactive momenta (*saṃskáras*).

The function of sensory organs is to receive inferences; the function of motor organs (vocal cord, hands, legs, anus, and genitals) is to transmit vibrations with the help of the internal sense; and the function of vital airs is to conjoin objectivity with mind-stuff (*citta* or ectoplasmic mind). The organs are comprised of:

1. Gateways like ears, eyes, skin, tongue and nose;
2. Nerve fibers, which react to the waves of inferences;
3. Nerve secretions, which further transmit the waves to the nerve cells; and
4. Nerve-cell points in the brain where the inferential waves are finally conjoined with the unit mind.

Thus, for example, the optical nerve, optical fluid, and the optic point of the nerve cell (in the brain) that are active behind the scenes are what we commonly call the organ of sight. When a particular set of neurons (brain cells) are activated, the ectoplasmic mind plate (*citta*) adopts the vibrational forms of what is seen. Such a process is experienced by one and all daily even in the dream state. In the dream state, the leftover impressions continue to play on the ectoplasmic mind long after they have been dissociated from the organs of sound, touch, form, taste, or smell. The activation of ectoplasmic mind can take place by a host of physiological or psychological factors such as gases produced by the digestive system, nervous tensions, and past reactive momenta. The sensory and motor organs maintain link between the physical world and the psychic world. Thus, sensory organs facilitate carrying information to the brain and mind.[8]

The mind consists of *citta* (ectoplasm), *aham* (doer "I" feeling), and *mahat* (pure "I" feeling) and is the controller of the ten motor and sensory organs. Vital energy (*prána*) is the controller of the mind in the physiological stratum. The mind does not contain any inferential waves and therefore cannot be heard, touched, seen, tasted, or smelt. It has the qualities of grasping an idea, thinking, and feeling. Some robots are being programmed to capture some of the attributes of this mental phenomenon but the human mind is unique in its ability to master emotions. The mind is, therefore, a suitable candidate for pursuing the realization of highest consciousness.

The mind—a very peculiar entity—moves within the domain of the abstract material world. Breathing is the nexus between the body and the mind. *Práńáyáma* (a breathing exercise in yoga) slows down the breathing, thereby establishing control over vital energy (*práńa*) and thereby over the motor and sensory organs and, in turn, over the body.

Science Behind Virtual Reality

The existence of mind may be found in the pure "I" feeling. This itself does not perform any action but remains involved with the sense of an action. Doer-I feeling is really the doer of actions and enjoyer of the fruits of the actions. The ectoplasmic mind actually takes the form of the object of our ideations, mental actions. The external application of *citta* (mind plate) only comes about with the help of the 10 motor or sensory organs. While imagining London, for instance, the help of none of those organs is required, because London may be physically far away and therefore beyond the reach of perception. Thus the *citta* loses its contact with the sensory organs and takes the shape of London on its own. When *citta* loses contact with the sensory organs, they become nonfunctional, and a person loses his or her sense of relationship and distinction of place, time, and person. As soon as the imagination of *ahaṁtattva* (doer "I" feeling) ceases, *citta* (mind plate) also loses its shape, and, at the same moment, the sensory organs start functioning. Then alone does a person realize that the London, that he/she had been seeing, existed only in imagination. It is due to this process that the imagined object appears factual as long as the spell of the imagination lasts. The moment that spell is broken it appears to be imaginary and not real. This is what happens during the process of virtual reality (VR). VR blurs the line between digital and physical worlds, thereby generating a sense of being present in the virtual environment for the consumer. According to 2018 Mordor Intelligence Report,[9] the global VR market was valued at $3.13 billion in 2017 and is expected to reach $49.7 billion by 2023, at a compounded annual growth rate (CAGR) of 58.54 percent over the forecast period (2018–2023).

Mind–Spirit Realm and Psycho-Spiritual Training: A Yogic Perspective

According to yogic science, *cakras* or plexi act as the substations of the mind from which vibrational expressions occur. They constitute the metazoic (multicellular) structures. The attractive force of supreme consciousness when passing through these metazoic structures, gives rise to scores of propensities, which may increase with the growing complexity of the human mind. Each plexus is a collection of certain glands and sub glands. The plexi are situated at the intersecting points of *iḍa*, *suṣumṅá*, and *pingala nāḍiis* (nerves). The vibrational expressions of propensities such as anger, fear, hatred, jealousy, and greed cause hormones to secrete from the glands, which, in turn, set in motion different actions and reactions in the human body. The existence of the mind to a large extent depends on the existence of its propensities, which is the result of inherent *saṁskáras* (reactive-momenta) carried by a living being over its evolutionary cycle.

Higher plexi control the lower plexi and the Supreme Self functions directly through the higher plexus known as *Guru Cakra* (multi-propensive plexus) and *Sahasrara Cakra* (seat of unit-consciousness). Supreme Self is the rudimental cause of all diversities, creating and controlling the crude, subtle, and causal worlds. It is the material cause, the efficient cause, and the witnessing entity. The entire colorful panorama of the universe is a condensed form of countless inferential waves emerging in the stream of the macrocosmic imagination and reverts to its ultimate owner by the cosmic will. Thus, the unity of Supreme Consciousness lies beneath the endless diversities of nature.

The unending flow of consciousness and bliss takes different forms, depending on whether it is mind, organs, or inferences. The difference in peoples' thoughts, ideas, manners, customs, dress, and food habits are all due to their varying *saṁskáras*. The moment individual *saṁskáras* are removed, the mind loses its independent existence and only the soul or spirit remains. Differences are nothing but the divine play of the Supreme Consciousness. This play can come to an end in individual life but never collectively. Thus, universe continues in its eternal journey according to the will of macrocosm.

The stages through which the cosmic force manifests itself in a unit body are called *kośas* (sheaths, layers). *Kośas* are like layers of the plantain flower, ranging from crude to subtle. They are all embodied in the *citta* (crude mind). The outermost layer is called *Annamaya kośa* and represents the body layer. The food we take, the water we drink, the air we breathe, and whatever our senses are exposed to directly affect this layer. Conscious mind is the *Kámamaya kośa* and is intimately connected with sense perceptions. *Manomaya kośa* is sometimes called the subconscious mind and is responsible for all deep cognitive functions, memory, logical thought, problem solving, decision-making, and so on. The other three *kośas* are part of the causal mind and termed *Atimánas kośa, Vijinánamaya kośa,* and *Hirańamaya kośa.*

These layers of mind display a wide spectrum of psychic phenomena, consisting of thinking, remembering, meditation, transmutation, and diversion of psychic sustenance, rationalization, para-psychology, and sublimation of mind to the Higher Consciousness. All past, present, and future knowledge remains stored in the causal mind, so it is not unusual to predict the future by delving into the causal mind. Phenomena such as telepathy, omniscience, clairvoyance, and transference of thought are all products of the causal mind. Supreme Consciousness is the subtlest state of consciousness and remains beyond the ambit of the unit mind. It is the Supreme Consciousness alone that can establish one in the meta-empirical omni-telepathic stance of Nonattributional Consciousness.

As indicated earlier, human beings are born with dominant inborn instincts, strong propensities for immediate and ensured pleasure, and future happiness. However, the path of evolution requires that lasting bliss can only be achieved if mind is elevated to higher levels of consciousness. For this, one's lifestyle must include sentient diet, proper training for restraint in diet and dealings, regular exercise of body and mind, right occupation, and adherence to codes of conduct representing higher values of life. Hence, the need to undergo proper psycho-spiritual training is paramount to the achievement of progress and happiness in life.

Overall Progress Through a Balanced Approach

Everybody thinks, but not every thought brings about individual progress or universal welfare. Hence, it is important to know how to use the power of thought for nurturing individual and collective peace and happiness.

In order to control one's thoughts, one must engage in cognitive exercises and meditative practices. What the cosmic mind has done to date will continue to be done by unit minds or their robotic assistants in slow and gradual steps. The changes come about at the personal level (personality–charisma effect), organizational level (strategy effect), and the mythical ideological level (narrative effect), and each level interpenetrates the others at both the "macro" and "micro" levels to accelerate the process of transformation.

Nunez[10] has explored the complexity of changes at the "micro" and "macro" levels in the following manner:

> Wars, religions, and national economic and political policies are large-scale phenomena that act top down on individuals at small scales, who then act bottom up on the larger scales, as in the prominent examples of Jesus, Darwin, Marx, Einstein, and Hitler. Modern complexity science explicitly recognizes such circular causality; that is, interactions across multiple levels of organization in both directions. The brain's neural networks, which can form nested hierarchies at multiple spatial scales, may act in an analogous manner to produce various conscious, preconscious, and unconscious processes.

Progress is about management of change. There is nothing constant in the universe. Changes in broader collective psychology lead to new systems of social and economic management. Sometimes far-sighted individuals spearhead the changes and at other times changes are the product of initiatives of grassroots movements. Technological developments are hastening the advent of distributed authority with a clear and transparent structure of roles and accountabilities. The emphasis is likely to shift from "who is right?" to "what is right?" Thus, the purpose is likely to dictate organizational culture and pave a way for progress at all levels.

Human beings sometimes forget that their sojourn on this earth is a transitory one. We live for a hundred or at most a hundred and twenty years. We must never forget that we grow only with the help of nutrients provided by Mother Earth, begotten of the Cosmic Operative Principle. All that we have borrowed will one day be returned to Mother Earth.

We are born only for a single purpose: to unite with the source of All-Universal Consciousness, and to pave the way for all other creatures to attain the same stance. In order to achieve this goal, we need to adopt a dual approach: use of cosmic ideation (subjective approach) and objective adjustment (utilizing all faculties for all-round welfare).

Thus, we cannot lead a secluded existence in some cave or on some mountain top. We need to live like a lotus, which has its roots in the mud and yet stays above the water. I am very hopeful that we will take all necessary steps in order to establish a world where everyone is respected as the embodiment of divinity, where all get the opportunity to utilize their capabilities for imparting joy and happiness to all around, and where all stay engaged in blissful realization of Universal Consciousness. That would be the path of subjective approach and objective adjustment.

The Journey to Inner Space

Nothing is as old as the Truth and nothing is as new as the Truth. It requires wisdom to discover the *élan vital*, the embodiment of Eternal Absolute Truth and to keep adjustment with the relative truth, subject to eternal change.

A little reflection will remind us that every creature and every nation longs for freedom, good health and happiness, material prosperity and abundance, progress and justice for all. Yet, these ideals remain elusive for us. Unless we develop and awaken our inner higher consciousness, we are likely to fall short of achieving these goals.

We are more than mere body and mind. We are not just "limited" creatures to be molded by our societies and the natural environment. We are the embodiment of a life force (*élan vital*, unit-consciousness): something much greater and more precious, with which every one of us is endowed from birth. Information may be stored in the cloud, in computers, or in books, and is easily accessible to anyone today. Knowledge may be extracted from the patterns of information contained in databases. Yet, there will always be a need of wisdom masters. And wisdom can only be drawn from within.

A question we need to ponder in every age is what type of society or development we want, and why. This question is as relevant to business and government as it is to citizens like you and me. We should also consider which aspects of our past we need to hold on to, and what should be released. We do indeed live in a rapidly changing world, but the modern notion of "development" tends to reduce everything to a commodity. These are questions to be answered as much from the heart or spirit—intuitively—as from the intellect. The diversity of nature is fast disappearing. The clock is ticking and immediate action is needed.

The experience of old civilizations amply demonstrates that there is great worth in the old cultures. For instance, the Vedas, Upanishads, and Tantras in India were the products of intuitive knowledge, linking us to the spirit within us. The Greeks also affirmed the message of "know thyself." And the Chinese pursued Tao. This knowledge is not mere information, but life-transforming wisdom. It is trans-disciplinary and transcendental and imbued with the tender sweetness of universal love. It is the basis for human longings.

Human longings are multifarious, ranging from the physical to the spiritual. The exclusive pursuit of pleasure-seeking physical longings consumes the lives of most people. There is nothing wrong with the pursuit of pleasure; it is indeed built into our biology. The drawback is that pleasures do not provide permanent happiness and carry the seeds of unbridled desire for accumulation. This creates unreasonable disparities and causes unneeded sufferings to many creatures.

Today, just one percent of the population controls the bulk of the resources in almost every country. The thirst for power is an expression of a deep inherent longing to ensure lasting peace and happiness. However, lasting happiness cannot be found in individual gain but can be attained only by balancing personal desires with the yoga of restraint. Herein lies the secret of integrating the psychology of self-enrichment with the desire and endeavor for broader flourishing. The long journey toward bliss (*ananda*) is both an inner journey and an outward journey. When the inner and outer are integrated, bliss is within reach.

The inner journey is thus no less of a challenge than reaching distant stars. We place high value on "book knowledge"—the type of knowledge that can take us to the farthest fringes of outer space—but much less on that which can take us into the deepest mysteries of inner space. We need to nurture the spiritual as well as the material. Spiritual here is not an expression of religion, but of the life force that resides in each one of us, and yet remains so distant from our everyday consciousness. On the path to fully expressing our individual potentials, we are the repositories of a great invisible treasure, which we can manifest to empower good over evil, rationality over dogma, culture over brute force, truth over falsehood, selflessness over selfishness, peace over war, and spirit over matter.

The future of humanity lies in which of our longings we will prioritize. A happy blending of intuitive knowledge and mundane knowledge can ensure harmony between the inner and the outer spheres of life, and offers great promise to create a progressive society, a world where there is inner tranquility as well as a compassionate, just, and sustainable civilization. The spirit of empathy, discrimination, and altruism needs to be cultivated from an early age so that the coming generation can deal with the challenges of the age. The support of wisdom teachers is required to impart this impulse. The central task of educational renewal is: how to create such wisdom teachers with a holistic vision?

Summary

Humans are born with an ability to question their own existence: its origins, its evolution, its possibilities, and its purpose. Scientists, philosophers, and lay people are endowed with the curiosity to know and experience all that there is. The ultimate answers to reality may perhaps never be readily available for all, yet that has not stopped us from speculating and exploring pathways to achieve better answers. We know more today than we knew even a hundred years ago. Of course, there is also knowledge that was available a few thousand years ago, which has remained hidden from the general masses.

In this chapter, we have taken an inner journey that shows that answers lie not only outside of us but also within us; and the journey to Higher Consciousness is as fascinating as the journey to the farthest reaches of outer space. The science of bio-psychology leads us to understand the important roles of a sentient lifestyle and meditation in helping us to control our emotions and experience and lift the mind through different states of consciousness to the highest state.

The goal of meditative pursuits is not merely to better understand our inner urges or control our emotions but also to develop attitudes that enable us to control technology and function as better leaders or role players—whether in business, at home, in politics or in any other public domain. What emerges from this pursuit is a new mindset, which can bring inner peace as well as a progressive social, economic, and political order. In a world where violence is rampant, it is even more important to build a peaceful mind from an early age. In order to achieve this, we must have a subjective approach and objective adjustment. That is, we must never lose sight of our absolute goal of uniting each unit consciousness with Supreme Consciousness, while building a compassionate, sustainable, and progressive world where needs on all levels of one and all are met.

To make such a society possible should be the goal of our educational system and the socioeconomic system. We cannot let emotionless technology bereft of higher consciousness convert future human society into a world of robots as envisioned by science fiction writers and affirmed by some scholars. The world requires wisdom teachers and enlightened leaders at all levels and science, technology, and arts must be guided by higher consciousness and not baser propensities. Let "arts and sciences for service and blessedness" be the slogan of our generation! Let the universal economic renaissance minimize all disparities while preserving all diversities!

References

[1] Maslow, A.H. 1943. "A Theory of Human Motivation." *Psychological Review* 50, no. 4, pp. 370–96.

[2] https://en.wikipedia.org/wiki/Purusartha

[3] Spross, J. 2018. http://theweek.com/articles/717294/wealth-inequality-even-worse-than-income-inequality. UK: The Week Publications Inc.

[4] Suzanne, H., A. Cooper, J. Lee, and M. Harris. 2015. *Biological Psychology*, 439–79. New York, NY: Sage.

[5] Panksepp, J. 2004. *Affective Neuroscience: The Foundations of Human and Animal Emotions*, 101. New York, NY: Oxford University Press; and Klavdieva, M.M. 1995 "The History of Neuropeptides." *Frontiers in Neuroendocrinology* 16, pp. 293–321.

[6] Ramachandran, V.S. 2004. *A Brief Tour of Human Consciousness*. Serbia: Pi-Press.

[7] Ramachandran, V.S. 2007 "The Neurology of Self-Awareness." The Edge 10th Anniversary Essay, The Third Culture , USA: Edge Foundation Inc. https://edge.org/3rd_culture/ramachandran07/ramachandran07_index.html

[8] Sarkar, P.R. 1959. *Idea and Ideology*, Calcutta: A.M. Publications; and Shambhushivananda. 2018. "Body-Mind-Spirit Spectrum." In *Thoughts for a New Era*. Sweden: Gurukul Press.

[9] Mordor Intelligence, Industry Report, Virtual Reality Markets. April 2018. https://mordorintelligence.com/industry-reports/virtual-reality-market

[10] Nunez, P.L. 2016. *The New Science of Consciousness: Exploring the Complexity of Brain, Mind, and Self*. Amherst, New York, NY: Prometheus Books.

PART V

Economic Issues

CHAPTER 11

Reviving the American Dream by Restoring the Balance

Navin Doshi

Introduction

On March 11, 2011, a massive earthquake, as high as 9 on the Richter scale, shook Japan for over two minutes, causing unprecedented destruction in its wake. A powerful tsunami followed a few hours later, sharply deepening the gloom and destruction. It was the latest example of what can happen when a vast imbalance occurs in nature in the form of shifting tectonic underneath a country's surface.

I believe similar, but human-made imbalances designated later, are rocking global economic system. They have already generated a violent storm in terms of what is called "the Great Recession" that started in late 2007 and has lingered till this day in the form of low-wage jobs, degrading money flow, increasing wealth gap, and much more. But since the imbalances are getting bigger, we are now headed toward an economic earthquake that could be as disastrous as tremor that hit Japan.[5, 6]

These imbalances include:

1. Huge budget deficits
2. Huge trade deficits
3. Massive printing of money controlled by a top few
4. Because of deregulation, banks enjoying vast profits with reduced lending

5. Income and wealth inequalities not seen in capitalism before

6. Manufacturing jobs not increasing substantially in spite of President Trump's efforts

An interesting article was written by an unknown Indian economist about how crazy and imbalanced world economy is.

Japanese save a lot. They do not spend much. Also, Japan exports far more than it imports. The country has an annual trade surplus of over $100 billion. Yet Japanese economy is considered weak, even collapsing. Americans spend, save little. Also the United States imports more than it exports and has an annual trade deficit of over $400 billion. Yet, the American economy is considered strong and trusted to get stronger.

Americans borrow from Japan, China and even India. Virtually others save for the Americans to spend. Substantial Global savings are invested in the United States, in dollars. India itself keeps its foreign currency assets of over $50 billion in U.S. securities. China has sunk over $160 billion in U.S. securities. Japan's stakes in U.S. securities is in trillions.

The United States has taken over $5 trillion from the world. As the world saves for the United States. It's the Americans who spend freely. Today, to keep the U.S. consumption going, that is for the U.S. economy to work, other countries have to remit $180 billion every quarter, which is $2 billion a day, to the United States!

Who has invested more, the United States in China, or China in the United States? The United States has invested in China less than half of what China has invested in the United States. India has invested over $50 billion in the United States. But the United States has invested less than $20 billion in India.

Why Is the World After the United States?

Americans hardly save. In fact they use their credit cards to spend their future income. That the United States spends is what makes it attractive to export to the United States. So, the United States imports more than what it exports year after year. The world has become dependent on U.S. consumption for its growth. By its deepening culture of consumption, the United States has habituated the world to feed on U.S. consumption.

But as the United States needs money to finance its consumption, the world provides the money.

It's like a shopkeeper providing the money to a customer so that the customer keeps buying from the shop. If the customer will not buy, the shop won't have business, unless the shopkeeper funds him. Who is America's biggest shopkeeper financier? Japan, of course. Yet it's Japan that is regarded as weak. Modern economists complain that Japanese do not spend, so they do not grow. To force the Japanese to spend, the Japanese government exerted itself, reduced the savings rates, and even charged the savers. Even then the Japanese did not spend (habits don't change, even with taxes, do they?). Their traditional postal savings alone is over $1.2 trillion. Thus, savings, far from being the strength of Japan, has become its pain.

Saving Is Sin, and Spending Is Virtue

This is an illusion that does not follow the laws of economics and the nature, disregarding the symbiotic relationship between men and nature. We cannot just keep consuming and creating infinite garbage polluting our own environment. Creators of this illusion are "professional maggots" feeding on the declining empire. When corruption, monopoly, and the price distortions that they create become too large of a component of GDP, the economy is headed for a collapse.[1, 4]

When "finance" becomes too large of a component of GDP, the economy is heading to collapse. Manufacturing and delivery of tangible, productive services must be a major, growing component. Finance is a support function to allocate capital.

Every "app" and "black box" with multibillion-dollar market caps, every loan issued for the purpose of share buy backs, all of this garbage is an inefficient deployment of capital. The Fed and the banks keep printing it up.[2, 3]

Government has failed in monitoring and regulating all of the important things and piled on regulations in areas that kill small businesses (the #1 job creator) establishing large barriers of entry for new firms that won't play "the capital markets game."[1]

Becoming more hawkish wanting to go for "regime change" in Iran, Trump has lurched America drastically forward on the path to a monumental financial catastrophe. That is because taken together the warfare state and the welfare state are also the fiscal demise of the state.

Giant Budget Deficits

The whole world is now awash in giant budget deficits. Most economists attribute them to the popularity of Keynesian economics, but that is not accurate. Keynes never preached relentless deficits, which were needed in recessions and depressions to raise aggregate demand, but the deficits were to be matched with surplus budgets when boom came around. There would then be deficits and surpluses over the course of the business cycle, but not a debt accumulation. U.S. debt pile, which was below a trillion in 1980, has grown into a mountain. The federal debt, as of December 2017, is over $20 trillion, and it is rocketing at the rate of $1.5 trillion per year. In addition, almost all states, especially California, Illinois, and New York, have large deficits and debt. They either have to raise taxes or trim government spending or do both.

All Fed chairmen seem to be unaware that nature dislikes imbalances, and somewhere things could go wrong unexpectedly to create misery for the borrowers, lenders, and the economy. Things have not changed much during last 16 months of Trump's presidency. Political wisdom has been that the government can borrow unlimited quantities of money, stabilize the economy, and face no undesired consequences. The laws of nature have been thwarted again.

The United States indeed has been able to borrow trillions from abroad, because it is a military superpower, a consuming powerhouse, and a world reserve currency nation. This practice has decimated its manufacturing and lowered real wages for millions of workers. Foreign countries accept U.S. bonds for their surplus goods exported to the United States. Some Euro-zone nations have been as reckless as the United States in their foreign borrowing. Greece, Spain, and Portugal among others have borrowed trillions as if there is no tomorrow. But since 2009, they have faced the so-called sovereign debt crisis.[10, 12]

The sovereign debt crisis emerged in full swing in mid-2010, when Greece was on the verge of defaulting on its foreign debt. Greek budget deficit had turned out to be larger than expected and it was not clear if the nation could service its giant debt. The clustering property of nature simply means that upward or downward trends occur for a while because events occur in a cluster. Otherwise there would be no discernible trends, but only random fluctuations, because a number of events with similar effects have to occur before a trend is formed. When Greece appeared to be on the verge of default, Portugal, Ireland, and Spain (PIGS) also appeared to be in the same boat. This illustrates how events tend to occur in clusters. As the saying goes, *when it rains it pours.*

When imbalances occur and natural laws are violated, some Black Swan event occurs and destroys the house of cards. People are then caught off-guard and lament their earlier recklessness, but by then it is already too late. Only way out of this huge burden is either to declare bankruptcy or through increasing the rate of inflation and reducing government spending and the budget deficit until we are on a right trajectory.

Nobel laureate Paul Krugman of Princeton University and President Trump's economic advisers believe that the U.S. government should spend even more, raising the budget deficit for infrastructure and defense spending. On paper the argument sounds good, but the recent experience from the sovereign-debt crisis suggests that unlimited budget deficits have their costs in terms of higher interest rates and potentially bigger problems. Japan's experience since 1990 suggests that postponing genuine reforms by relentlessly increasing government spending is no sure way to prosperity. In fact, the opposite has happened. Japan has been stagnant for over two decades in spite of its debt pile.[12]

Huge Trade Deficits and Loss of Manufacturing

The other major imbalance in the world is that few nations have balanced trade. United States and Australia have large deficits and other countries, such as China, Asian tigers, and Germany, have large surpluses in their foreign accounts. When the gap between labor productivity and the real wage increases, supply exceeds demand and then the country keeps its currency artificially low to generate a trade surplus to fill the supply–demand gap and keep its factories running. It keeps its employment high but only by exporting unemployment to trade-deficit nations. The United States also has a large wage–productivity gap, but it has encouraged so much consumer borrowing that its demand has consistently run ahead of its supply; this excess demand is its trade deficit.

American trade deficit also stems from the fact that cheap imports from abroad have all but destroyed the U.S. manufacturing base. The nation just does not produce the variety of goods that it did during the 1950s and the 1960s. So, there is not much the country can export. Diminishing manufacturing base implies diminishing living standard, because the manufacturing wage normally exceeds the average wage in service industries that employ over 75 percent of the U.S. workforce. This is because with manufacturing industry, a nation builds products, whereas in services industry, those products are repaired. And the repair work is far less valuable than the production work.

The havoc caused by American trade debacle on manufacturing cannot be exaggerated. According to the Economic Report of the President, some 11.5 million people out of a labor force (of 150 million) worked in manufacturing in 2010. This turns out to be less than 8 percent. Now compare this to the situation in 1800 when the nation was primarily an agrarian economy. At that time about 6 percent of the workforce was employed in manufacturing. Not surprisingly, the nation's living standard is also moving back toward the pre-industrialization days. One of the causes for the reduction in manufacturing jobs is attributed to the development of computers and Internet. For example, Apple (market cap $1 trillion) employs about 60,000 people, as opposed to General Motors (market cap $45 billion) employing over 200,000 people.

Early proponents and founders of the free trade doctrine did not envision giant trade deficits. They believed in balanced trade, which was produced by the gold standard. A deficit nation had to pay for excess imports with gold; this trimmed its money supply, which was also linked to its gold stock pile. The fall in money supply lowered its prices, and in turn stimulated exports, until the trade was in balance. Today everything is topsy-turvy. Money supply is no longer linked to gold or anything else; nations are happy to accept dollars for their surplus production. There is no compulsion for disciplined economic policies. So, imbalances keep growing.

In order to revive manufacturing, trade surplus nations must be compelled to follow free trade just as the United States and Europe do. Currency manipulation violates free commerce. A "beggar-thy-neighbor" policy implies a competition among countries to trash their currencies to increase the export. Asian tigers and China are the main manipulators. They should be so declared, and then under the World Trade Organization (WTO) rules that prohibit subsidies, the United States will be able to impose trade restrictions on these nations. That should help revive American manufacturing, create high-paying jobs, and trim unemployment.

Gottfried Haberler, a Harvard economist, proved in 1950 that tariffs raise the nation's living standard when there is large-scale unemployment. He was generally in favor of free trade, except in the presence of high joblessness. Evidently President Trump is trying to follow this course to increase the manufacturing base.

Excessive Money Printing

Another irresponsible policy today is the uncontrolled money printing by the world's central banks. Any time the Fed buys anything from the private sector, it creates money either by printing it or by writing a check for the purchase, because the check is eventually deposited in a bank, creating more money. There is no transparency in what central banks are doing around the globe. But it is common knowledge that trillions have been printed or created to bailout several banks that had offered cheap, no-down payment loans to homeowners in the past, thereby generating a housing bubble all over the planet. The banks and their employees reaped large fees and bonuses, but then their loans soured and generated a housing and banking crisis, as well as a serious recession.

The Fed is not worried about inflation, and in justification it points to the muted rise in the consumer price index (CPI) since 2007. However, the CPI is not the only gauge of soaring prices. There are two types of inflation—commodity inflation of the CPI, and asset inflation. Both produce worrisome consequences. Asset inflation, whereby prices soar for bonds, shares, and commodities, is just as bad as the rise in the cost of living. Stock markets have rocketed up as if the United States is in the midst of a boom. Even though GDP growth averaged less than 3 percent, the Dow has soared very close to its all-time high. Something that goes up sharply also comes down sharply, and when it falls, it really hurts and sours the economy. So asset inflation can be really harmful, and when money supply soars to generate it, the policy is wrong and the end result can be very painful. Ask Alan Greenspan, who presided over stock market bubbles and their crashes in 2000 and then in 2008. There are no free markets, more so after the 2008–2009 market crash. Markets are manipulated by institutions often with the blessing of the government for political and economic advantage.

The main reason for the failure of the laws of supply and demand in many commodities is huge speculation by financial institutions, thanks to the deregulation during Clinton years, along with a much larger money supply, which has been fostered by all that money that the banks have received from their bailouts. The banks are unwilling to lend much in a weak economy, but with so much cash piling up in the vaults of financial institutions they, along with hedge funds, are busy using it in speculation, especially in oil, gold, and copper. The prices of such assets soared once the stock market recovered after March 2009, and then fell after 2013 again due to market manipulation. Indeed, institutions and funds made a lot of money, creating dislocations in commodity markets. The point of it all is that there are other costs to excessive money creation, which Fed chairmen have not recognized.[2, 3]

There is also hidden inflation that many have not noticed. The cost of essential goods and services that includes cost of food, housing, health care, and education has risen much faster than the CPI. Google search shows that the annual price of wheat, oats, pork, and cotton has gone up 60 percent, while the price of canola, sugar, copper, heating oil, gasoline, coffee, and beef has surged over 20 percent.

What then should be the annual growth in money supply to maintain a good monetary discipline? Milton Friedman gives us the answer. He used the classical economists' quantity theory of money to offer a monetarist rule. The theory relies upon the well-known exchange equation:

$$MV = PY$$

Here M is money supply, V, the velocity of money in circulation, P the average price such as the CPI, and Y the real GDP. Friedman believes that normally V remains constant as it depends on bank lending and how much money people want to keep as cash in their valets. If P is to be kept constant, that is, if the inflation rate is to be zero, then M should grow at the same rate as Y or the GDP. It can be shown from the equation that if P and V are constant, then

$$\text{Money growth} = \text{GDP growth}$$

The GDP growth rate has been about 3 percent per year over the long run. Hence annual money creation, according to Friedman, should not exceed this figure. But money growth has far exceeded this rule, and that is why there has been asset inflation as well as a strong surge of food and housing prices.

Another type of money growth rule is offered by the proponents of gold and silver standard, where money supply is linked to the nation's stock of gold and silver. Since this stock does not grow fast, money growth is also restrained. In addition, the gold and silver standard, as argued earlier, does not permit unlimited trade deficits. This is then another argument in its favor, and I believe reversion to this standard will go a long way in restoring price stability and the revival of U.S. manufacturing. It is precisely for some of these reasons that even the newly evolving financial technologies such as blockchains as discussed in Chapter 3 should have a gold standard so that these new technologies are also self-regulated such that supply and demand grows and falls in proportion to maintain an economic balance.

Historically gold standard provided a stable debt to GDP ratio in the range of 10 to 30 percent, except during the years of World War ll. This ratio started to rise uncontrollably after 1971 when the gold standard was removed, and currently it is over 100 percent. A more detailed analysis as to why the U.S. dollar should be restored to gold standard can be read in 2014 book by economist Apek Mulay titled *Mass Capitalism : A Blueprint for Economic Revival.* Anchoring currency (think of it as blood flowing in the economic body) to gold and/or silver regulates the currency flow and provides nutrients efficiently to the economic body.[8] Unanchored fiat currency flow often accelerates to the level of uncontrolled velocity creating the economic boom and bust. This is what happened in the late 1970s in the United States. Similarly, hyperinflations of the past, such as those in Germany (1920s) and Brazil (1980s and 1990s), occurred because of a sharp rise in the velocity of money, so much so that people tried to spend money the moment they received any cash, fearing that their cash could lose value the next day, or even the next hour. But anchoring currency to gold and silver would remove the threat of such high inflation.

Excessive Deregulation

Ever since 1981, many industries have been deregulated, some with positive results and some with negative consequences. When this policy encourages competition among firms, the effects are positive, but when it stimulates speculation, the impact is mostly negative. Thus, deregulation of airlines and telecommunications done in the early 1980s increased competition in these areas; as a result airline fares fell sharply, and so did phone charges. I remember the days when I had to pay $2 per minute to speak to my family in India, but now I can do this for less than a quarter dollar. I also remember when I used to cringe while flying from Los Angeles to New York. The economy class air fare ran into thousands, at least in terms of today's prices. Now you can fly the same route for as low as $500. This type of deregulation has had a strongly positive effect for the consumer as it increases competition.

However, deregulation was also extended in the 1990s to the financial sector, especially with the repeal of the Glass-Steagall Act (GSA), which had barred commercial banks to conduct investment banking activities. Until the act's repeal the banks were not allowed to deal with stocks and their derivatives, but now they were able to do what they had done during the 1920s, that is, delve in stocks and then create a stock market bubble, with disastrous consequences in the 1930s. This time also bubbles dutifully followed the financial deregulation, only to climax into crashes. The point is that industrial deregulation is good, but the financial deregulation, particularly when products developed by Wall Street are totally opaque like those in Las Vegas casinos, is bad for the economy.[11]

There were also some unintended consequences of the GSA's repeal. It led to international financial deregulation as well. Until 1995, when the WTO displaced the General Agreement on Tariffs and Trade (GATT) of 1944, individuals in many countries such as Japan were not permitted to transfer money abroad. The financial institutions could do that, but not individuals. International finance's deregulation changed it all, with unexpected effects on America's foreign commerce, because the dollar could not fall in spite of the rising trade deficit. Such was not the case during the 1970s and the 1980s, when a nation's trade deficit would routinely result in currency depreciation, which in turn eliminated the deficit. This, however, is no longer true.

Once international finance was deregulated, individuals and institutions in trade-surplus nations increasingly invested their dollars into U.S. government bonds and other assets. Countries like China, Japan, Korea, and Saudi Arabia purchased these bonds in great quantities, thereby preventing the needed fall in the dollar. So, the trade deficit could not correct itself, and kept rising with no end in sight. The deficit in turn decimated U.S. manufacturing. Thus, financial deregulation, domestic and international, had deleterious, though unintended, consequences.

There is a fundamental reason why banks should not be allowed to dabble in risky ventures. If they were dealing with their own money, they would not be so fearless, but they are when dealing with other people's money (OPEOM), which we know is quite addictive. When they are reasonably certain that they will be bailed out in case of major losses, they tend to be reckless, and when their bets misfire, results could cause havoc in the economy. The world learned this lesson painfully during the Great Depression and the United States enacted the GSA in the 1930s, but in 1999 this was all forgotten as the GSA was repealed under the leadership of President Clinton, Fed chairman Greenspan, and the secretary of treasury Rubin. Why we repeat our mistakes is unfathomable. The biggest problem deregulation has created is the ballooning of a very opaque derivative market. The national value of the derivative market (January 2013) is over $1,200 trillion, over 17 times the total world GDP of about $70 trillion. The problem associated with the elephant size derivative market has also been described as financial instruments of mass destruction.[4] America should put an end to all financial deregulation, but deregulation of productive industries should be given a top priority, especially in energy.

There were more than 2600 mergers in the oil industry in the 1990s. Mergers among large companies are what generate cartels. When there is a decline in competition, prices generally rise. If deregulation were to occur in domestic oil, and some of the firms were broken up to increase competition, the way AT&T was broken in 1983, then just as phone charges fell, the oil price will fall. In fact, no new laws need be passed; only the existing anti-trust laws should be enforced and *New Macroeconomics* by economist Apek Mulay is a great book to understand why enforcing anti-trust laws needs to become a top priority. The United States can follow its own precedent in the way Standard Oil was broken up in 16 independent companies in 1911, only to be followed by a visible decline in the price of gasoline. The size of a corporation matters. I believe there should not be any institution that has become "too big to fail."

One more devastating result due to the deregulations has been the destruction of small and medium size businesses that creates majority of jobs, thanks to the involvement of banks with deep pockets competing and taking it over for themselves.

Growing Income and Wealth Disparity

The biggest problem in the world today is rocketing inequality in income and wealth. Historian Arnold Toynbee attributes the collapse of 21 different civilizations to just two causes: concentration of wealth, and inadequate response to changing circumstances including changing environment. Today, the inequality is the highest in the history of capitalism and cannot be ignored anymore. Barely 1 percent of families own more than 40 percent of wealth in the United States; the bottom 20 percent have just 3 percent share of income. Not only does this disparity have social consequences such as crime and divorce rates, as the low-income family finds it hard to cope with day-to-day pressures of life, it also has very harsh economic consequences. A very likely cause of Donald Trump's victory was his voter base from the Rust Belt. They had lost their high-paying manufacturing jobs, many of them losing their wife and kids because they could not support the family and losing the house due to mortgage default.

Professors Raghuram Rajan and Ravi Batra[2, 3, 12] have argued that consumer debt problems arose because of growing inequality in the 1990s and 2000s. They both were critical of Alan Greenspan who ignored this development and fostered a culture of reckless indebtedness. As wages stagnated and Greenspan brought interest rates down to fight the onslaught of stock market crashes, consumers and homeowners increasingly borrowed money in a desperate attempt to maintain their lifestyles. The end result was a credit binge, a housing boom, and eventual housing collapse. But because of stagnant wages, profits went sky-high, and so did executive compensation and income and wealth disparities. Financial institutions and their executives profited the most by creating casinos on Wall Street, literally.

Conclusion

I am not sure if we could come out of the current abyss employing the conventional methods unless we have some sort of revolution. Some of the reforms I have outlined earlier should reduce inequality, if it is done with discipline and strong will.

For instance:

- Balancing our trade by compelling trade-surplus nations to follow free trade, and revalue their currencies, will revive U.S. manufacturing and create high-paying jobs. As the middle-class salaries goes up, inequality would fall.
- Restraining money growth will reduce inflation and the cost of living, which in turn should maintain the purchasing power more or less unchanged.
- Repealing financial deregulation will induce banks to pay attention to their real purpose, which is to lend money to needy businesses. This will stimulate investment as well as high wage employment and the economy. When banks no longer are able to make money from financial derivatives, they will have to go back to lending, to make a profit and lubricating the economy.
- Oil and commodities speculation will fall if banks are not permitted to use people's deposits for nonlending activities. This will also help the middle class. Thus, the reforms suggested previously should tend to mitigate income and wealth disparities.

I need to explain few important attributes of nature, pertinent to this chapter. Formation of clusters, usually for self-preservation, is a natural phenomenon. Blood clots at microlevel, tribalism at macro level, and galaxies at astronomical level are examples of clusters. Clustering is an uneven distribution of elements or events. Clustering is the cause of likes, dislikes, hate crimes, old boys club, and empire building. Clusters are therefore, not only material but also psychic patterns. Nature's nature, within clusters, is also to create pairs of opposites, in every field of human endeavor. The objective in life for everyone is to learn to bring harmony, balance, and complementarity between the opposites to transcend to higher level. Another way to express is to build bridges to remove hard polarization. This is basically the same as Buddha's middle path discovered several millennia ago.[6, 7]

These attributes of nature suggest that we should not allow imbalances to occur, and if they do emerge, we should not wait till a calamity arises, bringing misery for a long time.

The federal deficit no longer generates the return it did in the 1960s. At that time a 1 percent deficit was associated with an annual GDP growth of 4.5 percent. From Bush-Cheney to Obama-Biden, the deficit has exceeded 10 percent of GDP, yet growth has averaged below 3 percent.

From March 9, 2009 to now there has been a relentless rise in share prices, spawning yet another bubble, which is nothing new as such events have been occurring with regularity in the United States and the rest of the world. There were stock market bubbles in the 1980s, then in the 1990s, and then between 2004 and 2007. They had all crashed, but major investors had been bailed out.

The Dow Jones Index (Dow) has almost quadrupled in about seven years, from about 6,700 to above 24,000. Is the economy booming? No. What separates this bubble from all others is:

- It happened in an environment of around 2.5 percent GDP growth.
- It is happening even as General Motors and Chrysler declared bankruptcy and had to be bailed out.
- However, share markets are ignoring all these negative factors and keep rising.

The Dow and S&P 500 peaked this year (2018) around 26,000 and 2,800 for this cycle. The plunge protection team, PPP (plunge protection team that includes officers of Fed, stock exchanges, and the U.S. Treasury secretary was established in 1987) has been increasingly manipulative to keep the market within a certain band. It was devastating to all big investors (nongovernmental organizations (NGOs), retirement funds etc.) after the 2008 crash (S&P low was around 700) when PPP lost the control. Treasury Secretary Paulson had to bend down to his knees begging speaker Pelosi for a huge Quantitative Easing (QE). They have done well during last nine years helping top 5 percent at the expense of small savers, wage earners and "small" retirees with the zero interest rate (ZIRP) and negative interest rate (NIRP) policy.

So the question is, with "volatile" Trump geopolitics and so many black swans floating around, I am not sure how long PPP can maintain the market without substantial correction. Needless to say, black swans include the increasing deficits and debt that causes increasing cost on the debt of over $21 trillion, uncontrolled Medicare and social security cost, and the trade war. It appears that the latest bubble, and perhaps the worst in history, will also burst like all others before, and then the economy will be even worse.

What will the Fed do when there is another crash, which is inevitable, because every bubble bursts eventually? It is clear that we need to reduce the federal deficit, restrain money growth, enforce anti-trust laws, end financial deregulation, perhaps even return to gold standard, and, above all, eliminate the trade deficit, as Trump is trying hard to do, by declaring China and other trade surplus areas as currency manipulators. We need to introduce competition wherever possible, including and specifically the functioning of the government as they have done so in Scandinavian countries. We need to have gold and silver as competing currency to check money printing. When such reforms are introduced, global imbalances should decline, and economic policy will conform to the infallible laws of nature. U.S. manufacturing base will revive. Prosperity will then return and the living standard will rise for all, not just for the wealthy few.

I would also like to see more balance and harmony between the opposites of every pair that would ultimately complement each other.[9] More needs to be done to avoid polarization and build bridges between feuding opposites. The modern world is dominated by a Western world-view, as a result of Western jingoism. But the legacy of both, the East and the West, has been the power of knowledge and the growth within through intro-spection. For a solution to inequalities, a clear perception of the problems is first necessary. It seems every pair: liberals and conservatives, labor and management, paper currencies and inflation hedges, and many more—all seem to be out of balance. Then there are problems of corruption at the highest levels and Gaponomics implying widening gap between the rich and the poor in Western countries, featured in the March 12, 2012 issue of *The Economist*.

What we need is life education, not merely professional education without morality, which has led us to an exploitative world of today. We need education of the heart. I hope greater emphasis is put on such education at every level. Education that unifies humanity, but maintains individual autonomy, which stimulates the highest level of creativity, should become our universal currency, the currency of the mind, together with the currency anchored to gold and silver needed for a sound econ-omy and a healthy body—with hopefully very positive results.[5, 6, 7]

References

[1] Baker, R.W. 2005. *Capitalism's Achilles Heel*. Englewood Cliffs, NJ: John Wiley & Sons.

[2] Batra, R. 2005. *Greenspan's Fraud*. New York, NY: Palgrave Macmillan.

[3] Batra, R. 1996. *The Great American Deception*. New York, NY: John Wiley & Sons.

[4] Das, S. 2010. *Traders Guns & Money*. London: Pearson.

[5] Doshi, N. 2009. *Transcendence, Saving Us from Ourselves*. New York, NY: Ithaca Press.

[6] Doshi, N. 2011. *Economics and Nature*. Los Angeles, CA: Nalanda International and New Delhi: DK Printworld.

[7] Doshi, N. 2016. *Light with No Shadow*. San Diego, CA: Balboa Press.

[8] Jastram, W.R. 1977. *The Golden Constant*. New York, NY: Ronald Press Publication, John Wiley & Sons Inc.

[9] Jung, C.G. 1942. "A Physical Approach to the Dogma of the Trinity." *CW* 11, no. 1958, pp. 169–295

[10] Koch, R. 1998. *The 80/20 Principle*. New York, NY: Doubleday.

[11] Mandlebrot, B., and R. Hudson. 2004. *The (Mis) Behavior of Markets*. New York, NY: Basic Books.

[12] Rajan, R.G. 2010. *Fault Lines*. Princeton & Oxford: Princeton University Press.

[14] Rajan, R.G., and L. Zingales. 2003. *Saving Capitalism from the Capitalists*. New York, NY: Crown Business.

[15] Taleb, N.N. 2007. *The Black Swan: The Impact of the Highly Improbable*, 2 vols. New York, NY: Random House.

CHAPTER 12

Free Markets in a Fully Automated Economy

Apek Mulay

Introduction

In my 2018 book *New Macroeconomics*, I discussed about a revolutionary new wage-gap theory for ensuring a sustainable progress of the economy. There, I called upon new business models to ensure fair competition, cooperation, and collaboration between different entities in an ecosystem. Eventually, as everything gets automated, machines will take over most of the work done by human beings. Additionally, it will be the big data that will be driving the growth of the economy. From automated cars to wearable Internet of Things (IoTs), a huge amount of data will be generated—some data will be structured but a lot of data would remain unstructured. Given the exploding growth of data generated in recent years, *The Economist* magazine concluded that "the world's most valuable resource is no longer oil, but data."[5]

Data analytics will revolutionize the entire global economy reforming the existing business models and supply chains. However, just like antitrust laws have not been enforced in recent past, which resulted into huge mergers and acquisitions (M&As) in every industry, the present business models in today's data-driven economy have also resulted in oligopolies such as Amazon, Facebook, and Google. Hence, *The Economist* rightly concludes that the new data economy demands a new approach to antitrust rules.[5] This chapter educates the reader about significant aspects of this new data economy, the new business models that are reshaping the new economy, and most importantly, how should the new business models be structured to bring about a next golden age in global economy driven by artificial intelligence (AI). This would bring about a renaissance in global economy.

The Big Data Business: From Business Intelligence (BI) to Artificial Intelligence (AI)

The combination of intuition and domain knowledge has and will always be instrumental in driving businesses forward. However, data-based decision making makes it more accurate. As more and more data get generated, this data is used for obtaining BI. The term "business intelligence" (BI) refers to technologies, applications, and practices for the collection, integration, analysis, and presentation of business information. The purpose of BI is to support better business decision making. The main challenge with BI is that there is no closed loop formation whereby the generated insights leads to changes in key performance indices (KPIs).[9] Business analytics (BA) fills up this gap by forming a closed loop by means of integrating BA output and models as interventions into business processes, thereby permitting measurement of business benefits.[9]

Statistical analysis is performed on data to get inferential statistics and these are used to improve and to optimize decisions and boost performance of a business. The profession of business analytics is not restricted to just seeking BI but to perform advanced analysis like predictive analytics and prescriptive analytics. It becomes critical that management assumes full responsibility for a business analytics initiative in collaboration with relevant business units.[9] The cooperation of the latter is crucial, because operations and outcomes of such an initiative will have a direct impact on the operations of respective business units. This highlights the importance of a cooperative and collaborative ecosystem for success of any business analytics initiative because business analytics relies on defining business objectives that often affect more than individual departments, and because it is useful to use data from across the organization. Business analytics champions are those who understand the business environment and the fundamentals of the discipline. Failure is an important part of business analytics process, which helps the analytics team to learn from failures.

In business analytics, it is important to note that data mining capabilities and methodologies can be applied to structured numerical data but can also be applied to text data, called as text mining.[9] Insurance companies make use of text mining to identify fraudulent insurance claims. In text analytics, sometimes negative documents are written in positive language and vice versa. Hence, it becomes necessary to measure sentiment analysis to understand how language is used especially if the text is too long to read and make that judgment manually. Identifying customer sentiment could also help in identifying opportunities for cross-sell and upsell.[9] Also, having a positive sentiment toward a brand or company increases the likelihood of success.

Roy H. Williams, a marketing consultant and author, says "the first step in exceeding your customer's expectations is to know those expectations." Analysis of social media data provides insights about mood swings and changing preferences of users.[9] Based on these behavioral characteristics, companies can provide relevant services and provide tailored products to social media users. In this way, effectiveness of marketing strategy can be measured by its ability to maximize the number of customers who buy in, while minimizing marketing costs. With the help of big data, the first and perhaps most crucial step in devising any marketing strategy is understanding customer's profile and behavior as well as uncovering insights of preferences and choices across those specific types of customer segments using predictive analytics.

Predictive analytics (which is a part of big data analysis) makes use of linear regression, tree analysis, cluster analysis, and multidimensional analysis to perform advanced statistical analysis on data to obtain predictions like customer churn rate, survival analysis, lifetime value analysis, and so on.[9] With predictive analytics, marketing divisions can perform up-sell, cross-sell, market basket analysis, and elasticity modeling to increase revenue from their existing clientele. Thus, data analytics offers new ways of generating additional insights to the businesses to increase their bottom-line profits from operations. On the other hand, prescriptive analysis performs optimization of data using linear programming and simulations on the existing data set to predict the most likely behavior to make next best offer, to optimize the inventory of business, to find the least costly path of transporting goods from source to destination, and so on.[9] The U.S. Internal Revenue Service (IRS) uses its predictive analytics tools and applications as a first step in investigating potential tax evasion, fraud, under-reporting, tax preparer noncompliance, and money laundering.[9]

The concept of AI has already been extensively covered in Chapter 2. With so much intelligence obtained from data analytics, with the help of machine learning, it is possible to make the machines intelligent enough to perform those tasks that in past were thought to be possible only by human beings. Today, companies are holding a lot of data called as "dark data" and trying to make some sense out of this data to draw some intelligence out of this data. As the field of business analytics is still evolving, many companies have already collected huge amounts of data even if they don't get much information from it with some hope that this collected data would prove to be a valuable resource for them in the near future. In next section, we shall try to understand the logic behind this massive data collection by data-driven companies.

Two-Sided Network: Data Platform Business Model

A two-sided network or data platform brings together user groups in a two-sided network. This new business model provides an infrastructure and rules that facilitate transactions between the two groups. As compared to a traditional value chain where value moves from right (cost) to left (revenue), a two-sided network incurs cost and revenue on both left and right. It incurs costs in serving both sides and can collect revenue from each side as well, although one side is always subsidized (pays much lower cost than the other). The value proposition for data platform for any user largely depends on number of users on the network's other side. The value grows as the platform matches demand on both sides. The users are willing to pay more for access to a bigger network, so the margins grow as user bases grow in a data platform business model.

Some of the examples of two-sided network indicating the subsidized side of the data platform is mentioned in the following.

As shown in the Table 12.1, both sides of a two-sided network receive and provide something. To elaborate further and to make it clear, the following figures show the data platform business model for a computer

Table 12.1 Examples of Two-Sided Network indicating subsidized and unsubsidized where unsubsidized side refers businesses, consumers, advertisers, clients, and so on, which have to pay money to support the business platform and the subsidized side refers to the users of platform who are subsidized in order to increase value for the platform by increased use of the platform resulting in more data available for analytics

Two-sided network	Subsidized side	Unsubsidized side
Windows/Macintosh PC operating systems	Application developers	Consumers
Google Inc., Yahoo Inc.	Searchers	Advertisers
Monster, Indeed, Recruit	Job seekers	Employers
AMCAT (Aspiring Minds Computer Adaptive Tests)	B2C clientele (job seekers, test takers, etc.)	B2B clientele (employers, universities, etc.)
Amazon.com	Shoppers using Amazon.com	Businesses advertising with Amazon.com
PatientsLikeMe (PLM)	Patients sharing health conditions	Pharmaceutical industry

adaptive test (CAT) company called *Aspiring Minds*. The business model of Aspiring Minds has enabled its corporate clients to scientifically assess, using machine learning and other advanced algorithms, the potential match between a job seeker and open positions with an employer.[6]

Aspiring Minds has experienced its success as business-to-business (B2B) entity, creating and selling technology products geared toward industry verticals. The company has designed adaptive tests to help its corporate clients make decisions based on these test results. Its B2B clients pay Aspiring Minds a fee for every candidate assessed or hired. Aspiring Minds also has a business-to-consumer (B2C) clientele and the company has been successful in generating revenues from its B2C clients equal to those from B2B clients by charging test takers a $15 fee at universities and technical institutes and at its own testing facilities throughout India.[6]

Thus, B2B strategy involved pursuing clients that had large hiring needs and servicing their human resources groups and hiring departments with skills assessments. The B2B clients would provide a demand for the assessment. Its B2C strategy involved convincing job seekers that Aspiring Minds skills rating would arm the job seeker with credentials that would ultimately enable them to find jobs above and beyond their conventional resume and experience.[6] It would boost their resume just like some accredited certifications recognized by the industry.

As shown in Figures 12.1 and 12.2, the data platform depends on a large number of subscribers to get more data and the number of subscribers is higher when the subscribers see a perceived value for them by means of contributing their data. Also, the non-subsidized side observe a lot of value in this business model when they can get more reliable understanding of data from its bigger sample size that provides better statistical measurements. Given these requirements of a two-sided network, we can understand why the companies like Facebook, Amazon, and Google are collecting as much data as possible and lot of that collected data is categorized as "dark data." Internet users freely and openly share personal sentiments, opinions, and complaints, either behind anonymous pseudonyms or even with real identity. The advantage of data platforms like Facebook and LinkedIn is that the data from these social media provides information about relationships between customers and even between customers and noncustomers. This way social network data adds a layer of connectivity information to the relationship of customers, noncustomers, and company as compared to just one-to-one relationship with customers.

These two-sided networks make use of consumer-driven data to offer analytical insights to the unsubsidized side. However, In today's existing corporate business model, the majority shareholders of these businesses are primarily external shareholders, or the company shares are concentrated into the hands of a very few company employees at the C-suite level, these businesses have a fiduciary obligation to provide high returns on investments (RoI) to their fewer numbered internal majority shareholders or large number of external shareholders. Hence, we have observed a lot of mergers and acquisitions (M&As) in big data business and formation of huge oligopolies in a very short time, resulting in a decrease of competition. Additionally, we have also observed insanely high valuations of some of these data companies at their initial public offering (IPO). I have already elaborated in all my previous books how monopoly capitalism is responsible for bringing the technological progress of Moore's law to a standstill. Hence, for a big data business to achieve its full potential, the tech industry must learn from the mistakes made in past and reform their

Two-Sided Platform Business Model

B2B Clients Value

- HR officers of Corporations were able to measure not only skills and knowledge but also personally and behavior traits of job seekers.

- Quantified employability based on better hiring decisions based on English Language, Analytical Skills, Subject Knowledge and personality traits of job seekers.

- Comprehensive assessment with customized scoring received based on needs.

B2B Clients Contribute

- Provided the required skills needed for prospective job applicants to succeed in work place.

- Paid for each job offer extended through AMCAT database, depending on hiring difficulty in a particular market.

Data Platform Business Model

B2C Clients/Job Seekers Contribute

- Pay $15 for taking Aspiring Minds Computer Adaptive Test (AMCAT)

- Tests taken at University or AMCAT testing centers.

Clients Value

- Students and job seekers secure jobs after graduation. Overcome low GPA barriers.

- University got access to Companies that did not recruit on campus leading to relationship between Universities and Employers.

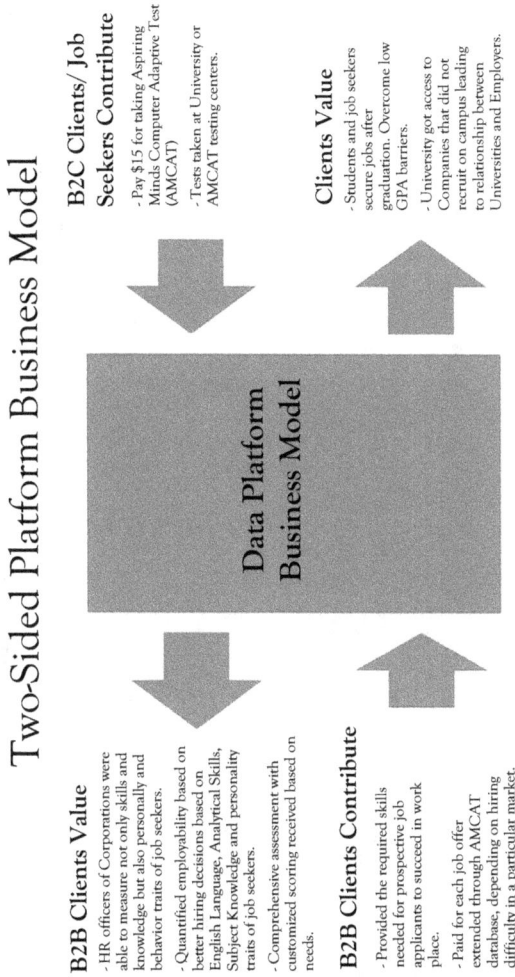

Figure 12.1 A two-sided network business model for 'Aspiring Minds'

Client Engagements

B2C Clients Contribute

- Current employees in corporations as well as prospective employees provide assessments to their managers as well as prospective employers.

B2C Clients Value

- Higher retention rate of employees due to higher success in their workplace (95% among large clients in India)
- Get assessment about their strengths and weaknesses and areas to develop for success.
- More chances of hiring at good companies irrespective of brand name of educational institution.

Aspiring Minds platform

R & D Team
- Refine algorithms based on how employees fared

B2B Corporate Clients Value

- Analytics results engage the B2B clients and show how they are benefitting from this assessment.
- Better hiring decisions based on better improvised machine learning algorithms.

B2B Corporate Clients Contribute

- Feedback on employees hired through Aspiring Minds Database.

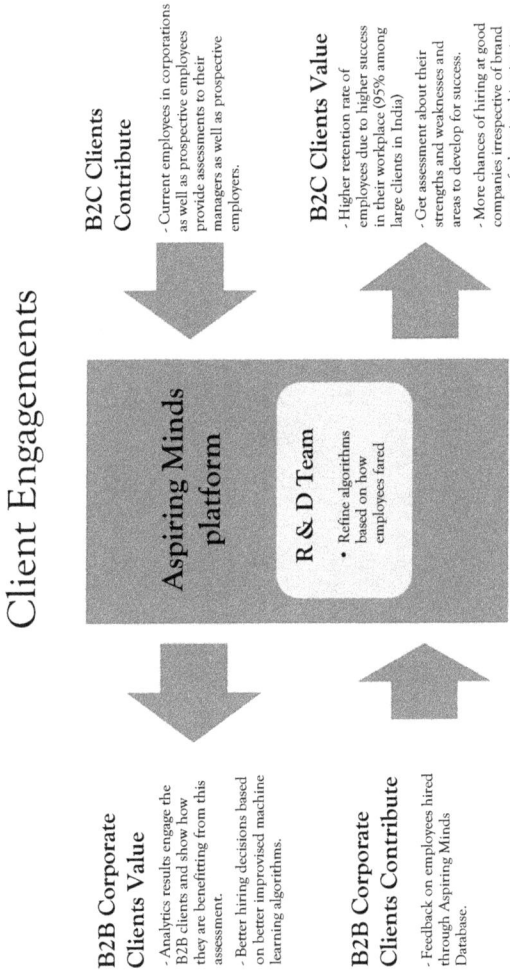

Figure 12.2 A two-sided network business model for Aspiring Minds for engagement with clients

business model. The data platforms should also comply with the existing macroeconomic parameters to ensure sustainability.

Two Key Factors Transforming Existing Business Models in Big Data Business

1. **Business Strategy and Its Relationship to Technology.**[7]

   In November 2013, Phillip Evans, in his speech at the TED institute (in partnership with Boston Consulting Group), made a bold prediction about the future of business strategy and he said that it starts with big data. Evans started off with the origins of business strategy with the thoughts of Bruce Henderson and Michael Porter. Henderson focused on doing more of same thing to get better and hence Henderson focused on the idea of concentrating mass against weakness, of overwhelming the enemy. This way, a military concept of strategy was introduced into the business world by Bruce Henderson. This is one of the key drivers behind the M&As that are happening in today's corporate world.

   Although Michael Porter agreed with what Henderson had to say, Porter believed that every business is composed of individual components and each of those entities must cooperate to minimize the transaction costs through improved efficiency. He called this as value chain of what holds the business together. Porter's idea of minimizing transaction costs through value chains have been the key drivers in the phenomenon of globalization where the high-cost manufacturing operations were moved offshore to the low labor-cost countries (LLCs) to minimize transaction costs, thereby making the value chains more efficient. According to Phillip Evans, it is primarily from these two intellectual giants that the whole premise of business strategy has evolved. One point to be noted is that the impacts of these two strategies on macroeconomics were not analyzed by either Bruce Henderson or Michael Porter.

   However, Evans argued in his speech that the glue that holds value chains together can break up (allowing them to separate) due to falling transaction costs due to a rapid progress of Moore's law and exponentially decreasing communication costs due to exploding growth of the Internet. This is causing vertical structure of organizations, resulting from business strategy practices recommended by Bruce Henderson and Michael Porter, to transform into a horizontal one because of plummeting transaction costs. Additionally, according to Evans, the polarization of scale economies allows for scalable communities to substitute traditional corporate production. Evans mentioned that the big data economy needs industry structures that will accommodate very different motivations, from the amateur motivations of people in communities to maybe the social motivations of infrastructure built by governments, or, for that matter, cooperative institutions built by companies that are otherwise competing, because that is the only way that they can get to scale in the big data business.

I would agree with Phillip Evans and also say that because Bruce Henderson and Michael Porter's business strategy did not take the consideration the operation of a businesses within parameters of macroeconomics, it has resulted into formation of oligopolies resulting into a loss of free markets as well as unsustainable trade deficits. But, for Evans suggestions of horizontal scalability to hold true, macroeconomic policies must ensure reorganization of supply chains and reforming the existing data platform business models such that free markets can thrive. This would also have to ensure that there is a robust growth of scalable communities and existing businesses are able to cooperate more rather than compete in this big data business.

2. General Data Protection Regulation (GDPR)

The European Union's (EU) GDPR took effect on May 25, 2018 and created new rules around users' consent to provide their data online and how that data is stored.[8] Prior to GDPR, a fast-spreading epidemic of data misuse incidents was largely overlooked by lawmakers, including breaches and data misuse at Yahoo, Facebook, Target, Equifax, and so on. Though each incident generated its own round of hearings and regulatory fines, basic privacy law has remained unchanged. GDPR is more of a hint at protectionism in EU technology policy since 2015 in a plan for "digital single market."[8] Under GDPR, data collection for European users, for example, would require frequent and explicit consent ("opt-in"), which could be withdrawn at any time "without detriment." So far, mining social media buzz has been increasingly used by governments, political parties, and other organizations, both commercial and noncommercial, to know what certain audiences think about them. The 2017 Cambridge Analytica scandal has exposed how this feature could be misused to bias 2016 U.S. presidential election results in world's richest democracy—the United States.[12]

Consumers have been granted a new right to take with them data deemed as personal, with the costs borne by the entity that collected it. The new rules also include an extended version of the so-called right to be forgotten (or "right to erasure," as it's now being called). The person to whom any information refers can demand removal of that data under a variety of conditions, including that the subject "objects" to further processing. GDPR definitions are vague but fines are astronomic (20 million Euros or 4 percent of annual global revenue, whichever is greater, for violations of most provisions).[8] While GDPR is certain to improve choice, control, and transparency for EU consumers, these new powers come with new responsibilities and new costs for users, not least of which are ballooning budgets for government data management and enforcement bureaucracies worldwide. More directly, users will face frequent interruptions to the flow of their online lives, forced to review, decide, and reconsider each element of information they enter.[14] In economic terms, every new mandatory disclosure, user control, and privacy "dashboard" introduces transaction costs into interactions that previously didn't have them.

Articles 7 and 8 of GDPR discuss about seeking consent of the subject's data, Articles 15 and 16 discuss about the accessibility of this data, Article 17 discusses about erasure of data and Articles 25 and 32 of GDPR cover the security and encryption of subject's data.[18] As shown in Figure 12.3, before GDPR became a law in European Union, it was possible for a company headquartered in Bangalore, India, and having its satellite office in Berlin, Germany, to make use of a third-party data server or its own server located in Seattle. However, after May 25, 2018, under the existing business model, companies that are not careful about handling the data of

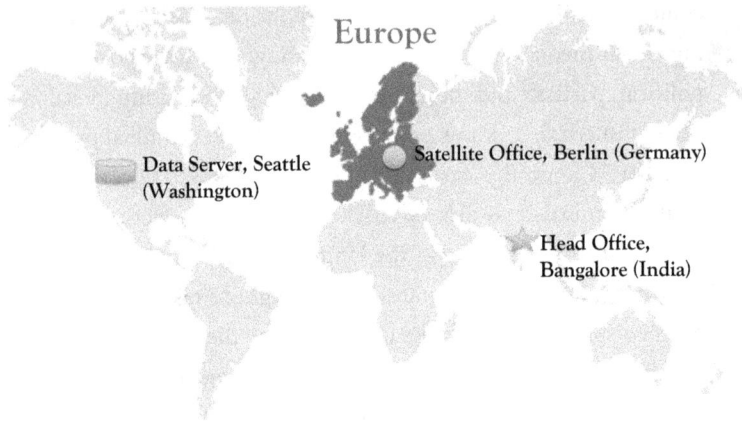

Figure 12.3 Globalized business model of MNCs prior to GDPR

Figure 12.4 Localized business model of MNCs post GDPR

their EU clients would be facing hefty fines. As a result of GDPR, in order to avoid huge penalties, data companies would prefer to keep the data of European consumers local as well as have local servers and analytical teams to draw insights from this European data as shown in Figure 12.4.

GDPR was the necessary evil to stop the MNCs like Facebook, Google, and LinkedIn from violating the macroeconomic parameters and transfer the most valuable resource ("data") from crossing borders and making monetary gains from it without knowledge of the platform users. Now that GDPR has become a law in Europe, it is just a matter of time that such a legislation would also become a reality in the United States and other parts of the world because of abuse of data privacy. Hence, regulations on Internet companies are one way to stop such unethical practices of sharing client's personal data with outsiders to do targeted marketing. However, free market capitalism calls for a smaller government size and lower regulations.[1] In that case, restricting the flow of data from EU citizens to move across EU borders and forcing the data companies to invest heavily in the EU to do business in Europe would result in data localization as compared to data globalization. Hence, such a move should be welcome by EU citizens with regards to protection of privacy of their personal data.

GDPR was a necessary step to prevent the rampant abuse of data privacy on data platforms effectively bringing about an end of industry self-regulation and there is an evidence of such abusive practices in the United States too. To give an example, in a recent court filing against Facebook in the Supreme Court of San Mateo, it was mentioned that Mark Zuckerberg weaponized the data of one-third of the planet's population to cover up his failure to transition Facebook's business from desktop computers to mobile ads before the market became aware that Facebook's financial projections in its 2012 IPO filings were false.[12] This was possible for Mark Zuckerberg due to his control over the Facebook platform being the sole owner of huge number of shares (like a dictator) at Facebook. Hence, the existing platform business model of Facebook must transition to a free market economy such that control goes into the hands of majority of company employees as compared to a few minority in the company. This is because the majority of employees would take decisions in best interest of their majority shareholders and hence the company.[1] The decision making would become more democratic.

However, under GDPR the additional disclosure information might become overwhelming information for the users of data platform and the questions that matter most could get lost. The consumers might eventually just accept everything or reject everything, effectively achieving exactly opposite of what was intended to be achieved out of this new law. Additionally, GDPR compliance would become a huge burden for data companies and changes the way data platforms could have in fact benefitted the users of platform by means offering a solutions through targeted marketing. GDPR requires that companies send e-mails to people on their mailing list who have never bought anything and seek their permission in order to continue sending them e-mails.[8]

This certainly affects the businesses that depend heavily on gathering and tapping customer data. GDPR will prove to be a burden in terms of compliance for data companies in the EU. Additionally, because of globalization, it would be difficult for platforms operating in other parts of world to not face fines for their operations in EU unless they begin decentralizing their global operations and segregating data as per compliance requirements of GDPR. In one way, GDPR is a blessing because it could lead to focus on making best use of local data for local economic development. However, because of larger bureaucracy from government regulations, the full potential of data analytics cannot be unleashed. According to internal research from a digital marketing firm Huge Inc., about 38 percent of Americans are ignoring the permission e-mails, and 23 percent have used them as an opportunity to unsubscribe. As a result, some e-mail marketers stand to lose 80 percent of their marketing lists due to GDPR.[14]

There is a high possibility of law suits between EU citizens and the big MNCs such as Facebook and Google. On top of everything, the advancements in data analytics through the power of Google Analytics or Adobe Analytics cannot be fully utilized for the growth of a business as well as to meet the needs of the consumers. Hence, new ideas are needed to unleash the potential of new advancements in the field of data analytics but at the same time protect data privacy and achieve self-regulation. This is precisely what I discuss in the subsequent section because GDPR has enforced a kind of self-regulation in the economy as chief information officer (CIO) and chief compliance officer (CCO) of data platforms would be required to constantly monitor the compliance policies in order to avoid hefty fines. In order to unleash the power of data analytics, data platforms must be scalable such that the majority shareholders should be able to make decisions in the best interests of subsidized portion of the data platform, which contributes data to the platform in order to offer better and more accurate analytical capabilities for the business.

For data platforms to be able to provide more value to their users, they need to have more users. By means of having a neo-cooperative outlook of an organization where majority shareholders of big data platforms are employees as compared to outside investors, these employee-owned businesses would not only have much better framework to protect data privacy but at the same time such a business model has potential to observe an increase in the number of users due to an increase in the trust of their users. As a result, it would be possible to draw better analytics because of a larger pool of users on these neo-cooperative business platforms as compared to their competitors who may not follow the neo-cooperative business model. Hence, there would a fair competition among data business platforms to compete for consumer data by having an employee-owned business model.

On June 28, 2018, California governor Jerry Brown signed data privacy legislation aimed at giving consumers more control over how companies collect and manage their personal information.[17] Under this proposal, large companies, such as those with data on more than 50,000 people, would be required, starting in 2020, to let consumers view the data they have collected on them, request deletion of data, and opt out of having the data sold to third parties.[17] Additionally, companies would be required to provide equal service to consumers who exercise such rights under the law. Each violation would carry a $7,500 fine.[17] Although the law applies to only users in California, it is surely going to have ramifications on data companies doing business across the state borders. In fact, I would consider this law to be GDPR version of United States. This calls for more decentralization of business practices as well as neo-cooperative business model for data-driven companies. Additionally, the law in California would encourage companies to have data of less than 50,000 people providing an incentive to have a smaller size of data companies.

Mass Capitalism's Business Model for a Fully Automated Economy

While AI is a very broad field, the investments that would drive the near future of global economy would be primarily in machine learning. One of the applications of machine learning has been very briefly elaborated in the Aspiring Minds data platform.[6] Because of a tremendous need of machine learning algorithms in future enterprise applications such as natural language processing (NLP), image recognition, fraud detection in the financial industry, classification, and so on, the global semiconductor industry is expected to make significantly huge investments in chips that can deliver such machine learning applications. The semiconductor chips should be able to store and process such large amounts of data. This would give a further incentive to increase yield on semiconductor wafers at sub-nanometer technologies. Although the AI applications are the software applications, they must be able to function effectively with hardware. Hence, the holistic technology ecosystem should focus on sustainable progress of both hardware and software capabilities. While software development will drive technological progress, the semiconductor industry can make huge contributions to produce state-of-the-art chips that help in machine learning applications such as field programming gate arrays (FPGAs) and graphic processing units (GPUs). This is a clear evidence of upcoming growth in labor productivity from the use of machines.

As shown in Figure 12.5, the productivity gains significantly outpace compensation in the tech industry. This has caused the progress of semiconductor industry to come to a standstill as elaborated in my previously published books.[1, 2, 3] However, with further increase in productivity from AI applications, the gap between wages and productivity is expected to grow even further. The horizontal line is a reference line noting the range where productivity equals compensation. There are also industries where productivity lags compensation. The industries that have lower growth in productivity as compared to growth in compensation should make heavy use of AI and automation to raise employee productivity. However, tech industry where rising productivity significantly outpaces wages should follow three-tier business model to ensure that wages keep pace with productivity and they can reduce the working hours of employees progressively or devote excess hours toward research and development (R&D)

Avg. Annual Productivity v/s Avg. Annual Compensation by Industry (1987–2015)

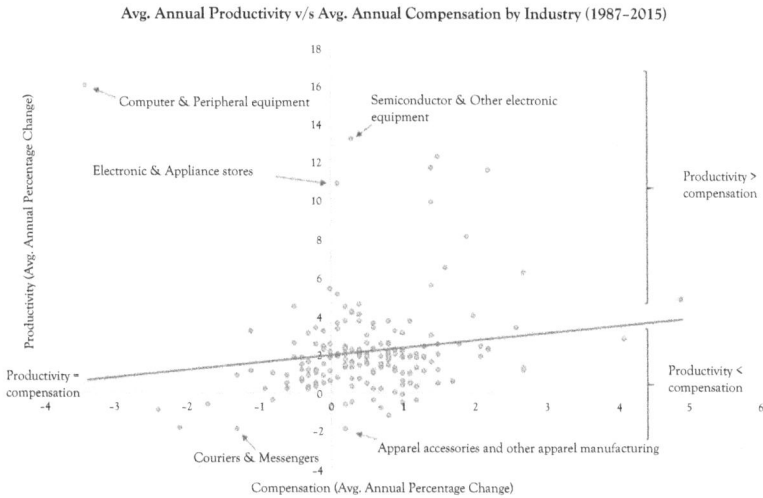

Figure 12.5 Average annual productivity and average annual compensation by industry, 1987–2015

Source: U.S. Bureau of Labor Statistics.

for furthering technological progress. This way economic balance can be maintained so that supply and demand grow and fall in proportion.

In my 2014 book *Mass Capitalism*, I presented a three-tier business model for the economy, which would ensure that wages would catch up with productivity with a minimal government intervention. Coming from semiconductor industry background and having a solid understanding of macroeconomics, I was able to present a detailed picture of how the entire industry should be structured for a sustainable economic progress. I expanded this model to cover the Internet of Things (IoT) in my 2015 book *Sustaining Moore's Law*.[2] In my 2016 book titled *How Information Revolution Remade Business and the Economy*, I presented an overall picture of how the entire technological ecosystem should function for ensuring that automation can progress sustainably for the overall economy.[3] Later in my 2018 volume titled *New Macroeconomics*, I presented to readers how free markets are feasible despite automation and there is no need of doles such as universal basic income (UBI) in an automated economy if true free markets are made a possibility.[13]

In this chapter, I envision how data platform business model should fit into the overall technological ecosystem such that progress of artificial intelligence (AI) and robotics would become a boon for a bright future of humanity. This business model presents a holistic picture of how businesses should function in a fully automated economy to have minimal government regulation and maximum job creation. As a matter of fact, business analytics derived from business operations would be adding a tremendous value to this three-tier business model, which primarily focuses on ensuring a steady growth of both supply and demand, to restore an economic balance.

Professor Robert Kaplan at Harvard Business School says that the consistent alignment of capabilities and internal processes with the customer value proposition is the core of any strategy execution.[9]

While marketing analytics focuses on the customer-facing aspects of benefits derived from implementing business analytics, the operational analytics provides the benefits of business analytics by marrying the customer-facing "front office" business analytics with internal or "back office" business analytics.[9]

As a founder of a cooperative e-commerce start-up Calcutta Handicraft (http://calcuttahandicraft.in/), our inventory management team as well as shipping team in India faced their most challenging roles in the optimization of exact inventory for the business. E-commerce businesses are today worried about outrunning their existing inventory due to demand spikes or not being able to sell all the inventory adding to the inventory costs and hence resulting in significant drop in profit from operation. The main goals in inventory management are optimizing the inventory so as to minimize the inventory holding costs and wastage, while ensuring that right items are available when needed to ensure that there is maximization of potential profits from operations and minimization of any negative impacts such a delays for prospective customers. This challenge is because of an increased demand uncertainty during periods of rising demand whereby there was a growth in orders for downstream participants due to an increase in the number of orders. On the other hand, during periods of falling demand, orders decreased or stopped, thereby not reducing inventory. This is a well-known business challenge for any e-commerce business. In business terminology, this is called a "bullwhip effect," which describes the amplification in the demand uncertainty as one moves upstream in supply chain and farther away from the consumer.[9]

While operational analytics can help in flattening out the 'bullwhip effect' as much as possible, I believe that there would still be significant amount of overproduction without the presence of three-tier business model as described and demonstrated in Figure 12.6. While predictive analytics can forecast the required stock level as well as type of inventory, prescriptive analytics can help integrate forecasts within larger ecosystem to optimize the logistics for any data driven business. The AI, robotics, and chatbots would help right from interacting with customers to fetching orders. However, as explained in my previous books, to avoid layoffs for businesses, there should be no overproduction for businesses. Business analytics can help in adjusting inventory, but business analytics cannot handle the cyclical nature of economy. Economy goes in cycles and even with an added knowledge of operational analytics, an astute judgment in business should always consider the "unknown unknowns," also known as "act of God" or "black swans," which are unpredictable by humans and machines alike.[9] However, by restructuring the entire business model of industry to fit into the three-tier business model, it is possible to minimize the overproduction and hence layoffs by taking proactive measures with the help of data analytics.

This three-tier business model would also be able to shorten the timeframe from failure detection to intervention, as well as maximize the ability to detect true events and to minimize false alerts with use of data analytics. In addition to failure detection, predictive maintenance is possible using data analytics by analyzing the various conditions of a single asset such as sensors, logs, ongoing operations, and so on, to predict when failures are likely to occur. Besides, since the data platforms are neo-cooperatively owned, they would earn the trust of their customers and provide more value to their users while protecting privacy of their data with a minimal necessity of any kind of government intervention.

In the three-tier business model shown in Figure 12.6, on the right-hand side for the "manufacturing sector," we have a lights-out wafer fab where all the semiconductor manufacturing steps from dicing and cleaning wafers to lithography and metal deposition are completely automated from the start to the finish. With the use of data-analytics, key performance indices (KPIs) can be set-up to meet key business requirements (KBRs) to improve the efficiency of operation of a lights-out wafer fab.

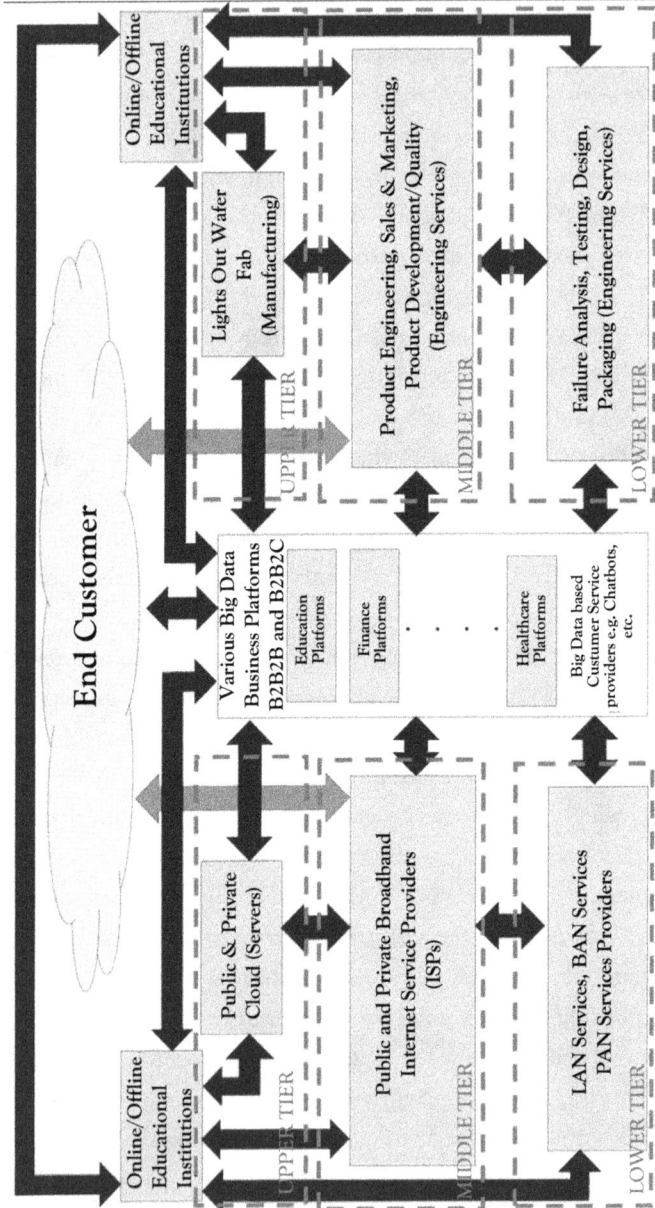

Figure 12.6 A Three-tier (tiers identified by dashed lines) business model for a fully-automated economy based on Mass Capitalism

The robotic automation that would move the production of wafers from the beginning to the end will generate a lot of data, which can be processed to obtain operational analytical insights in order to streamline the business operation. More details about the upper tier business model can be referenced to my book *Mass Capitalism*.[1]

The middle industrial tier will consist of robots, which would use the analytical insights from lights-out wafer fab to tweak process improvements as well as feed into the specific customer's (B2B or B2C) needs of the wafer fab. The middle industrial tier will use historical user data to derive marketing insights that would help companies perform customer analytics and help in the growth of business. While most operations would be automated, marketing is one aspect of the business that cannot be completely automated as it needs some human interaction, but marketers can use web analytics to increase the conversion rate of their customers as well as to analyze the changes in consumer behavior. The middle-industrial tier will also feed the customer requirements to the designing, packaging, and testing facilities at the lower industrial tier.

At the lower industrial tier, there are small businesses that do custom design based on the needs of the middle industrial tier. The small design facilities bring about innovations in their designs. The assembly and packaging facilities help to put together the chips inside a package. Robots would be replacing many of these operations too in the near future. Additionally, there would be testing facilities that would do on-demand testing on packaged chips and feed the generated test data to the middle industrial tier. In this way, in a fully automated economy, the middle industrial tier will be the most critical tier holding together the upper and lower industrial tiers. Additionally, the middle industrial tier would also be able to connect with rest of the economy.

On the left-hand side of this three-tier business model, we have the three-tier model for the "services sector." In this sector, we have the public as well as private cloud servers at the upper tier. This layer plays an important role in the storage and retrieval of large amount of digital data into and out of the servers, database management technologies such as MySQL, MongoDB, and HDFS (Hadoop Distributed File System) could be used depending on the business scenario as every technology

262   ECONOMIC RENAISSANCE IN THE AGE OF ARTIFICIAL INTELLIGENCE

has its advantages and disadvantages when used in a specific scenario. We have covered these technologies in a detail in Chapter 2.

The middle industrial tier would consist of broadband network of fiber optic cables as well as several IoT gadgets, which would help in collecting huge volumes of data from businesses and clients (B2B and B2C).[2] There would be a decentralized economic planning to not just comply with the future requirements such as GDPR to protect consumer data but also make it possible for local data to be analyzed to gain insights and drive local economic development. The Internet of Things (IoT), computer networks such as local area network (LAN), body area network (BAN), personal area network (PAN), and so on, form the lower tier of the service sector. This tier can feed data from IoT to middle industrial tier as well as get inputs from B2B and B2C clientele. The classification of different tiers in economy can be done by breaking up giant oligopolies by enforcing anti-trust laws.

The big data platforms are sandwiched between the manufacturing sectors and service sectors. As explained previously, the various big data platforms provide a lot of value for a fully automated economy. In fact, data platforms will play a major role in helping consumers drive the growth of the economy. These big data platforms will revolutionize every sector of the economy. Some of the different of B2B2B and B2B2C data platforms are:

1. Aspiring Minds, which uses machine learning for quantifying employability;
2. Modak Analytics, which uses data analytics to offer affordable analytical services to SMEs;
3. PatientsLikeMe (PLM), which offers a better a trustworthy platform to improve care for patients, and so on.

However, for the aforementioned data platforms to become sustainable, it is essential that they focus not just on data inputs from customers that drive decisions but at the same time these data platforms make decisions that are in the best interests of their clientele rather than a few outside investors. Hence, the platform business model should be structured such that the majority of shareholders are the employees of the platform. This would also ensure that the employees take decisions for the company, which are in the best interests of the company employees first and then the outside investors. This would also ensure that majority shareholders would be unwilling to share confidential and private information of data platform users with any third party for short terms monetary gains. Additionally, the owners of data platform (majority of employees) would ensure maximum customer satisfaction and customer retention leading to the growth of the business.

This three-tier business model would enhance more collaboration between the different participants of an ecosystem. Even if the economy is fully automated, the three-tier business model would minimize overproduction of goods into the economy and hence minimize unemployment. The services offered by data platforms would ensure maximum customer satisfaction. When robots do most of the work, it is obvious that the need for human labor would be minimized. Hence, human beings would have ample of free time and with this fully automated economy, the economy would always remain in balance.

However, not all human beings will quickly find no work to do. The purchasing power of a person would greatly depend on what value he or she adds to the society. As mentioned in my 2016 volume, *How Information Revolution Remade the Business and the Economy*, the minimum necessities and maximum amenities would play a major role in deciding the purchasing power of individuals in a free market economy.[3] Hence, people with high purchasing power would be able to afford robots to do most of their work and find more free time. However, the human society should gradually also increase the purchasing power of other members of society for them to be able to afford to buy robots in order to increase their leisure.

Economic Model for Accurate Predictive Analytics

On a microeconomic level, the goal of any model building is to shorten the time from failure detection to intervention, as well as to minimize false alerts. Lagging proactive indicators are measurements that indicate partial failure by means of sensing a failure in braking performance. Predictive maintenance is based on analyzing the various conditions of a single event such as sensors, logs, ongoing operations, and so on, to predict when failures are likely to occur. Predictive maintenance capabilities lead to maintenance optimization, considering risk, required skill sets, required service parts, and various other considerations, while minimizing maintenance costs and/or downtimes.[9]

By analyzing past problems, it is possible to optimize maintenance schedules to account for risk and required skill set with the end goal of minimizing operational costs and disruption and of maximizing performance and operating conditions. Unknown events might have precursors of unusual behavior to indicate a change in the normal mode of operation. Modeling normal behavior for a business is traditionally done using methods such as survival analysis.[9] However, economists have also derived equations to take into consideration the impacts of macroeconomics.

The following model is obtained from the Appendix section of Professor Ravi Batra's 2015 book *End Unemployment Now*.[4] This model is extremely useful for regression analysis as well as other advanced econometric analysis to make forecasts using data with a high accuracy. It is possible to develop a forecasting model based on these equations that can help build chatbots to proactively provide intimations to businesses and government organizations to take precautionary measures to estimate the rate of profits as well as to minimize the problems of overproduction in the economy. The Appendix of *End Unemployment Now* covers a logical derivation of these equations. These equations have a lot of business value for economic forecasting using big data analytics. They can be used for operational analytical purposes.

Any business or government would greatly benefit from having an accurate forecast of overproduction in an economy. Having knowledge of overproduction can help minimize the layoffs or act proactively to minimize the unemployment in the economy through quick economic reforms. Businesses can cut down on production requirements if they gauge that there is an overproduction in the economy. In Chapter 6 of my book *New Macroeconomics*, I offered a concrete evidence of how wage-gap theory is a complete economic theory and includes best ideas from both classical and Keynesian models making *New Macroeconomics* novel.[13] According to the wage gap theory of Professor Batra, the overproduction in a closed economy can be estimated with best accuracy using the equation

Overproduction, $X = AS - AD = wL\ [\beta - (1 + \alpha)] - CB - GD$ (1)

where A = average Product of Labor

L = level of employment

w = real wage

α = response of investment to consumer spending

$\beta = A/w$ = wage gap

CB = consumer borrowing

GD = government debt

AS = aggregate supply

AD = aggregate demand

The overproduction in an open economy can be estimated using the equation

Overproduction, $X = wL\ [\beta - (1 + \alpha)\ (1 - \sigma)] - CB - GD + \sigma T$ (2)

where A = average product of labor

L = level of employment

w = real wage

α = response of investment to consumer spending

σ = a positive fraction, which is a function of exchange rate, foreign GDP, and so on.

$\beta = A/w$ = wage Gap

CB = consumer borrowing

GD = government debt

AS = aggregate supply

AD = aggregate demand

T = trade deficit

There is also an equation to measure the profits in a macroeconomy and observe what is needed for profits to rise in wake of growing wage gap. The profits can be calculated using

$$\text{Profits} = AL - wL - \text{Unsold Goods} \qquad (3)$$

where A = average product of labor
L = level of employment
w = real wage

Science and Technology: An Unmixed Blessing

In previous chapter 11, the author has illustrated an important aspect of nature that something positive must be associated with something negative. Why must any positive development must be associated with a negative movement? The reason lies in the very nature of this universe, which exists in a vibrational flow balanced by positive and negative forces. Our earth and the atmosphere surrounding it are finite. Any positive waves in this finite realm will have to be counterbalanced by a negative wave. Therefore, any invention, creating a positive wave of physical comfort is matched by a corresponding negative wave leading to discomfort. In view of the interdependent nature of the physical world, it is not surprising that the results of new technology will be exactly counterbalanced by its side effects. Therefore, if life becomes easier in some respects, it will become harder in other aspects. No one can laud science and technology as an unmixed blessing.

Today, we see that human beings are suffering several mental and emotional issues. Mass shootings in the United States have become extremely common. Just by May 17, 2018, there have already been over 100 mass shootings in the United States in the year 2018 alone.[10] This shows growing mental health issues in one of the technologically most advanced countries on this planet and there is an urgent need to address this issue without any further delay. Hence, it was important to have readers understand how to overcome these mental health issues in our human society with a proper understanding of biopsychology and role that psycho-economics plays in overall macroeconomic stability. The author has elaborated on this topic further in Chapter 10 on meditation and consciousness. The real barometer of progress in the ultimate analysis must be the mental pleasure, which is really nothing, but a mental vibration expressed through the relaxation of the nerves; that is, pleasure is nothing but a mental vibration emitted by relaxed nerves. When the nerves are under tension, the vibration generated in the mind is called pain. In evaluating the impact of science, people usually focus on the convenience it has provided, while ignoring the nervous tension it has created in our lives. Hence, even pleasure in mental realm is accompanied by its negative aspect of pain in that realm.

According to late Shrii Prabhat Ranjan Sarkar's philosophy of neohumanism, in the inner psychic movement of human beings, their existential awareness is completely rhythmic.[15] Some of what happens in outer world is adjusted in inner physic existence and some is not. Whenever there is a maladjustment between the two, one feels some distress. Sometimes people feel more comfortable in the company of some people and feel uncomfortable in company of others. When external rhythm is in sync with internal rhythm, then people feel comfortable; else they feel distress. There exist a lot of mental disorders when there is a lack of adjustment between the internal and external worlds. The technological advancements achieved by humanity have resulted in maladjustment of speed between their internal and external world causing a clash. As the clash is felt more on psychic realm than physical realm, an increasing number of people are losing their mental balance.

Integrating Spiritual Progress with Scientific and Technological Progress[11]

In Chapter 10, the author has elaborated on the importance of meditation and higher spiritual practices. I do not wish to delve into that topic. However, I would like to offer my two cents on why there is an ever-increasing need for the profession of economics to integrate spiritual progress with economic progress. *Mass Capitalism* gives an impetus to take into consideration overall human progress—physical progress, intellectual progress as well as spiritual progress. Spirituality is an inherent trait in all human beings. No one can deny that human thirst for happiness is unquenchable. We all want more and more from life; seldom are we satisfied with what we have. There is hardly anyone content with his or her circumstances. The human thirst for happiness is infinite, but material things are all finite; hence they can never quench the infinite human thirst. Human beings all seek unlimited joy, but material objects, being limited, can never offer that. The limited cannot yield the unlimited.

Only an infinite entity can satisfy the infinite human hunger for enjoyment. Spiritual pursuit is simply a pursuit of that infinite entity.

While physical and intellectual activities deal with the limited, spirituality is concerned with the unlimited. Hence the goal in the spiritual arena is not the finite but the infinite. Therefore, the feeling of pleasure resulting from spiritual activity is not accompanied by pain, or happiness by misery. Spiritual activities include meditation and selfless living. Without providing help to the needy, the forward movement to the infinite is considered to be impossible. And since the mind's goal is infinitude, the spiritual life results in an expansion in the volume as well as the mass of the mind. As a result, the mental conflict declines and the nerves get relaxation. The person becomes broad-minded. He or she seeks to serve others, to share in their pains. A community that respects the selfless beings and attempts to emulate them also then experiences increased happiness without corresponding pain. That is when true progress occurs in the entire society.

Science and technology have tremendously increased the pace of life. More decisions than before have to be made in a relatively short span of time; one must move fast from place to place to cope with the speed of machines. All this adversely affects the nerves, and in turn puts stress on the brain and the heart. Heart failures and mental agonies are the inevitable by-products of scientific and technological progress. Spiritual practices, which calm the nerves, are therefore indispensable if we intend to master the science and not be mastered by it.

Spiritual Practices to Develop Creativity in Human Beings

According to the author of the landmark best-seller *Think and Grow Rich*, a "genius" is developed through the sixth sense and understanding of sixth sense comes only by meditation through mind developed from within. The author further believes that sixth sense is the medium of contact between the finite mind of individuals and infinite intelligence.[16] As sixth sense is a point at which the mind of an individual contacts the universal mind, it is a mixture of both mental and spiritual.

As quoted from *Think and Grow Rich*,[16]

The "sixth sense" is the faculty that marks the difference between a genius and an ordinary individual. [p. 211]

The more this faculty is used, the more alert and receptive the creative faculty becomes to vibrations originating outside the individual's subconscious mind and more the individual relies upon it and makes demands upon it for thought impulses. This faculty can be cultivated and developed only through use. [p. 211]

That which is known as one's "conscience" operates entirely through the faculty of the sixth sense. [p. 211]

Ideas received through the creative faculty are much more reliable because they come from sources more reliable than any available to the reasoning faculty of the mind. [p. 213]

The author of *Think and Grow Rich* also states about the faculty of "creative imagination" through which the humankind has a direct communication with infinite intelligence. According to the author.

This faculty [Creative Imagination] functions only when the conscious mind is vibrating at an exceedingly rapid rate, as for example when the conscious mind is stimulated through the emotion of a strong desire. [pp. 98–99]

In this way spiritual practices of meditation would help in developing creative genius in all human beings and would help in the rapid advancement of physical, mental, and spiritual progress of all human beings in the age of artificial intelligence.

Conclusion[11]

Scientific change and intellectual transformation, unaccompanied by spiritual advancement, would lead not only to degradation in the physical arena such as our environment, but also to racism, bigotry, and social conflicts such as gun violence. Spirituality is the foundation of a sustainable human progress. During the last few centuries, thousands of remarkable inventions and new theories have almost totally transformed our way of life. But spiritually, we have stagnated and even moved backward due to complete materialistic approach toward life. Consequently, battles and wars have been deadlier in the current century than ever before. Rising greed, crime, drugs, and environmental pollution threaten to overwhelm the delicate thread of life on our finite planet. The moral is that change in the physical and mental sphere, without spiritual advancement, is ultimately self-destructive. Hence, I conclude that AI and robotics would become a boon to human progress if there is a spiritual advancement in our society. A lack of it would lead to many deleterious side-effects, which could even collapse of our great human civilization.

References

[1] Mulay, A. 2014. *Mass Capitalism: A Blueprint for Economic Revival*. Book Publishers Network.

[2] Mulay, A. 2015. *Sustaining Moore's Law: Uncertainty Leading to a Certainty of IoT Revolution*. Morgan & Claypool Publishers Network.

[3] Mulay, A. 2016. *How the Information Revolution Remade the Business, and the Economy: A Roadmap for the Semiconductor Industry*. Business Expert Press, LLC.

[4] Batra, R. 2015. *End Unemployment Now: How to Eliminate Joblessness, Debt and Poverty Despite Congress*, 209–23. Palgrave Macmillan.

[5] *The Economist*. 2017. "The World's Most Valuable Resource Is No Longer Oil, but Data. The Data Economy Demands a New Approach to Antitrust Rules." May 6, https://economist.com/leaders/2017/05/06/the-worlds-most-valuable-resource-is-no-longer-oil-but-data

[6] Lakhani, K.R., M. Iansiti, and C. Snively. REV May 6, 2016. "Aspiring Minds Case Study." *Harvard Business School* 9-616-013.

[7] Philip, N. November 2013. *How Data Will Transform Business*. TED@ BCG, San Francisco. https://ted.com/talks/philip_evans_how_data_will_transform_business?utm_source=linkedin.com&utm_medium=social&utm_campaign=tedspread

[8] Downes, L. April 9, 2018. "GDPR and the End of the Internet's Grand Bargain." *Harvard Business Review*. https://hbr.org/2018/04/gdpr-and-the-end-of-the-internets-grand-bargain

[9] Hardoon, D.R., and G. Shmueli. 2015. *Getting Started with Business Analytics—Insightful Decision-Making*. CRC Press, Taylor & Francis Group.

[10] Jeffrey, C. May 18, 2018. "Mass Shootings in the U.S.: When, Where They Have Occurred in 2018." *abcnews*. https://abc15.com/news/data/mass-shootings-in-the-us-when-where-they-have-occurred-in-2018

[11] Batra, R. 2016. "A New Concept of Progress." *Renaissance Universal Magazine.* http://ru.org/index.php/economics/372-a-new-concept-of-progress

[12] Cadwaladr, C., and E. Graham-Harrison. May 24, 2018. "Zuckerberg Setup Fraudulent Scheme to Weaponize Data, Court Case Alleges." *The Guardian.* https://.theguardian.com/technology/2018/may/24/mark-zuckerberg-set-up-fraudulent-scheme-weaponise-data-facebook-court-case-alleges?CMP=Share_iOSApp_Other

[13] Mulay, A. 2018. *New Macroeconomics.* Business Expert Press, LLC.

[14] Castillo, M. June 15, 2018. "No One Is Opening Those Emails about Privacy Updates, and Marketers Are Getting Nervous." *CNBC.* https://cnbc.com/2018/06/15/gdpr-emails-going-unopened.html

[15] Sarkar, P.R. *The Liberation of Intellect: Neo-humanism.* Calcutta: A'nanda Ma'rga Praca'raka Sam'gha.

[16] Hill, N. *Think and Grow Rich: Revised and Updated for the 21st Century,* Revised and expanded by Dr. Arthur R. Pell. London: Penguin.

[17] Dave, Paresh. June 28, 2018. "California lawmakers approve data-privacy bill opposed by Silicon Valley." *Reuters.* https://www.reuters.com/article/us-california-privacy/california-lawmakers-approve-data-privacy-bill-opposed-by-silicon-valley-idUSKBN1JO35Y

[18] PPAI White Paper. January 2018. "The General Data Protection Regulation". https://www.ppai.org/media/2941/gdpr.pdf

CHAPTER 13

Summation and Conclusion

Introduction

Dear Reader, We are now at concluding chapter of this book. As technological progress continues unabated, the progress of human society does not seem to be on par with the progress of technology. This is sure to have an adverse impact on our human society. High unemployment, mental issues such as depression, anger, mass shootings, and so on, have become a norm in the U.S. economy today. As mentioned in Preface, our human civilization has an intimate relation with science and technology and hence both (civilization and science) should progress together. But where scientific progress supersedes civilization, there civilization meets its Waterloo. If artificial intelligence and robotics are utilized properly, they have a potential to reduce the working hours of all human beings and make our lives much easier. The surplus labor available could be in turn beneficially utilized for the progress of our human society.

In order to achieve an economic balance, total restructuring of the economy is essential so that technological progress can continue in a sustainable way. Instead of creating imbalances and huge unemployment, the economy should be restructured to achieve full employment. Human beings desire an unlimited happiness that cannot be satisfied with material things, which can provide only limited happiness. Only a something infinite in nature can quench the thirst of the human urges for infinite happiness. Hence, a scientific approach to spirituality could bring about a harmony and balance in our individual as well as in our collective life in this human society. In this book, we transitioned from upcoming technological revolutions of IoT, AI, and blockchains to newer business models and better planning to future cities to make them sustainable and eco-friendly. We further discussed the new ways to protect our environment as technology progresses and understood the necessity to collaborate and cooperate to reap the benefits of AI and robotics.

Later we discussed how surplus human labor that would be freed up from technological progress could be applied to deeply nurturing of our symbiotic ecosystems. Further, we discussed how the development of a global constitutional framework may prove more effective as global economies start implementing AI-related technologies and without much needed constitutional reforms, AI could potentially violate even the basic rights of human beings. Subsequently, we also discussed an important role quantum computers and quantum communication will play for advancements in the field of AI and robotics to solve complex problems and do a better forecasting. Later we also understood the importance of scientific aspects of a quantum wave function and offered a convincing argument to discard materialism and accept a universal spiritual ideology. We also offered a detailed explanation about how biopsychology could be used to understand the science of virtual reality, which is expected to become a $49.7 billion industry by 2023. We also understood, how bio-psychology could be used to also explain a scientific way to achieve a happy blending of intuitive knowledge and mundane knowledge to ensure a harmony between the inner and the outer spheres of our life. We concluded by analyzing how the present economic crisis came into existence and why it is important to impart a moral education along with professional education to members of our society to avoid such crisis from happening anytime in future.

Summation of all Chapters

In Chapter 1, we discussed about the IoT, which is a network of connected devices. As more and more devices get connected, they generate a lot of data. We understood about the need for the technological sector to undergo rapid transformations in its business models to bring about a dawn of a new industrial revolution. These devices can help ease the lives of human beings by automating a lot of simple and complex tasks with machine learning. However, for IoT revolution to come about, the growth in purchasing power of human beings without indebting the consumers should also be taken into consideration. If people have to go into huge debt in order to make use of these new advancements in technology, then the resulting technological progress will also become unsustainable.

Chapter 2 explains the importance of big data and AI in offering a unique customer experience for all organizations trying to obtain new customers and retain existing customers. It explains different technological aspects of AI and how machines can be trained to converse with humans as receptionists, store assistants, and clerks. Hence, AI would have a huge impact on blue-collar jobs in the economy. While education would prove to be an asset for the workforce, the ones who are intellectually backward will find it difficult to find decent jobs in an AI-driven knowledge-based economy. Does this mean that "doles" such as universal basic income (UBI) should be provided to the unemployed? The technological progress that will come with big data and AI has a potential to revolutionize the entire economy. However, its growth would become unsustainable if there is huge human unemployment and necessity of too much government intervention into the economy to offer doles to the unemployed.

In Chapter 3, we discussed how emerging financial technologies such as blockchains could revolutionize the financial industry within the next decade with a decentralized approach. We also observed how the new technology is much more secure and cost-effective as compared to present banking systems, which have shown no innovation in almost 50 years. We also discussed how adoption of gold standard by cryptocurrencies can help restore a sound financial ecosystem, which would eventually uplift the humanity from clutches of poverty.

In Chapter 4, the author illustrates how the economic preference for "humans first, nature second" has resulted in adverse consequences on the environment and created an overall instability on our planet. Recent technological developments and upcoming innovations with AI and big data radically reduce the costs for businesses to create yet another contradiction, in that their success destroys the viability of parts of the market place without creating new forms of activity that allows those human beings displaced, to find alternatives at the rates required to keep the system stable. Hence, along with technological advancements, it is important that the entire ecosystem should become sustainable and preference moves away from globalization toward an economic localization. In addition to all of the aforementioned, decentralized planning would create more jobs locally resulting in lower need for populations to migrate while providing a maximum value to local residents over nonlocal actors. It also offers many different ideas to give cities their unique local identity (that cherishes local customs and traditions) in order to liberate them from always being planned in a certain specific way like it happens today, in order to make the future cities sustainable and eco-friendly as well as to envision a completely different society than the one in which we live today.

In Chapter 5, the author illustrates the important steps to ensure that macroeconomics protects the environment as technology keeps advancing. He argues that there is not much of an economic problem as much of a design problem in today's economy. Here, we learn that it's not technological or industrial designs that are problems, it's our economic design that is the main problem. And once we transform the economy, then the environmental and technological designs will follow. Additionally, the purpose of "green revolution" should be not simply to produce more material things more efficiently, but rather to create the material means to support a society where people's basic needs are met and where they can prosper in communities, in harmony with nature, while pursuing personal and spiritual development.

In Chapter 6, the author educates the reader about the differences between cooperation and collaboration, mentioning that collaboration is a subset of cooperation. He also believes that the future of AI purely depends on the people in control of developing and programming AI, which could promote Power through Collaboration (PtC) or Predatory Power. He opines that the socioeconomic system should pass into the hands of people motivated to use AI to share productivity gains more equitably, as would be associated with the more collaborative PtC Types operating via the more collaboration-promoting PtC Motivation. The reader also gets introduced to evolving collaborative socioeconomic systems such as circular economy, conscious capitalism, sustainable capitalism, just capital, inclusive capitalism, compassionate capitalism, transformational company, benefit corporation, social business, and so on. These systems have lot of new approaches to collaboration. However, *Mass Capitalism* has a unique business model based on collaboration and competition to ensure economic balance, which is not offered by other socioeconomic systems that would solve the problems of unemployment making technological progress sustainable.

Chapter 7 offers thousands of years of research from history, archaeology and anthropology in prescribing solutions to the current environmental and climate change catastrophe that integrate technology and universal income (UI). Societies have thrived in symbiosis with their watersheds; paying attention to the flow of water, environmental mysticism, water-harvesting techniques, and emphasizing decentralized economies. They have perished when behemoth urban environments ignore this perennial truth and place power and greed above all else. This chapter argues that trillions of dollars can be freed up by returning to the watershed. In this process, UI can be used as a transition and integrated with advances in AI in a return to these ancient truths. AI and an eco-friendlier economy can transform human society to focus on realizing human potential and a life focused on human communities.

In Chapter 8, the author walks us briefly through the human history of horrors and revulsions at devastations caused by new technologies leading people to attempt to develop an international system that would end wars. The origins of constitutions lie in the rules that were developed to govern and manage economic affairs as well as to govern geographically dispersed populace. Although the Universal Declaration of Human Rights was released back in 1948, it did not have an effective mechanism for actually protecting or guaranteeing those rights. Because of defects in global constitutions, there is a huge level of inequality shaped by national policies and infrastructure in different countries. As compared to offering UBI, the author believes that when people have the opportunity to earn their own living, it creates a more positive sense of self-worth and overcomes any tendencies toward idleness. Automation and robots can play a role in either improving or worsening problems depending on the social, economic, and political choices made regarding them. Due to the slow and sometimes clumsy way with which such issues are dealt with through multilateral treaty negotiations, the author believes that the development of a global constitutional framework may prove more effective. As global economies start implementing AI-related technologies, constitutional protections will be required to prevent AI from creating violations of basic human rights.

In Chapter 9, the author elaborates on the important role that quantum computers and quantum communication will play for advancements in the fields of AI and robotics. In the future, quantum computers will be able to solve complex problems and do better forecasting than today's supercomputers. While there is some focus on cyber security in today's big data and IoT business as discussed in Chapters 1 and 2, with quantum communications, the integrity of data is protected by the laws of physics and hence there is no higher level of security. Author explains how the quantum wave function is one of temporal and spatial nonlocality and has been most effective in predicting and explaining scientific observations. He further elaborates on Albert Einstein's model of the universe, which has enormous scientific and philosophical implications that have been by and large ignored by the scientific community. He makes a strong argument that mind is nonlocal and nonmaterial and cannot be equated with brain. The author concludes his chapter by discarding materialism and supporting a spiritual ideology that consciousness, not matter/energy is the first cause of creation and serves as the ground substance of creation which is transformed into the material universe.

In Chapter 10, the author takes us through an inner journey that shows that answers lie not only outside of us but also within us; and the journey to higher consciousness is as fascinating as the journey to the farthest reaches of outer space. In the process of distinguishing between the activities of brain and mind, the author helps us to understand a link between mental functions, brain activity and the physiological processes involved in this bio-psychological neural dynamics. An understanding of bio-psychology is important to develop the field of augmented reality and virtual reality, which is expected to be a combined $108 billion industry by 2021. In addition to all the aforementioned, it is important to find solutions to exponential growth of mental health issues faced by our human society, with an understanding that such vibrational expressions of propensities such as anger, fear, hatred, jealousy, and greed cause hormones to secrete from the glands. Additionally, human beings need to undergo proper psycho-spiritual training to achieve progress and happiness in life. The author believes that meditation and spiritual practices would help achieve a happy blending of intuitive knowledge and mundane knowledge thereby ensuring a harmony between the inner and the outer spheres of life.

In Chapter 11, the author illustrates how present economic policies followed in the United States and across the world that make saving money a sin and spending a virtue, do not obey the laws of economics and laws of nature by disregarding the symbiotic relationship between human beings and nature causing imbalances resulting in "black swan" events. He briefly elaborates the different causes of huge trade deficits and budget deficits in the U.S. economy. He highlights the importance of a gold standard for country's currency for an overall economic stability. He argues that there exist no free markets anymore and markets are manipulated by institutions often with the blessing of the government for their political and economic advantage. He suggests several remedies to revive the American economy and makes a strong case by distinguishing good effects of industrial deregulation, which creates competition from the bad impacts of financial deregulation that stimulates speculation. He concludes about the need to bring harmony, balance, and complementarity between the opposites to transcend to a higher level. Last but not least, the author believes in imparting moral education along with professional education to all members of society.

In Chapter 12, we discuss the new business models for data driven economy. We also discuss about the recent regulations enacted for data-driven economy in order to protect data privacy of citizens and their impact on the existing business models. We understand the importance of having a three-tier business model in a data-driven economy in order to ensure that supply and demand both grow and fall in proportion. Additionally, this three-tier business model has an added advantage to get better and more accurate forecasts to prevent overproduction as well as to minimize layoffs in the new data driven economy. This way the problem of huge unemployment could be solved by reducing the working hours of employees with rapid growth in the productivity of machines. We concluded this chapter by highlighting the importance of integrating scientific progress with spiritual progress to make overall progress of humanity sustainable.

Law of Social Cycle

In February 2009, I came to know about my mentor, Professor Ravi Batra in a local event in Dallas, Texas, where he was invited as a keynote speaker. The event was organized after world had witnessed a huge crash of stock markets in year 2008 and the markets continued to fall to its lows of March 2009. At that event, I purchased an autographed copy of Professor

Batra's 1990 book titled *The Downfall of Capitalism and Communism: Can Capitalism Be Saved?*

I was intrigued with the title and to be honest, I have never read such a thorough analysis of last 5,000 years of recorded human history. Hence, the book is a masterpiece in itself and I was very impressed with the depth of Professor Batra's research. In that book, I came across Professor Batra's teacher and mentor named Shrii Prabhat Ranjan Sarkar. I read about two important things put forth by his mentor Shrii Prabhat Ranjan Sarkar, one was the law of social cycle and second was a new economic treatise called the progressive utilization theory. An analysis of last 5,000 years of recorded human history has been a remarkable work of Professor Batra's 1990 book, in which he has made some incredible economic and political forecasts for the U.S. and global economy based on the law of social cycle.

Let us understand the law of social cycle before we discuss about progressive utilization theory. The law of social cycle has its source in the concepts of macrohistory presented in Shrii Prabhat Ranjan Sarkar's philosophical treatise, titled *Ananda Sutram*, along with original concepts of metaphysics, epistemology, and ethics.[1]

According to Shrii Sarkar's writings on macrohistory in 1950s, in this movement of the social cycle, one class is always dominant. The movement of the social cycle in a clockwise direction in Figure 13.1 (shown by light gray colored arrows) constitutes an "evolution" if it occurs after a sufficiently long duration. If this clockwise movement occurs within a short duration, this is called "revolution." The movement of the social cycle counterclockwise in Figure 13.1 (shown by dark grey colored arrows) constitutes a "counter evolution" if it occurs after a significantly long duration. This counter evolution is extremely short-lived. However, if this counterclockwise movement occurs within a short duration, it is called "counter revolution." Counter revolution is even more short-lived than counter evolution.[1]

Professor Ravi Batra from SMU, Dallas, analyzes the successful operation of the law of social cycle in his 1978 book titled *The Downfall of Capitalism and Communism: A New Study of History*. Based on this analysis, Professor Batra correctly predicted the collapse of Soviet Communism 15 years before it occurred for which he received a medal of honor from the Prime Minister of Italy. As per the law, the control of society keeps

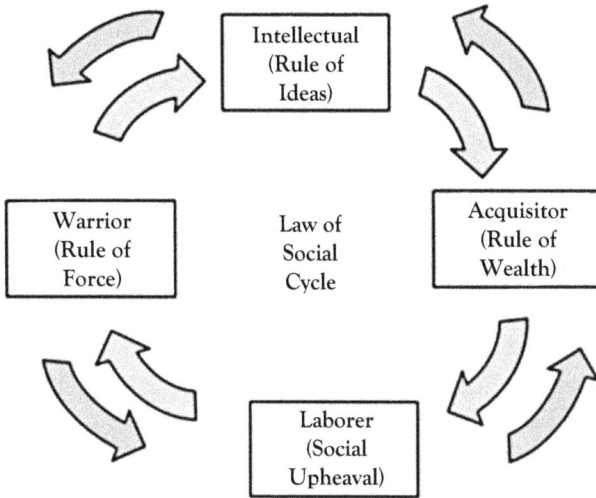

Figure 13.1 *Law of social cycle explained in pictorial form. As shown in the figure, control of society keeps moving from intellectuals to acquisitors to laborers to warriors in a clockwise or anti-clockwise direction depending on the domination of intellectuals, acquisitors, warriors, or laborers*[1]

moving from hands of intellectuals to acquisitors to laborers to warriors in order to complete one cycle.

According to this theory, people in any society are all relatively similar; they have generally the same goals, desires, and ambitions but differ in the way they go about achieving their goals. Based on their approach to achieve those goals, people could be classified into four different psychological categories, viz. warriors, intellectuals, acquisitors, and laborers.[2]

Warriors: Warriors are people with strong bodies, vigorous physical energy, and a sharp intellect. Warriors tend to develop the skills that take advantage of their inherent gifts of stamina, courage, and vigor. Their mentality is one that is not averse to taking physical risks. They all achieve success through their physical skills and a deep understanding of their profession. Examples of people in our society with the warrior mentality include policemen, firemen, soldiers, professional athletes, and so on.[2]

Intellectuals: Intellectuals have a more developed intellect than the warriors, but generally lack the physical strength and vigor. Intellectuals are happiest when they try to achieve success by developing and expressing their intellectual skills and talents. Examples would be teachers, writers, professors, scientists, artists, musicians, philosophers, doctors, and lawyers and above all, priests.[2]

Acquisitors: Acquisitors have a penchant for acquiring money. If money can be made, the acquisitors will find a way to make it. They are not considered as bright as the intellectuals, nor as strong as the warriors, but they are keen when it comes to making and accumulating money and material possessions. Such people are the traders, businessmen, managers, entrepreneurs, bankers, brokers, and landlords in our society.[2]

Laborers: Laborers lack the energy and vigor of the warriors, the keen intellect of the intellectuals, or the ambition and drive of the acquisitors. Their contribution to society is profound and no society could function without them. However, the other groups generally look down upon and tend to exploit them. The laborers, including peasants, serfs, clerks, short order cooks, waiters, janitors, doormen, cabdrivers, garbage collectors, truck drivers, night watchmen and factory workers, keep society running smoothly by working diligently and without complaint.[2]

The present stage of the U.S. economy with the election of Donald Trump as president was due to anger of the working-class Americans against the corruption of career politicians, which resulted in loss of their high-paying jobs. Hence, it marks the end of one cycle of "rule of wealth" in society and movement to "rule of warriors." This could mean that the economy could be in chaos and it would need the policemen and the army to take control and we can observe early signs of it in form of a border crisis with President Trump's demand for additional border patrol agents at its southern border with Mexico. However, if proper economic reforms are undertaken and the cycle moves to the "rule of intellectuals" with new ideas for revival of economy, then the resulting economic system can benefit all four classes of people.

However, Shrii Sarkar discusses about a fifth class of people called the benevolent intellectuals (*Sadvipras* in Sanskrit) who lie at the center of the social cycle. They are classless people who have characteristics of all the aforementioned four classes which means that they are physically strong (like warriors), intellectually sharp (like intellectuals), high business acumen (like acquisitors) and are spiritually elevated to care for all people in society including the laborers. According to Shrii Sarkar, these *Sadvipras* (benevolent intellectuals) control the movement of the cycle.[4]

It is to be noted that in his book titled *Human Society—Part II*, Shrii Sarkar mentions the following about the fifth class of individuals called as Sadvipras:

> Sadvipras will have no rest, ever. A time will never come in the life of a sadvipra when he or she will relax in an arm chair and say, "Ah, I have nothing to do today. Let me rest awhile." In this first phase of human history, the sadvipra society has not yet formed itself. In the absence of a sadvipra society the social cycle is moving on its natural round. In every age, the government of the predominant class becomes exploitative, and thereafter comes evolution or revolution. For lack of sadvipras' assistance, the foundation of human society is lacking firmness. Today I extend my earnest request to all reasonable, virtuous and moral fighters that they form a good, well-disciplined sadvipra society without further delay. These sadvipras will work for the good of all countries, for the all-around emancipation of all humanity. The downtrodden humanity of this disgraced world is looking up to the eastern horizon, awaiting the sadvipras' advent with earnest zeal and eagerness. Let the cimmerian darkness of the interlunar night disappear. Let the human being of the new day of the new sunrise wake up in the world.[4]

Progressive Utilization Theory

In 1959, Shrii Prabhat Ranjan Sarkar put forth a new economic treatise and called it progressive utilization theory. The economic system is quite different from existing economic systems of communism and capitalism, which we are familiar with. In his economic treatise, Shrii Sarkar believed that it was time to raise the bar of fundamental rights for human beings and believed that these rights should receive a constitutional guarantee. [8] He believed that all human beings should also have the right to the following necessities for basic human existence, which include things such as food, clothes, housing, medical aid, and education. However, He did not believe in European social democracy or American liberalism as a good way to achieve it. He believed that doles (such as UBI) would make people lethargic and demanding high income just because they exist. Hence, he believed in the welfare of the society through work rather than offering welfare for free.

Shrii Sarkar believed that diversity is law of nature and hence everyone cannot be equal. Hence, he believed that there should be special incentives offered to people who are extraordinary so as to encourage people to contribute their skills and intelligence for the betterment of society. Hence, he offered minimum necessities and maximum amenities. I have discussed this in detail in chapters of my 2016 book *How Information Revolution Remade the Business and the Economy.*

Shrii Sarkar also put forth his philosophy of neo-humanism and mentioned that all molecules, atoms, particles, positions, and neurons are veritable expressions of pure consciousness. By extending the spirit of humanism to both animate and inanimate worlds in his philosophy of neo-humanism, Shrii Sarkar believed that neo-humanism would elevate humanism to universalism. He believed that neo-humanism will help human beings to progress beyond selfishness in their individual and collective lives.

As discussed by several contributing authors to this book, there needs to be some important and radical changes in the global economy as AI and robotics could potentially lead to loss of jobs of several members in human society, which is not restricted to just laborers but also intellectuals, acquisitors, and warriors. Hence, it is very timely for all thought leaders to take a look at Shrii Sarkar's economic treatise called as progressive utilization theory for an all-round development of humanity. My previously published volumes such as *Mass Capitalism, Sustaining Moore's Law, How Information Revolution Remade the Business and the Economy,* and *New Macroeconomics* offered an innovative approach establishing a socio-economic system where there is a progressive utilization of technology for ensuring a sustainable technological progress.[7] Those books along with the ideas presented in this book offer a comprehensive solution to the problems faced by global economy and offers a sustainable path ahead for the U.S. and global economies based on Shrii Prabhat Ranjan Sarkar's progressive utilization theory.

According to Shrii Sarkar, it is incorrect to say that advanced scientific technology is the root cause of unemployment. This is rather misinformation or propaganda, carried out by leaders having little knowledge of socioeconomics. We observe this misinformation in the form of wider support for UBI from tech titans like Mark Zuckerberg and Elon Musk. The question of unemployment arises only in the today's capitalistic framework, where industry is only for profit at all costs. In an economic structure based on cooperative collaboration, where industry stands for consumption over pure profit, the question of unemployment will not arise. Automation and other advances in technology such as AI will not reduce the number of laborers; rather, working hours will be reduced and the remaining hours used in nonwork pursuits as discussed in some of chapters in this book. A reduction in working hours depends not only on productivity, but on the demand for commodities and the availability of labor. With the ideas presented in this book, the progress of AI and robotics could be utilized to bring about an all-round development of humanity.

In today's economy, those who want to promote public welfare without antagonizing the owners of capital will have to oppose AI and robotics. This is because when the productive capacity of machinery is doubled, the human labor required is decreased by half, such that large numbers of workers are retrenched from their factories. A few optimists may say, "Under circumstantial pressure other ways will be found to employ these surplus laborers in different jobs, and the very effort to find these alternatives will accelerate scientific advancement, so the ultimate result of mechanization is, in fact, good." This view, though not useless, has little practical value, because it is impossible to arrange new jobs for retrenched workers as quickly as they become surplus laborers in consequence of rapid automation.

What Makes Progressive Utilization Theory a Completely New Economic Treatise?[3]

Progressive utilization theory differs from existing form of capitalism and communism as follows:

1. The business model in this new economy is three-tiered. The neo-cooperative corporations occupy the middle industrial tier; Extremely capital-intensive industry such as semiconductor manufacturing is run with partnership of local government at upper industrial tier. The upper industrial tier may also include huge and complex industries that are focused on the extraction of raw materials; and lower industrial tier consists of small, private enterprises conduct business too small in scope for the other two sectors to run, where entrepreneurship is to be encouraged. This neo-cooperative ownership of middle industrial tier was outlawed under communism. Capitalism is committed only to the interests of the private sector.

2. The approach taken by progressive utilization theory for middle industrial tier is based on voluntary, not forced, cooperation. Of course, the economic system believes in offering special incentives in the form of tax breaks to businesses that have this kind of neo-cooperative framework. Under Soviet Communism, farmers were forced to join agricultural cooperatives, which was extremely un-psychological, and not paid according to their individual output, which was nonproductive. In today's capitalism, high-paying jobs are offshored to low labor-cost countries (LLCs) to minimize the costs of production in order to maximize their profit. This has resulted in unsustainable trade deficits for U.S. economy. Additionally, in the United States, for example, the businesses have used millions of illegal immigrants, who are paid only a fraction of the wages of legal workers, in agriculture and other labor-intensive industries. This adds to the unemployment of local citizens and permanent residents in the United States.[5]

3. The industrial approach of communism was centralized, with huge factories producing one item to be widely distributed, whereas capitalism's approach is to move the production facilities to LLCs through centralized supply chains in order to maximize the profit at headquarters of the company. Progressive utilization theory has decentralized supply chains, which not only improves the efficiency of supply chains but also results in a complete and wholesome decentralization of economy that relies on local self-reliance.[6]

4. The decisions are made top-down in communism, which included five-year plans for industry. Communism was, in fact, a party dictatorship. All economic planning was highly centralized and controlled by the state in case of communism. In today's capitalism, majority of multinational corporations (MNCs) have centralized supply chains that span multiple continents resulting in unsustainable trade imbalances in the global economy. Progressive utilization theory believes in a bottom-up governance where local people have a voice when it comes to the development and utilization of local resources, and so on. The supply chains are decentralized to a level at which people are most aware of economic problems and potentialities, and therefore best able to plan for their own local economy.

5. The employees in factories and corporations in both communist and capitalist economies feel alienated due to lack of ownership and sufficient control of their workplaces. As discussed in detail in *Mass Capitalism: A Blueprint for Economic Revival*, the majority shares of Fortune 500 corporations would be owned by their employees and this increases the motivations and possibilities for personal fulfillment for these employees. As employees are the majority shareholders of large corporations and private properties on a massive scale, the system effectively becomes *Mass Capitalism* because it would ensure that capitalism works for masses.[5]

6. The five-year planning under communism resulted in a command economy, which was responsive to production quotas. This did not keep pace with ups and downs of the economy. In case of capitalism, the profit seeking resulted in offshoring of high-paying jobs and illegal immigration resulting in a huge wealth disparity and lack of sufficient purchasing power for majority of the population. The new economy under progressive utilization theory believes in increasing the purchasing power in proportion to productivity of employees with a minimal government intervention. Hence, there is a balance between supply and demand of goods in the economy. The approach of new economy is aimed at undertaking reforms toward increasing consumers' purchasing power and the availability of consumer goods in order to meet the basic and amenity needs for local residents to maintain an economic vitality.

Conclusion

I am an eternal optimist that it will be the *Sadvipras* (benevolent intellectuals) from around the world who would be implementing the ideas presented in this book as well as my previously published books to help establish *Mass Capitalism* based free market economic reforms in order to bring about an all-round development of every individual in our human society as we march toward a technological advanced economy with automation and AI-driven innovations. Thus, economic renaissance in the age of artificial intelligence is about to become a reality in the very near future with the help of *Sadvipras*.

References

[1] Mulay, A. 2014. "Defending the IP of the US Semiconductor Industry." *EBN*. February 27. https://ebnonline.com/author.asp?section_id=3315&doc_id=271858

[2] Mulay, A. 2014. "Arab Spring in Middle East and Its Impacts on US Semiconductor Industry." *Apekshit Mulay's Blog*, January 18. https://apekmulay.com/arab-spring-in-middle-east-and-its-impact-on-us-semiconductor-industry/

[3] Susmit, K. 2009. "Differences Among Prout, Capitalism and Communism." *Susmit Kumar's Blog*. http://susmitkumar.net/index.php/us-economy?id=105:differences-among-prout-capitalism-and-communism

[4] Mulay, A. 2015. "In the Quest of a Sadvipra." *Apekshit Mulay's Blog*, June 6. https://apekmulay.com/in-the-quest-of-a-sadvipra/

[5] Mulay, A. 2014. *Mass Capitalism: A Blueprint for Economic Revival.* Book Publishers Network.

[6] Mulay, A. 2015. *Sustaining Moore's Law: Uncertainty Leading to a Certainty of IoT Revolution.* Morgan & Claypool Publishers Network.

[7] Mulay, A. 2016. *How the Information Revolution Remade the Business, and the Economy: A Roadmap for the Semiconductor Industry.* Business Expert Press, LLC.

[8] Susmit, K. 2009. "Fundamental Rights." *Susmit Kumar's Blog*. http://susmitkumar.net/index.php/us-economy?id=106:fundamental-rights

About the Authors

Satinder Paul Singh is a technologist at heart and has an excellent track record in accurately predicting how new technologies will play out in the coming years, including how they will compete with or complement existing technologies, enhance devices, and change the competitive landscape. Satinder Paul Singh brings more than 17 years of driving cutting-edge technologies from definition to profitable business with experience in the semiconductor industry as an executive and strategy consultant for companies focused on Automotive (Connected Cars), Industrial IoT and Wireless Semiconductor technologies. Satinder delivered breakthrough semiconductor products with combined projected long-term revenue greater than $500M and total investment costs more than $100M.

Satinder has strong Exposure to entire IC/SoC Design Process from Specification, Microarchitecture analysis, Silicon implementation, Silicon Evaluation until Final mass production activities in Automotive, Communication, Industrial, and Computing markets. Satinder drives Continuous operational excellence through lean and agile practices in the development and flow methodologies for improving quality and efficiencies across business units under aggressive market schedules.

He has chaired technical sessions at International Symposiums like SNUG, CDN Live, GSA and key-note speaker there since 2009. He has also authored several papers and articles showing this wide expertise in macroeconomics, semiconductor technology, supply chains, business models, microeconomics. He contributes to recognized publications such as EBN, SEMI.org, EFY, LinkedIn, and so on.

He is an expert presenter and negotiator; able to forge solid relationships with partners and build consensus across organizational levels. He works on multiple projects with various departments to advise them and jointly determine their strategy (e.g., in which end-markets to participate, what technology and commercial partnerships to prioritize, what approach to follow for mergers and acquisitions).

Satinder advised customers globally on various SoCs and Mixed Signal IP and patent applicability and support their make/buy or create/

license decisions analytically. He championed new process development, improvement, integration and deployment, and performance measurement to improve organizational and operational efficiency quality.

Satinder Paul Singh worked with Corporate Management in the Internet-of-Things (IoT) segment to create a "beyond silicon" strategy to pursue new profit opportunities beyond the core business.

Satinder is well versed in data and analytics approaches including Big Data, Data Mining, and Data Science tools to enable information assessment. He is also an expert in Machine Learning and Deep Learning applications. With his expert knowledge of Machine Learning, he helps in the development of predictive models using machine-learning platforms for prediction of yield and equipment reliability in the high speed, low power semiconductor devices.

Satinder is the Robert Plant of the semiconductor world. He works heavily with Hedge Fund managers on consolidation in the semiconductor sector. He has numerous professional affiliations worldwide.

Sreenivas Adiki is currently working with large Telecommunication Network OEM as Analytics Solution Architect. During the last 20+ years he has played various roles in different organizations in the areas of software development, design and architecture in various industry domains such as Telecommunications, Banking and Financial Services, Insurance and Retail. His experience of having worked with fortune 1000 customers across the globe helped him understand the business and technology perspectives that are common and specific to the markets. The global experience has helped him immensely in writing this chapter to put thoughts on how technology may impact the jobs, services and therefore the economy. He has joint patent issued on "Dynamic Data Dimensioning achieved by Appropriately Bootstrapped FPGAs for Partial reconfigurations" in the year 2014.

Sreenivas holds Masters in Computer Science and Engineering with Bachelors in Electronic and Communication Engineering. He is a TOGAF Certified Enterprise Architect, PMP Certified Project Management Professional and Partnerworks Certified Technical Sales Professional from Hortonworks.

His favorite past time include going for long walk, watching motor racing, reading philosophical texts and watching thriller movies. Sreenivas likes to experiment cooking new vegetarian recipes and sometimes they turn out to be good. He believes that

Excellence is not a battle with others; it is battle you play with yourself, by constantly raising the bar and stretching yourself

Shrikant Shete is very passionate about global macroeconomics and microeconomics, the global financial systems, and its interconnectedness with the global banking systems. He is passionate about the disruption in banking systems as he believes that there has not been much innovation within the banking system for more than 50 years. He believes that digital disruption in Banking and Finance can be the biggest disruptions in this new age, where all the principles of Banking will be redefined.

Global Stock Markets has always caught his attention, since as he says bulk of the monetary transactions run through the Markets and lot of work needs to be done for regulation of markets. He is the founder, MD and CEO of Eazybillpay Payment Technologies, Australia. Shrikant believes that there will be a complete change of the banking systems within the next decade. Shrikant holds an undergraduate degree in mechanical engineering from Walchand College of Engineering, Sangli, India. He has several professional awards from Wipro to his credit.

Michael (Mike) McAllum is the inaugural Chief Steward of the Centre for the Future's Academy of Scholars. The purpose of this global Academy is to reflect on and reconceptualize the nature of diverse world systems that extend beyond and outside the structure that frames our current collective world view. This work is integral to the Centre's intent to help design and realize a world that works for everyone and in so doing enables humanity to evolve more consciously.

A New Zealander, now based in Melbourne, Australia, Mike is internationally recognized as a critical thinker in the systemic shift from a dominant mechanistic socioeconomic world to an emergent networked, diverse, postnormal, and sustainable future. As a speaker, author, and facilitator consultant, he works predominantly with Asia-Pacific organizations, cities, and regions as they confront conditions of increasing uncertainty and complexity. He seeks to explore in plain language the nature of issues that have created such situations and the potential pathways available. One of the early examples of his work was the design and leadership of a future "options and directions" process known as the NZ Foresight Project.

Mike's PhD is the only critique of Jeremy Rifkin's *Third Industrial Revolution* and the socioeconomic transformational possibilities of time, form, and space it proposes. As part of this work, his theorizing on the nature of macro social transformation and postcapitalism has attracted significant global interest. He was one of the originators of the concept of strategic foresight and the articulation of both the theory and practice that converged futures and strategic thinking. This groundbreaking thinking was developed into two books *Strategic Foresight: The Power of Standing in the Future*, 2002 (co-authored with N. Marsh and D. Purcell) and *Designing Better Futures: Rethinking Strategy for a Sustainable World*, 2008. In addition, he has authored a number of book chapters, academic journal articles, and other reflective essays.

Mike is part of the Oxford Futures Forum and was a foundation member of the Association of Professional Futurists, and he has been an expert commentator in a number of global reports and documentaries including Discovery Channel's *The Future Makers*. He previously occupied leadership positions in the NZ Dairy Industry and was an Executive Board Member of the Global Council of YMCAs with a special interest in development and refugee programs.

Roar Bjonnes studied agronomy at Vinterlandbruksakademiet in Oslo. He is currently a researcher and writer with the PROUT Research Institute in Copenhagen, Denmark. The co-founder of the Prama Institute, a holistic retreat center in North Carolina, he conducts retreats and workshops on holistic health, yoga and alternative economics. He has written numerous articles on economic and environmental issues for magazines, newspapers and books. He is the author of two books on economics, *Growing a New Economy* and *Principles of a Balanced Economy*.

Dr. Stephen Willis, PhD (powerthroughcollaboration.com) is the developer of the "Power through Collaboration Formula" for managing collaboration in challenging situations. He is the author of two books: *"Power through Collaboration: When to Collaborate, Negotiate, or Dominate"* and *"Power through Collaboration: The Formula for Success in Challenging Situations."* His third Power through Collaboration book will be published in 2019—*"How Leadership Failure to Collaborate Created a Hurricane Katrina Mega-Disaster."*

Stephen's wide-reaching career includes: consultant and coach to Fortune 500 companies, startups, and nonprofits; instructor for Harvard University; CEO of AIB Business Consulting Inc; and psychologist with the Veterans Administration. Stephen's work building collaboration and resolving conflict has been funded by Packard Foundation, Marin Community Foundation, San Francisco Foundation, and Pante Rhea Foundation. Stephen earned a PhD in Psychology from Purdue University, a BSc in Mathematics from Manhattan College, and trained in Group Dynamics & Facilitation at the Stanford University Graduate School of Business. He is a member of the American Psychological Association and its Society of Consulting Psychology.

Matt Oppenheim, PhD has had a passion for social transformation; holding neighborhood festivals and breaking down the barriers of inequities. Much of his youth was spent hiking the watersheds of Southern California. His BA at the University of California at Santa Barbara focused on indigenous rituals of transformation. For fourteen years he served as an Eastern Mystical monk throughout the Pacific Region and finished his service with the co-creation of an ecological and spiritually based primary school in Australia. His MA was an ethnographic study of an urban village in a minority community in Los Angeles. Writing grants for the project, he became the community education coordinator. Then in his PhD at the California Institute of Integral Studies, he worked side-by-side with youth leaders in a Mayan village, creating Freirean curriculum about the suffering and transformation of their community. Next, his focus was facilitating service learning in school districts and universities, as well as research and interventions into school reform. He researched education programs for refugees and a successful intervention at a low-performing high school. Later he served as the parent; family and community coordinator at Albuquerque Public Schools. His passion for teaching at the university level over twenty years combined a love of service-learning, experiential learning and student engagement. Now he facilitates diversity training and serves as a patient advocate, helping people through the crazy maze of the U.S. healthcare system.

His endearing lifetime dedication now is to assist the reversal of climate change and environmental damage by reviving the world's watersheds. He is currently writing a book: *"People of the Watershed"* for people to understand that watersheds have been and always will be fundamental to human existence. The book will review 12,000 of archeology; indigenous practice; religions and myths of the watershed, as well as ancient practices of water-harvesting. This long history demonstrates the eternal tenets of sustainable civilization: following them has always guaranteed social and environmental resilience. Work against them and civilizations always fail, as ours is failing now. Oppenheim is a Fellow at the Society for Applied Anthropology; a graduate of the Stanford University Service Learning Institute and a member of the Board of the Prout Research Institute.

My greatest inspiration for this work is P.R. Sarkar and Prout (The Progressive Utilization Theory); mentioned in his chapter and often in this book.

Craig Runde, J.D., is a speaker, trainer, and coach in the field of conflict management and resolution. He is the former Director of the Center for Conflict Dynamics and Mediation Training Institute at Eckerd College. Craig is the co-author of several books on workplace conflict management including *Becoming a Conflict Competent Leader, Building Conflict Competent Teams, and Developing Your Conflict Competence*. He is also the author of the LinkedIn Learning course, *Improving Your Conflict Competence*. Craig received his BA from Harvard University, an M.L.L. from the University of Denver, and a J.D. from Duke University. He has practiced law in Colorado and has taught at the University of Minnesota Law School and Wake Forest University.

For over thirty years, Craig has also studied and written about developments in global governance, civil society, economic justice, environmental sustainability, world peace, and developments toward the creation of a world or global constitution.

Steven Richheimer, PhD attended Lehigh University in Bethlehem, PA where he obtained his Bachelor of Science degree in chemistry in 1968. He then enrolled in the graduate program in chemistry at Stanford University where he earned his Master of Science degree in chemistry in 1971 and his PhD in bio-organic chemistry in 1974 working under two-time Nobel Prize winning chemist Linus Pauling.

After completing his PhD at Stanford, Steven worked as a chemistry instructor at colleges in California, Missouri, and finally in Denver, CO. There he met his wife, Jeanne, and they were married in 1980. They had two daughters, and currently four grandchildren. From 1980 to 1990, Steven worked at Pharmaceutical Basics in Denver, CO as Director of Quality Control and Research and Development, and in 1990, he joined Hauser, Inc. in Boulder, CO as a staff senior chemist in research and development. He specialized in the isolation and purification of valuable drugs from natural sources, project management, analytical methods development, and scale-up and process development. During his 28-year career in pharmaceutical and natural products chemistry, he authored numerous scientific papers and patents.

Steven began practicing yoga in 1968 after graduating from college. While at Stanford, he began experimenting with mind expanding drugs and searching for a spiritual teacher. In 1970, he attended a lecture by an acharya (monk) of Ananda Marga (Path of Bliss) and decided to be initiated into the practice of Tantric meditation. That summer he went to Ranchi, India to have personal contact with the guru of Ananda Marga, Shrii Shrii Anandamurti (Baba). During the 4 weeks there, he had daily contact with Baba and attended classes in the spiritual and social philosophy of Anandamurti. This experience led to a profound change in his life and he became a devoted disciple of Baba. He continues to practice meditation daily.

Baba taught that Consciousness is primary and that mind and matter evolve from Consciousness. Since Consciousness creates reality, in essence

everything is simply a manifestation of the One. Being a scientist by training, Steven quickly realized that the spiritual ideology of Ananda Marga
was both rational and completely consistent with scientific principles. He
developed an interest in how evidence from the physical and behavioral
sciences confirmed the spiritual worldview. This led to his first book: *The
Unity Principle, The Link between Science and Spirituality.* The purport of
the book was that modern science confirms that there is a subtle unifying
principle that transcends space and time and that this "ground substance"
of creation is Consciousness. His second book is *The Nonlocal Universe,
Why Science Validates the Spiritual Worldview.* In this book, he shows why
the materialistic explanation for reality is negated by nonlocality observed
in the physical sciences including quantum physics and relativity theory;
and by overwhelming evidence from the behavior sciences indicating that
mind is nonlocal and cannot be equated with brain.

Steven retired in 2008, and he and Jeanne moved into their home in
Steamboat Springs, CO. His summers are fully occupied playing golf,
fly-fishing, hiking, biking, and soaring. During the long winter, he enjoys
downhill skiing, cross-country skiing, snowshoeing, and snow removal.
He also serves as a volunteer ski instructor with Steamboat Adaptive
Sports and Recreation (STARS).

Dr. Acharya Shambhushivananda Avadhuta PhD (Wharton School,
University of Pennsylvania) is the current Chancellor of Ananda Marga
Gurukula and Global Neohumanist Education Network. He coordinates
over 1200 educational projects in over 70 countries and a spokesperson of Neohumanist Movement worldwide. As a meditation teacher, he
has taught meditation to thousands of persons over the past 40 years in
over fifty countries. He is also the recipient of International Mahatma
Gandhi Award and a celebrated speaker on "Yogic Tradition and Contemporary Problems". He has been a key note speaker at Kyoto Forum,
Parliament of World Religions and scores of other forums around the
world. He is the author of *"PROUT-Neohumanist Economics," "Mystic
Verses," "Thoughts for a New Era- a Neohumanist Perspective."* In 1970's he
served on the faculty of Drexel University, Rutgers University, University
of Scranton and Philadelphia College of Textiles and Science in Eastern
United States. He is a gold-medalist of Punjab University, India and

also currently building an educational township called Ananda Marga Gurukula at Anandanagar in West Bengal, India.

Navin Doshi, Navin Doshi grew up in Mumbai, India and came to the United States in 1958 after completing his undergraduate studies in India. Navin completed a second bachelor's degree and a master's degree in Electrical Engineering at the University of Michigan, Ann-Arbor. He worked as an Aerospace Engineer at Northrop, where he was the recipient of NASA awards and U.S. patents. Navin and his wife, Pratima, started a business involving bedspreads in mid-seventies. They also engaged in real-estate and in financial investments.

Success in these ventures enabled Navin to become an active philanthropist, promoting value education and world peace, supporting fund raising activities and offering consultancy for projects relating to Indic traditions and world culture. In 1999, Navin and Pratima endowed the Doshi Chair of Indian History (now migrated to Indian Archaeology) at UCLA.

As with UCLA, Navin has a close relationship of patronage with the Loyola Marymount University (LMU) in Los Angeles. In 2006, Navin and Pratima Doshi endowed a Professorship for Indic Traditions at LMU which also administers a $10,000 annual Bridge Builder Award program, meant to honor eminent personalities who have worked toward world peace and harmony. Currently the Indic Traditions chair at LMU is occupied by Professor Christopher Chapple, a prominent scholar of Indian Religion and Yoga. The recipients of the Bridge Builder Award include Dr. Deepak Chopra, Conductor Zubin Mehta, writer and Buddhist Monk Thich Nhat Hanh, world religions pioneer Huston Smith, eco-feminist Dr. Vandana Shiva, bio-systems theorist Dr. Rupert Sheldrake, U.S. Congresswoman Tulsi Gabbard, and the President of Maharisi University and highly acclaimed physicist Dr. John Hagelin.

Navin has been a regular contributor to local newspapers on subjects of global economics and philosophy. His books, titled *Transcendence, Saving us from Ourselves*, published by Ithaca Press, *Economics and Nature*, published by Nalanda International and D.K. Print World in India, and the latest, *Light with No Shadow, a memoir My life Bridging Two Cultures*, braids human psychology based on Indic traditions with science, economics, spirituality, and his life experiences. He is one of the authors of an article in WORLD FUTURES, GLOBAL EDUCATION (2013 edition) edited by Ervin Laszlo and Sally Goerner. He also serves as a trustee in the board of trustees of university CIIS (California Institute of Integral Studies, San Francisco) and as a director in the board of Directors of South Asia Study Association, and a director of *Pranalytica*, a Quantum Cascade Laser manufacturer.

Apek Mulay is business and technology consultant at Mulay's Consultancy Services. He is also a senior analyst and macroeconomist in U.S. semiconductor industry. He is an entrepreneur with World Financial Group (WFG) and also co-founder of an e-commerce startup CalcuttaHandicraft.in. His first book *Mass Capitalism: A Blueprint for Economic Revival* (2014) is available as paperback, e-book (Amazon.com, Barnesandnoble.com, books.google.com) as well as an audio book (Audible.com). *Mass Capitalism* in Marathi language will be available for readers from Maharashtra, India, in 2019 published as *Samudayik Bhandwalshahi* by Utkarsha Publications, Pune, India.

Mulay has authored other books such as *Sustaining Moore's Law: Uncertainty Leading to a Certainty of IoT Revolution* (2015) with Morgan & Claypool publishers, *How Information Revolution Remade the Business and the Economy: A Roadmap for Progress of the Semiconductor Industry* (2016), *New Macroeconomics* (2018), and *Economic Renaissance in the Age of Artificial Intelligence* (2019) with Business Expert Press. He has also authored a monograph on technology with Lambert Academic Publishing titled *Improving Reliability of Tungsten Plug Via on an Integrated Circuitry: Process Flow in BiCMOS and CMOS Technology with Failure Analysis, Design of Experiments, Statistical Analysis and Wafer Maps* (2016).

Mulay pursued undergraduate studies in electronics engineering (EE) at the University of Mumbai in India and holds two master's degrees, one in electrical engineering from Texas Tech University, Lubbock, TX and other in business analytics from Naveen Jindal School of Management, The University of Texas at Dallas. Mulay holds a patent titled *"Surface Imaging with Materials Identified by Colors"* authored by him during his employment with advanced CMOS technology development team at Texas Instruments, Inc. He has chaired technical sessions at International

Symposium for Testing and Failure Analysis (ISTFA) in 2009, 2010, and 2016. He has also authored several articles showing this wide expertise in macroeconomics, geopolitics, supply chains, business models, socioeconomics, spirituality, personal finance, and microeconomics.

USCIS approved his U.S. permanent residency under the category of foreign nationals with extraordinary abilities in science and technologies even though he did not pursue a PhD degree in engineering or economics. He contributes to recognized publications such as EBN, Truthout.org, electronics.ca publications, EDFA magazine, NaSPA Magazine, PROUT Globe and Military & Aerospace Electronics Magazine (MA&E), SEMI.org, LinkedIn, and so on. He has appeared on national radio shows, national news in India, and some regional television shows too and has been featured on the cover in industry magazines for his ideas about *Mass Capitalism.*

Apek grew up as an athlete and loves to compete due to his athletic background. His hobbies include hiking, back-packing, photography and occasionally seeks pleasure in adventure sports like Bungee jumping, sky diving, white water rafting, and so on. He also believes in a healthy diet and lifestyle and practices meditation twice a day and loves to cook variety of sentient vegetarian food.

He has a well-visited personal blog (www.ApekMulay.com) with over 3 million hits since he started blogging in May 2013.

About the Editor

Apek Mulay is business and technology consultant at Mulay's Consultancy Services. He is also a senior analyst and macroeconomist in U.S. semiconductor industry. He is an entrepreneur with World Financial Group (WFG) and also co-founder of an e-commerce startup CalcuttaHandicraft.in. His first book *Mass Capitalism: A Blueprint for Economic Revival* (2014) is available as paperback, e-book (Amazon.com, Barnesandnoble.com, books.google.com) as well as an audio book (Audible.com). *Mass Capitalism* in Marathi language will be available for readers from Maharashtra, India, in 2019 published as *Samudayik Bhandwalshahi* by Utkarsha Publications, Pune, India.

Mulay has authored other books such as *Sustaining Moore's Law: Uncertainty Leading to a Certainty of IoT Revolution* (2015) with Morgan & Claypool publishers, *How Information Revolution Remade the Business and the Economy: A Roadmap for Progress of the Semiconductor Industry* (2016), *New Macroeconomics* (2018), and *Economic Renaissance in the Age of Artificial Intelligence* (2019) with Business Expert Press. He has also authored a monograph on technology with Lambert Academic Publishing titled *Improving Reliability of Tungsten Plug Via on an Integrated Circuitry: Process Flow in BiCMOS and CMOS Technology with Failure Analysis, Design of Experiments, Statistical Analysis and Wafer Maps* (2016).

Mulay pursued undergraduate studies in electronics engineering (EE) at the University of Mumbai in India and holds two master's degrees, one in electrical engineering from Texas Tech University, Lubbock, TX and other in business analytics from Naveen Jindal School of Management, The University of Texas at Dallas. Mulay holds a patent titled *"Surface Imaging with Materials Identified by Colors"* authored by him during his employment with advanced CMOS technology development team at Texas Instruments, Inc. He has chaired technical sessions at International Symposium for Testing and Failure Analysis (ISTFA) in 2009, 2010, and 2016. He has also authored several articles showing this wide expertise in macroeconomics, geopolitics, supply chains, business models, socioeconomics, spirituality, personal finance, and microeconomics.

USCIS approved his U.S. permanent residency under the category of foreign nationals with extraordinary abilities in science and technologies even though he did not pursue a PhD degree in engineering or economics. He contributes to recognized publications such as EBN, Truthout.org, electronics.ca publications, EDFA magazine, NaSPA Magazine, PROUT Globe and Military & Aerospace Electronics Magazine (MA&E), SEMI. org, LinkedIn, and so on. He has appeared on national radio shows, national news in India, and some regional television shows too and has been featured on the cover in industry magazines for his ideas about *Mass Capitalism.*

He has a well-visited personal blog (www.ApekMulay.com) with over 3 million hits since he started blogging in May 2013.

Index